LETTERCARVING IN WOOD

LETTERCARVING IN WOOD

A Practical Course

CHRIS PYE

GUILD OF MASTER CRAFTSMAN PUBLICATIONS LTD

First published 1997 by
Guild of Master Craftsman Publications Ltd
166 High Street, Lewes
East Sussex BN7 1XU

All photographs by Christopher J. Pye
unless otherwise stated.
All drawings by Christopher J. Pye
except: 5.33, 5.35, 5.37, 5.39, 5.40, 5.49, 5.60, 5.61, 5.62,
5.63, 5.66, 5.68, 5.69, 5.70, 5.90, 5.97, 5.101, 5.103, 5.105,
5.106, 5.108, 5.111, 5.112, 5.114, 5.116, 6.2 – 6.28, 6.35,
8.43, 8.50, 8.56, 8.63, 8.70, 8.76, 9.8, 9.9, 9.10, 9.13, 9.14,
9.15, 10.1, 10.3, 10.10, 10.23, 10.33 by John Yates.

Cover photograph by Zul Mukhida

ISBN 1 86108 043 3

Designed by Christopher Halls at Mind's Eye Design, Lewes.

Set in Trajan and Adobe Garamond

Printed and bound in Singapore under the supervision of
MRM Graphics, Winslow, Buckinghamshire, UK

Note
BCE (meaning 'Before Common Era') is used with dates otherwise identified as BC.
CE (meaning 'Common Era') is used with dates otherwise identified as AD.

Metric/imperial conversions
Although care has been taken to ensure that imperial measurements are true and accurate,
they are only conversions from metric. Instances will be found where fractionally differing
metric measurements have the same imperial equivalents. This is because, in each particular case,
the *closest* imperial equivalent has been given, usually to within $1/32$in either way.

For my son
Finian

CONTENTS

Acknowledgements   VIII
Introduction   1

PART ONE
GROUNDWORK   3

1 BACKGROUND   4
A brief history of lettering   4
What is 'good' lettering?   5
Light and shadow   8
Incised vs. raised lettering   9
The naming of parts   12
The modern roman letter style   14

2 SETTING UP   15
Carving tools   15
Other tools   19
Suitable woods   20
The worksurface and holding work   22
Lighting   22
Safety   22

3 THE PROCESS OF LETTERCARVING   23
Rough sketches to working drawings   23
Transferring the drawings   26
Carving   28
Finishing   28
Costing   29
Common mistakes   30

PART TWO
INCISED LETTERING   31

4 ABOUT INCISED LETTERING   32
'Stab' and 'stop' cuts   32
Depth and angle of cuts   32
Internal symmetry   33
Stabbing the root line   34
Alternatives to the V section   34
Alternatives to incising   35
Working with large lettering   36

5 INCISED LETTERING EXERCISES   37
Introduction   37
Exercise plan   37
Drawing out the letterforms   39
Exercises   39
   Straight letters   40
   ■1 Vertical stabbing with mallet and chisel   40
   ■2 Vertical stabbing with mallet and chisel, reversed hands   41
   ■3 Vertical stabbing with mallet, to a line   42
   ■4 Angled cutting with mallet   44
   ■5 Angled cutting with mallet, reversed hands   45
   ■6 Vertical trench with mallet   46
   ■7 Vertical trench, tidying by hand   49
   ■8 Serifs (I)   50
   ■9 Horizontal trenches   55
   ■10 Serifs (II)   57
   ■11 Letters H, T, F, L & E   59
   ■12 Oblique trenches   62
   ■13 Joining obliques – letters A, M, N, V, W, K, Z, X & Y   64
   Curved letters   70
   ■14 Vertical stabbing with mallet and gouge (I)   71
   ■15 Vertical stabbing with mallet and gouge (II)   72
   ■16 Vertical stabbing with mallet and gouge (III)   74
   ■17 Crescents (I)   76
   ■18 Crescents (II)   79
   ■19 Circles   81
   ■20 Letter O   83
   ■21 Letters C & S   85
   Straight/curved combinations   88
   ■22 Letters J, Q, D, U, G, P, R & B   88
   ■23 Using the V tool   92

6 CHARACTERISTICS OF INDIVIDUAL LETTERS IN MODERN ROMAN   95
Letters A–Z   95
Family resemblances   104
Summary of widths   104
Modifications to modern roman   106
Working with Roman and Arabic numerals   107

PART THREE
RAISED LETTERING 109

7 ABOUT RAISED LETTERING 110
Introduction 110
Guidelines 111
Carving 115
Letter shaping 116
Backgrounds 117
Routers 118
Common mistakes 119
Finishing 120

8 RAISED LETTERING EXERCISES 121
Introduction 121
Exercise plan 121
Exercises 122
    Basic techniques 122
    R1 Grounding using the deep gouge 122
    R2 Lowering the ground 126
    R3 Levelling the ground 128
    R4 Using the V tool 131
    R5 Grounding to an edge 131
    R6 Setting-in 135
    R7 Grounding within a counter 139
    Sample letters 142
    R8 I 142
    R9 H 144
    R10 A 146
    R11 D 148
    R12 B 150
    R13 S 152
    R14 Texturing ground 154
Summary 156

PART FOUR
LETTERFORM 157

9 LAYOUT 158
Introduction 158
Making a start 159
Family resemblances 160
Colour 162
Optical adjustment 169
Working parameters 170

10 LETTER STYLES 173
Trajan roman 173
Lower case roman 175
Versal 178
Uncial and half uncial 182
Gothic 186

PART FIVE
PROJECTS 191

11 INCISED LETTERING PROJECTS 192
Introduction 192
Inscripted post 192
House sign 196
Bowl 198
Small table 201
Dry transfer lettering 204

12 RAISED LETTERING PROJECTS 207
Introduction 207
Large, simple sign 207
Breadboard 210
Name stamp 213
Carved and lettered sign 216

PART SIX
RESOURCES 219

The Sheffield list 220
Glossary 222
List of suppliers 226
Further reading 228
About the author 228
Index 229

ACKNOWLEDGEMENTS

In the course of writing this book I have bothered more people than I meant to, and have a lot more individuals to thank by name than I am able. In this last group are all the carvers, both dead and alive, of the thousands of examples of lettercarving I have looked at over the years, whose inspiration both started me off, and keeps me going. Included amongst these is of course the late Gino Masero, who first showed me the rudiments of lettering technique.

Specifically, I would like to thank: my wife Karin, as always, for her sustaining tolerance and positive support; my commissioning editor Liz Inman, for her patience and encouragement which have been strengthening, and for her contribution to my writing efforts, which has been really appreciated; and Jonathan Ingoldby, my editor, for his hard work and the sensitive and confident way in which he moulded and polished the text.

I would also like to thank those lettercarvers, both here and abroad, who very generously and trustingly contributed photographs of their fine work: Wayne Barton (USA); Steve Eggleton; Ray Gonzalez; Deborah Hurst; Bridget J. Powell; Michael Rust; and Douglas Williams (USA). Now they have seen the result, I really hope that they are as glad to have been involved as I was to involve them. Thanks also to Rod Naylor for allowing me to use his photograph of a seventeenth-century lintel, shown below.

There are two contributors who deserve a particular mention: first, Gillian Maddison, not only for contributing her own lettercarving, but for all her generous work on my behalf, organizing the contributions of several others. Second, Tom Perkins, whose work in stone I nearly *didn't* include because I thought that, once seen, no-one would ever want to carve in wood! Although this book is about lettering in wood, I am very pleased to be able to represent the inspiring tradition of lettering in stone, and feature examples by Tom Perkins, whose work, to my eyes, comes as near to perfection as possible.

Finally, I would like to acknowledge the help I had from Elizabeth Walker and the National Museum of Wales, and thank the museum for the use of their Trajanic inscriptions.

Carved lettering on a seventeenth-century lintel. Photograph courtesy of Rod Naylor.

INTRODUCTION

I see this book as a workshop manual, aimed at anyone with an interest in carving letters into wood. I have assumed a basic knowledge of carving techniques, and therefore only discuss the fundamental aspects of areas such as tool grips and sharpness, but I have assumed *no* experience of lettercarving.

By working through the progressive series of exercises, you can learn to carve a basic and useful style of lettering in incised and raised forms, while acquiring lettercarving skills applicable to any other style.

At the same time, there is a wide enough variety of material, in enough depth, for this book to be of interest to existing lettercarvers who wish to improve upon, or expand, their skills.

Although it is a 'practical' course, theory is also a feature of the book, and is necessary in order to put the practical aspects into a context of design and appearance. It is a mistake not to pay attention to the design aspects of lettering, and you may well find that actual carving is the least of your problems when it comes to creating a successful piece of work! No matter how carefully carved, badly designed letters will never look good.

You may be wondering: why a whole book about lettercarving – surely it is dealt with elsewhere, in other carving books? This question is linked by some people to another: why bother to design letters when you can just use Letraset, and indeed why not just forget *carving* altogether and simply use a router? My experience as a woodcarving teacher is that lettering is a very popular topic with students. It is also a subject which I am frequently asked to demonstrate. There are many reasons for this interest, not least the pleasures to be had from lettercarving, from signs for one's own house, to presents for others. There are also financial incentives. Lettering in wood is a circumscribed skill: the product is easily defined, and it is obvious when it is finished – unlike a lot of other carving. Students who become competent letterers find at the same time that their general woodcarving skills improve enormously, because of the emphasis on carving tool manipulation and control involved in lettercarving.

So, there is a lot of interest in lettering but, at the present time, information is scattered in odd, brief chapters within books dealing with carving as a whole. As a result the subject is given fairly superficial treatment, which can be excellent as far as it goes, or may include poor methods of working. I know many students have found this 'scattering' of information both frustrating and uninspiring.

I came to lettering as a woodcarver, not as a letter designer, and like most other woodcarvers I undertake a lot of other work besides lettering. However, I have always enjoyed the challenge of lettering in wood – especially when it has paid a few bills here and there! I have been teaching lettercarving together with general carving for many years, and at one stage designed a scheme of work to help students make the best progress in the shortest amount of time. It is this practical scheme of work which has been developed here in this book. What makes this book different, and worthwhile, is not just that it deals exclusively, and in depth, with lettercarving, but that at its heart is a well-tried, structured course. For your ease of reference, all the incised lettering exercise numbers are prefixed by the symbol **I**, and all the raised lettering exercises by the symbol **R**.

As for Letraset and routers, I hope to show that there is nothing 'wrong' in using these if you prefer, but I think you will miss out on the joy and satisfaction to be had in the process of *hand* lettercarving. There are cases for using Letraset and similar transfer letters, and to this end I have included a project in Chapter 11 that demonstrates one particular technique.

Examples of lettering abound. The written word is an essentially human and ancient phenomenon, and the aesthetics of letters far-reaching. Stonecarving has played – and still plays – a tremendous part in lettering, hence my inclusion of examples of work in stone in this book.

I hope you will find here the practical groundwork of a subject which has enough depth to occupy a lifetime of study.

Opposite: roundel in beech (saxophone in lime) by Deborah Hurst.

PART ONE

GROUNDWORK

CHAPTER 1

BACKGROUND

AIMS

- To describe a little of the historical background to lettering and how it affects lettercarving today.

- To look at what you should be trying to achieve when you undertake the task of lettercarving.

- To discuss how carved letters differ from pen and printed letterforms.

- To compare the two main lettercarving approaches (incised and relief), and discuss their strengths and weaknesses.

- To define the parts of letters and the terms used in lettercarving.

- To introduce the letter style used in the core exercises in this book.

Fig 1.1　*An example of Trajan roman: a fragment of a Tuscan marble inscription, recording building work at the Roman camp in Caerleon around 100CE. (Photograph courtesy of the National Museum of Wales.)*

A BRIEF HISTORY OF LETTERING

The progenitor which inspired practically all the letter styles found in this book is known as the 'roman' alphabet. The most famous example, carved around 114–117CE, is to be found on Trajan's column in the Forum at Rome, and an example of this letter style is shown in Fig 1.1.

The development of the roman letterform, through Phoenician, Egyptian and Greek civilizations, is not particularly pertinent here. For carvers of letters the important point is that the roman letter style is the oldest still recognizable to us today. All previous alphabets are intelligible only to specialist scholars.

The alphabet shapes identified as 'roman', and epitomized by the Trajan carving, did not remain fixed, but changed and developed with the passage of time. Lettering still continues to change. It certainly has its 'classic' styles, but is essentially an evolving phenomenon, like language. Nowadays, for example, we have the letters **H, J, K, U, W, X** and **Y**, which would have been unfamiliar to the Roman carvers of Trajan's column. We now mix small, 'joined up' letters with capitals, and use Arabic numerals (i.e. 1, 2, 3), made to look like the roman style.

The many type styles with which we are now familiar have come about through work pressures in four areas over the years: on scribes with quill pens who needed to copy manuscripts accurately and quickly; on stonemasons having to cut the same pen-created letters into different types of stone with flat chisels; on the ingenuity and fancies of printers, right from the inception of the printing press; and, most recently, on the easy manipulation and creation of characters by computers or digital displays.

Fig 1.2   An example of contemporary lettering in stone: 'It Burns in the Void' from a poem by Kathleen Raine, lettered in Welsh slate by Tom Perkins. Letter height: 60cm (24in).

Carvers, whether in stone or wood, have always followed, or been influenced by, the printing and lettering styles of their times. They have also been influential on letter styles, themselves, their own styles being influenced by the restrictions placed upon them both by their tools and by the medium in which they work: wood. Differences brought about by the differing approaches of carvers, scribes and printers are fairly easy to spot in the lettering we see around us.

Unfortunately, space does not allow for a detailed look at the history of lettering, but if you want to learn more about this fascinating subject, there are many books available, some of which are included in the Further Reading section on page 228.

WHAT IS 'GOOD' LETTERING?

The word 'good', like the word 'art', is subjective. The very concept of 'beauty' is culturally conditioned and shared by consensus. However, there is no doubt that beauty is perceived in a fine example of lettercarving. Indeed, we cannot call it 'fine' without it having this sense of beauty.

The lettercarver needs to be aware of some of the basic criteria by which 'good' lettering is judged. In the past I have found it helpful to divide these into two parts: the point of view of the 'viewer' and that of the carver.

FROM THE VIEWER'S STANDPOINT

There are three uncontroversial aspects to be considered in *all* lettering. When designing and executing lettering, think of these three Cs:

1   **Clarity**
    The message must be readable – this is after all the purpose of most lettering. Unless the work is a deliberate puzzle, like a monogram, or deliberately playful or 'artful', with the words secondary in importance to the 'look', then the message should be easily understood. Simple letter styles are obviously easier to read than ornate ones.

2   **Communication**
    If part of the message embodied in any lettercarving is straight cerebral information, another part of what is communicated lies in the emotional response of the viewer. We can be affected by a fine example of writing from a purely artistic, aesthetic point of view, even if it is written in a language we don't understand, and uses symbols which we have no idea how to pronounce or interpret.

3 Congruence

There needs to be a connection between the style and presentation of the lettering, and the subject. Advertisers know that style is a large part of a message, sometimes the largest. By congruence I mean that the style should, if not enhance the message, at least work with it and not against it (see Fig 1.3). A parallel might be how body language supports verbal communication.

FROM THE CARVER'S STANDPOINT

Lettercarvers share the need for clarity, communication and congruence with calligraphers, but also have a practical need for letterforms which *carve* well, suiting the use of chisels and gouges in hard timber.

A competent carver *can* carve any alphabet which derives from the four main creative sources of lettering mentioned on page 4: carved, penned or brushed letters, printed letters and computer-generated letters. However, experience will show how some letterstyles (e.g. italic scripts) are awkward to cut, whereas other styles are far more suitable to carving (e.g. roman capitals).

A good letterform for carving will have an alphabet which:

- Can be cut in a clean and straightforward manner with carving tools.

- Will allow technical and artistic flair to develop easily *by virtue of the carving techniques required.*

- Will allow for speed and simplicity of execution, with a minimum number of tools required to generate the bulk of the effect.

- Will enable the carver to work to a rhythm or flow.

- Will benefit from the effects of light and shadow, rather than the contrast of black on white which applies to printed letterforms.

- Will work well in wood, taking into account the appearances, strengths and weaknesses of the grain.

This doesn't mean *only* having straight lines, or serifs, or forms which look like roman letters. Nor does it mean not taking on styles that are awkward to carve, although you may need to adapt elements of these for easier carving. Different styles will succeed or fail when these practical criteria are applied, and this will affect how you feel about the result, its appearance and how long it takes – which matters if you are being paid for the job! (see Figs 1.4 and 1.5).

Fig 1.3 'Fish' (from a poem by Rupert Brooke), carved in freely adapted roman-based letters by Gillian Maddison in mahogany. This is a good example of congruence, with the layout enhancing, and even illustrating, the message of the text. The dimensions are 66 x 23cm (26 x 9in) and the carving is mounted on a back board stained dark green.

Fig 1.4 *House name plate carved from solid English oak by Ray Gonzalez. 365 x 240mm (14¹/₂ x 9¹/₂in), letter height 38mm (1¹/₂in).*

Fig 1.5 *Plaque, 61 x 25cm (24 x 10in) in English oak by Gillian Maddison. A very formal massed layout for a formal siting.*

LIGHT AND SHADOW

All carving – and this includes lettercarving – is about manipulating light and shadow. What separates the carver of letters from the pen letterer or the printer, is the fact that the carver's letterforms are *three dimensional*. Without paint, carved letters are only visible because of the effect of light and shadow. This is easily observed if the lighting on a sample of carved letters is changed from side-on to straight-on (see Fig 1.6).

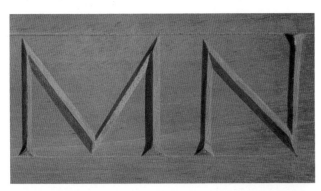

Fig 1.6   These carved letters have been lit straight-on (top), from a three-quarter angle (middle) and from the side (bottom), showing how the amount of shadow is increased in each case.

When you are carving a letter, it is the three dimensional cutting of the tools into a flat surface which creates the light and shadow effects, and the letter itself. As you carve the letterforms, think of your carving in terms of creating light and shadow.

The most important optical lines within any carved letter are those where there is a change of plane, especially a sharp one (see Fig. 1.7). In relief lettering this will be the corner lines created where the side walls join the surface of the wood above and the background. In incised lettering it occurs where the walls of the letter meet the surface forming a silhouette or outline.

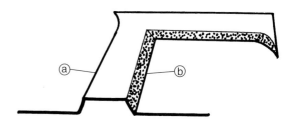

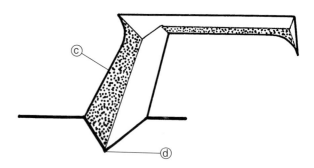

Fig 1.7   Optical lines produced through changes of plane, where (a) and (c) are surface edges, (b) the ground edge and (d) the root of the trench.

It is at such places that the eye registers the features of the letters most strongly and tells the reader's brain which letter their eye is looking at. As you cut the *edge* of a letter into the wood surface you are altering the letter shape more profoundly than by carving anywhere else within the letter. It is therefore very important, even if the walls of a carved letter are a little rough, that the edges lie precisely carved where you want them.

The centre line where the two angled sides of an incised letter meet is another important change of plane. An effect of light and shadow is created here which gives rhythm, a pleasing appearance, and sense to the letters. Here again, pay great attention to this centre line. Of course, the walls of letters should also be as neatly and precisely cut as possible.

Finally, remember that your lettering work is intended for residence somewhere. It may be a restaurant door, a simple garden gate, or around the lid of a box. Wherever, the letters will be subject to certain – usually changeable – lighting, and this must be taken into account as much as possible.

INCISED VS. RAISED LETTERING

There are two methods of carving letters in wood: incising and raising. These two approaches are rarely interchangeable and very infrequently mixed. Each has its strengths, its weaknesses and an appropriateness to a particular context.

INCISED LETTERING

'Incise' comes from the Latin 'to cut', as in incisor teeth or incisive comments. Incised lettering occurs when the surface of the wood is cut *into* in some way, but remains present, as a sort of 'foreground'. Good incised lettering is cleanly and 'incisively' cut.

Incised lettering has many of the qualities of 'chip carving', where patterns are made by removing chips of wood, and some letterers do use knives for light work (see Fig 1.8). Incised lettering is quicker to produce than raised lettering and can be readily cut freehand.

Incised letterforms can be far more delicate and fancier than raised letters, as the cuts are supported by the surrounding wood. It follows that there is a wider choice of styles appropriate to incising, making it useful in a wider context. Indeed, there are few places where incised lettering cannot be used, although it does work particularly well in a good cross light; in dull light it tends to disappear.

The height of an incised letter is measured between the cap and base lines – that is from the top to the bottom surface edges (see Fig 1.9), and they can easily

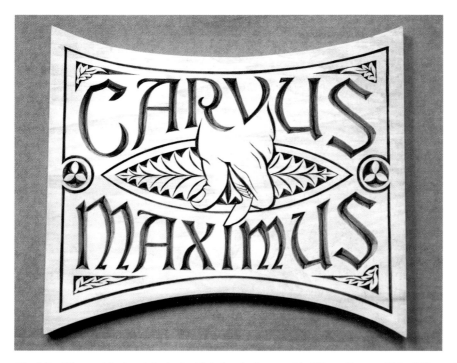

Fig 1.8 'Carvus Maximus': incised with knives in basswood by Wayne Barton, 356 x 205mm (14 x 8in).

9

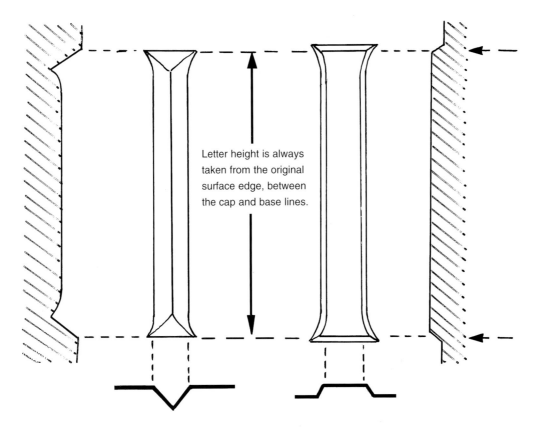

Fig 1.9   Measuring letter height.

be painted. For outside work the paint, being partially protected from the elements, will weather far better than it would if it were applied to raised lettering.

RAISED LETTERING

This is also known as **relief** lettering, and is in fact low relief carving, in which parts of a design are raised up and thereby separated from the surrounding area.

In practice though, it is not so much the letters which are raised up as the background which is carved away. The letters still end up projecting from the background plane, often referred to as 'the ground' (see Fig 1.10). Raised lettering normally takes much longer to carve than incised lettering, although removing the background can be speeded up by using a router (see page 118).

Short and cross grain in the wood can render some parts of a letter weak. This means that decorative flourishes are more difficult to achieve compared with

Fig 1.10   Kodak sign. Raised lettering in redwood by Douglas Williams.

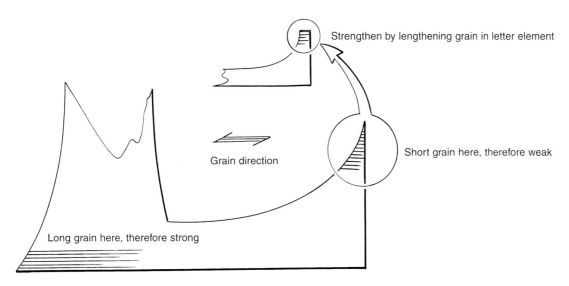

Strengthen by lengthening grain in letter element

Grain direction

Short grain here, therefore weak

Long grain here, therefore strong

Fig 1.11 *Areas of short or weak grain can be a problem in raised lettering.*

incised work (see Fig 1.11). As a result, relief letters tend to have larger, simpler outlines, and be bolder or heavier in style – serifs, for example, tend to be stubbier, smaller or absent altogether.

Raised lettering is often used where the lighting is poor or diffused – for example in churches. It is also possible to make raised letters stand out even more by texturing or tooling the background to create greater contrast with the letters.

Raised letters can be painted, but this requires greater dexterity with the paintbrush than with incised lettering. The paint is not protected at all from the weather, and the edges of the letters are also subject to water penetration and frost attack. Hence, raised lettering is best used indoors unless well sealed and maintained against the climate.

The height of a raised letter is measured on the original flat surface, from top edge to bottom edge, whether the sides splay or not.

SUMMARY

For your ease of reference, Table 1 lists the advantages and disadvantages of incised and relief lettercarving.

Comparative attributes of incised and raised lettering	
Incised lettering	**Raised lettering**
The wood is cut *into* in some way, but remains present.	Letters relieved as the surrounding ground is reduced.
Has many of the qualities of 'chip carving'.	Has many of the qualities of low relief carving.
Quicker to produce, and easily cut freehand.	Normally takes longer to produce. Use of a router speeds this up.
Support from wood grain makes fancier, more delicate letters possible.	Parts of letters tend to be weak because of short grain, resulting in the need for larger, simpler, bolder letterforms.
Wider choice of styles making it useful in a wider context.	Many alphabets are unsuitable for relief carving.
Needs a good cross light.	Better in poor or diffused lighting. Background texturing can be applied for greater contrast.
Height measured from top to bottom surface edges.	Height measured on the original flat surface.
Easily painted and more suitable for outside work.	Painting depends on dexterity with the paintbrush and is unprotected if used on letters outside.

Table 1

THE NAMING OF PARTS

Whatever method you use to carve letters, you need to be familiar with the nomenclature of lettering and letterforms. Fig 1.12 shows a selection of modern roman letters with the names of their various parts, or elements. These terms are fairly self-evident and are transferable between letter styles. Common alternative names for letter components appear in brackets. It also shows sections through incised and raised letters with their relevant terms.

Some terms only apply to letters worked in three dimensions and these need special attention. First, you need to be able to differentiate between the **internal angle** of an incised letter and its **root**.

- The **internal angle** is the angle at which the two side walls meet.

- The **root** is the actual *centre line* formed by the junction of the two walls.

There are two other terms that require a little more explanation: **stress** and **serifs**.

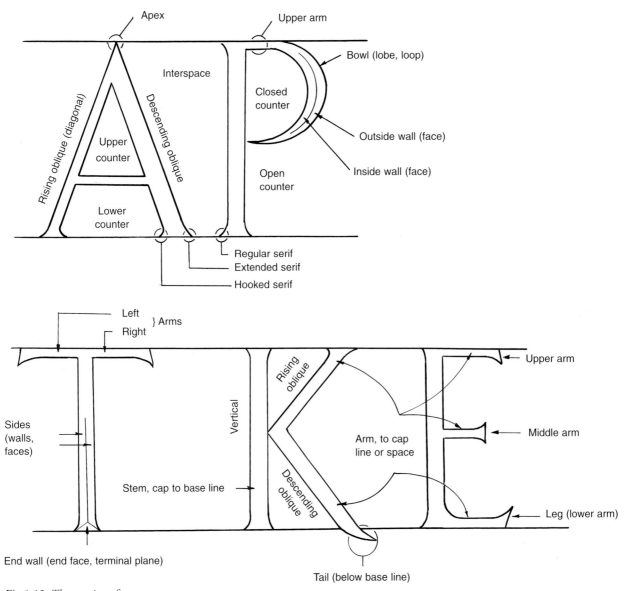

Fig 1.12 The naming of parts.

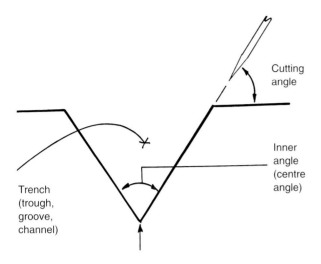

Cutting angle

Inner angle (centre angle)

Trench (trough, groove, channel)

Root (runs along centre line)

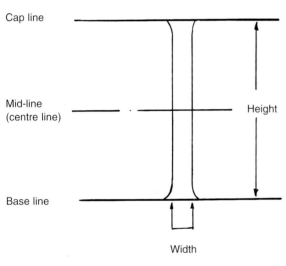

Cap line

Mid-line (centre line)

Base line

Height

Width

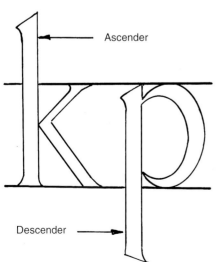

Ascender

Descender

STRESS

Stress relates *only* to rounded forms (curves and lobes). In some letter styles, curves vary between a minimum width and a maximum; i.e. from thin to thick. This is particularly obvious in the letter **O**, usually the exemplar for curves in an alphabet.

Stress is really the impact of 'weight' difference: thicker parts of a letter are optically 'heavy', and appear to have weight; thin parts appear to be 'lighter'. The more the difference between thick and thin strokes is emphasized, the greater the stress.

The 'line of stress' is taken across the *thinnest* points. Its angle of inclination, relative to the cap and base lines, varies with the style of alphabet. You must be consistent with the angle of stress in curves throughout a letter style in order to maintain the 'family resemblance' (discussed in Chapter 9). Roman letterforms with a vertical stress are referred to as **modern style**, to differentiate them from those with maximum tilt, called **old style**. Styles which fall between the two are known as **transitional** (see Fig 1.13).

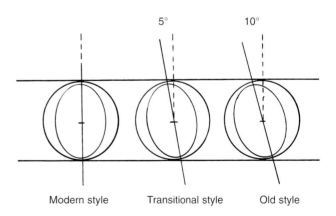

5°   10°

Modern style   Transitional style   Old style

Fig 1.13 Lines of stress in roman-based lettering.

SERIFS

Serifs occur at the end of a free letter limb, or stem, as a small cross-line. The word 'serif' is first recorded in English as late as the nineteenth century, coming from a Dutch word for a dash or line, but the serif itself goes back to the Roman period – we have no idea what carvers called them.

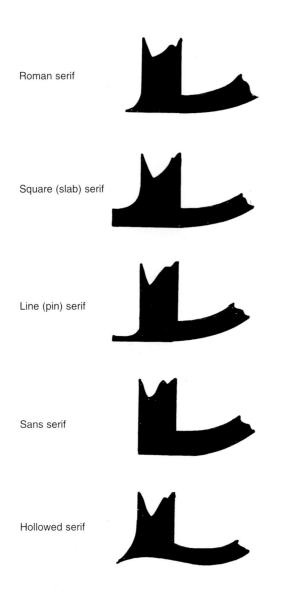

Roman serif

Square (slab) serif

Line (pin) serif

Sans serif

Hollowed serif

Fig 1.14 A few of the many variations of serif, including the effect of sans serif.

The serif probably came into being as stonemasons turned pen or brush letters into carved letters. They added serifs for two important reasons, still valid today. The first reason was aesthetic, and the results have been admired for centuries. The second reason was functional. A pen or brushed letter is read by ink or paint contrasting with the background. An incised letter is read by the contrast of light and shadow on either side

of the trench. As the wood surface is also lit, this can make the letter height more difficult to judge. The ends of a mixture of thick and thin strokes, in a variety of directions, tend to 'float' around the cap and base lines instead of lining up along them. Serifs *fix the optical length*, lining the ends of the letters firmly along the virtual cap and base lines and helping the eye to read along the text. Carved text without serifs is far more tiring to read than one with serifs, though not more difficult to carve.

Serifs vary in shape depending in part on the letter style and in part on the orientation of the limb from which they arise (see Fig 1.14). Some serif shapes are easier to incise, others carve more easily in relief. Of course, it is not *obligatory* to have a serif – many styles (mostly modern) are 'sans serif' – without serifs.

THE MODERN ROMAN LETTER STYLE

The style of letter I have chosen for the incising exercises (Chapter 5) and the raised lettering exercises (Chapter 8) is known as **modern roman**. This is a recent style bearing close resemblance to the original, 'classic' or Trajan style of roman lettering, more details of which appear in Chapter 10.

Trajan roman lettering exists only in capital letters, and it is this form of capital with which we are most familiar in the West. More analysis of Trajan roman has taken place than of any other letter style, and it forms the benchmark for laying out, optical spacing and family resemblances.

Modern roman is a little different from the classic style, being more geometric and less subtle. It is a clear, useful, functional script, being straightforward to lay out and quick and easy to work with. The most important difference from the classic style is a change in stress from the original tilt to the left, to a vertical.

This letterform will give practice in different sizes and orientations of straights and curves. If you can successfully carve these, you will find it relatively straightforward to move on to any other style.

CHAPTER 2

SETTING UP

AIMS

- To look at the tools required for lettering.

- To suggest the best woods for lettercarving and show what to avoid.

- To show how best to work on large panels.

- To examine different ways of holding work securely.

To carve anything successfully, including letters, you must have good quality, appropriately-shaped tools, correctly sharpened and maintained. You must be able to manipulate these tools correctly in order to achieve your aims. You need good wood to work with, which is held securely and safely while at the same time being adjustable for ease of access.

CARVING TOOLS

You don't actually need that many carving tools for lettering, and you will find that one tool can often be made to do the work of others. This is an important point, as many books state that *exact* curves of gouges are needed to match the curves of the letters. This is mostly *not* the case if the tools are manipulated properly.

Carving chisels are used for cutting straight components – incised straights or the sides of raised letters. The range of chisel widths you will need will depend on the size and style of letters you wish to carve. A corner or skew chisel is extremely useful for getting into tight recesses, and hence a must for lettercarving (see Fig 2.1). Whatever your ability, you will also find that, for mallet-work, a broad end to your chisel is always desirable (see Fig 2.2).

Fig 2.1   A simple range of carving tools used for lettercarving. From left: regular chisel; alongee chisel; deep gouge; flatter gouge; skew chisel; fishtail chisel; fishtail gouge; V tool.

Fig 2.2   The handle on the left, as supplied with the tool, has a small end and is less easy to hit with the mallet compared with that on the right.

The differing sweeps of carving gouges (see Appendix 1: the Sheffield list) are used to form the curved parts of the letters, and you will require a range of gouges, depending again on the size and style of the letters you wish to carve. Deep gouges are used for removing ground in raised lettering, and flat gouges for finishing it off. V tools (the commonest having an inner angle of 60°) are not used nearly as much in lettercarving as many people assume (in incised lettering hardly at all, although they are useful in raised lettering). Incised lettering, with rare exceptions, uses only straight carving tools, but raised lettering sometimes necessitates the use of shortbent gouges to clean up the background between the letters.

A fishtail chisel and gouge are needed, for cutting serifs. I have found that the best tool for cutting the end walls of serifs is a fishtail chisel with the cutting edge set to a small angle (or skew) of about 20°. The longer point gains extra access to a corner, while maintaining some of the flat feel of the chisel. If you do not have a skew chisel you can obtain them from manufacturers, but I find these to be skewed too much. It is better to get a normal fishtail and alter the angle yourself. I have included a conventional fishtail chisel in the recommended tools for incised lettering (see page 38) which will do the same job perfectly well. However, I suggest you change the shape if and when you feel confident enough to do so. You will also find spade tools and alongee chisels very useful shapes as they are lighter to work with and give greater visibility.

Shortbent flat gouges are preferable to shortbent chisels for clearing backgrounds in raised lettering, but a shortbent chisel with its blade skewed about 20° is useful for finishing the long outer curved walls of large raised lettering after the main work has been done.

KNIVES

As I have said, incised lettering has something of the beauty of 'chip carving', in which special knives are used to remove wedge-shaped slices of wood, and there are letterers who are successful entirely with knives in certain styles (for example, Wayne Barton, an example of whose work was shown in Fig 1.8). However, I only use woodcarving tools for lettering, partly because they are the tools with which I have long been familiar, and partly because I found knives far more tiring to use than carving tools when lettering to any depth, particularly with hard woods. This is because the work is concentrated on one hand, especially the thumb, and you cannot use a mallet with a knife. If you are interested in experimenting with knives, then there are books of instruction to be had, such as Wayne Barton's *Chip Carving Patterns*, details of which can be found in the Further Reading section on page 228.

HOLDING CARVING TOOLS

While you may be familiar with the correct techniques involved in holding carving tools, this aspect of the craft is so important for successful results that I feel it does no harm to go over the 'golden rules', and discuss the two principle grips used in the exercises and projects that appear in this book.

All carving is fundamentally about toolwork: holding and handling the tools correctly and getting them to make the cuts *you want*. Lettering is no exception, and involves a high degree of tool control. Ensuring you adopt the correct techniques and achieving good results with your lettered work will bring about an improvement in all your carving.

THREE GOLDEN RULES FOR HOLDING CARVING TOOLS

1   Hold all carving tools in *both* hands. The only exception to this is when you are using a mallet.

2   Make sure the front, or lowest hand, which is wrapped around the shank of the tool, is *always* resting on the surface of the wood being carved, or on the bench. This rule and the previous one ensure maximum tool control.

3   Keep your fingers *behind* the cutting edge, and never push the tool directly towards another part of your body. As only the sharp edge of a tool can cut, this will ensure you are always safe in your work.

TWO PRINCIPAL GRIPS

The two ways of holding carving tools described below give an excellent, safe and precise means of manipulating the corners and edges of chisels and gouges, and their adoption is highly recommended. For want of better terms, I call them the 'pen and dagger' grip and the 'low-angle' grip. I have assumed right hand dominance in my descriptions of them, so if you are left-handed, simply reverse the instructions.

PEN AND DAGGER GRIP

With this grip the tool is presented to the wood at a high cutting angle, making it the dominant grip in lettering, used for paring straight faces, making winding cuts in the curved parts of letters, stabbing and corner work. Refer to Fig 2.3. The blade is held rather like a pen in the *right* hand. The edge of the hand, or the lower knuckles, rest on the wood. The tip of your middle finger should rest behind the bevel and heel of the tool. This supports and guides the cutting edge from behind. This finger also runs along the wood with the tool, but never goes beyond the cutting edge. The index finger and thumb grip the sides of the blade. The handle of the tool is gripped with the *left* hand, with the thumb positioned near the top of the handle, as shown.

If this grip is used for heavy cutting or paring, you must bring your body in close to the handle, in order to put your weight behind the cut, and avoid strain on the arms, particularly the elbow joints. Applications of this grip are fully explored in the exercises.

LOW-ANGLE GRIP

This grip is not used nearly as much as the pen and dagger for lettering, but it is important, being used when making stab cuts into serifs, cleaning out the walls of large letters, manipulating the V tool, and removing background in raised lettering, so it must be mastered! Unlike the pen and dagger, you need to be able to reverse this grip (i.e. swap hands), so that you can cut from either direction without unnecessary contortions.

Refer to Fig 2.4. Hold the handle of the tool with your right hand, as if you were holding a screwdriver, and wrap the left hand around the shoulder of the tool so that part of the hand covers the blade, and part covers the handle. Extend the thumb of your left hand along

Fig 2.3 The 'pen and dagger' grip, showing how the blade of the tool is held rather like a pen, and the handle rather like a dagger. The starting position is shown above and the complete grip below.

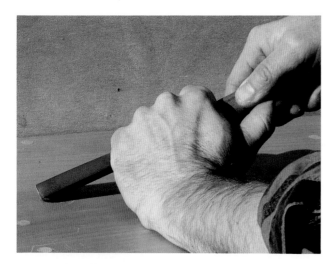

Fig 2.4   The 'low-angle' grip.

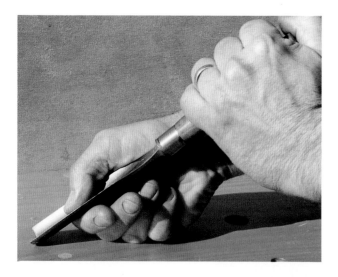

Fig 2.5   Two poor tool grips: the 'backcrank' and the 'snooker cue'.

the handle, to give extra control, and rest the heel of this hand on the wood. The right hand propels the tool forward against the resistance of the left hand, and rotates the tool as required. The left hand controls the forward push of the right, tensing, or breaking, against it. Once you have mastered the grip, swap hands and hold the tool in a reversed direction.

The 'front' and 'back' hands work *together*, controlling the cut in a precise way. The back hand propels the tool forward, while the front hand provides varying degrees of resistance to this, and hence control. Applications of the grip are also fully explored in the exercises.

POOR GRIPS

Poor carving grips can weaken the strength in the hands and wrists, cause inflexibility, and reduce tool control. Beware of them! There are two very common incorrect grips that you should guard against. The first is known as the 'backcrank', where the hand is cranked back and grips the blade palm uppermost. The second is the 'snooker cue' where the blade slides under a loose front hand, and is essentially only being controlled by the back hand rather than both (see Fig 2.5).

THE IMPORTANCE OF SHARPNESS

Whether carving tools are bought 'ready sharpened' or 'set only' (the bevel ground to an approximate angle but not sharpened), you cannot carve well unless your tools are kept *razor* sharp. Used on a piece of close-grained wood, a really sharp carving tool, with a cutting edge so thin you will not be able to see it, will leave a burnished, shiny cut, with no scratches. Dull tools, on the other hand, tear the wood fibres and are hard to control. No matter how good is your letter design and layout, your work will *always* be spoiled by using tools that are anything less than razor-sharp.

So, be rigorous in your sharpening regime, and never put a carving tool away in a state other than that in which you would like to get it out again. For detailed information on sharpening techniques and equipment, refer to Chapter 3 of my book *Woodcarving Tools, Materials & Equipment*, full details of which appear in the Further Reading section on page 228.

OTHER TOOLS

Besides carving tools (and the correct equipment to sharpen them!), you will need tools for:

- **Preparing the wood**
  Such as planes or belt sanders, unless you can get this done for you. **Routers** are discussed on page 118, and in the right place can be very useful and save time.

- **Drawing out letters on to paper**
  For this you will need pencils, erasers, set squares and rulers.

- **Drawing out letters on to wood**
  Once again you will need rulers, along with masking tape, a try-square, and for some tasks, a marking guage and an adjustable square.

- **Holding the wood**
  Such as clamps. However, there are various methods of doing this, and these are discussed on page 22.

- **Keeping the work clean**
  You will need a stiff brush to clear away chips enabling you to see how the work is progressing. *Do not* blow dust away, as it may get in your eyes, nor wipe the wood with your fingers, as this may dirty the wood.

MALLETS

Two mallets are illustrated in Fig 2.6. These are very useful tools, used when the work (or the wood) is too hard or demanding for pushing tools by hand. A **carver's mallet** is round, as opposed to a carpenter's mallet, which is square. The round shape will not deflect the chisel or gouge handle if the blow is out of alignment, as would a square shape. You *can* use a carpenter's mallet, but you will have to be extra careful, and I do not recommend it.

It is a good idea to have two weights of mallet: a lightweight mallet weighing about 0.5kg (1.1lb), for light, controlled tapping; and a heavier one weighing about 1kg (2.2lb) used for initial stab or stop cuts, and for taking out the bulk of the waste wood in the early stages of carving. If you have to choose between the two, then the heavier one (or an intermediate weight) will do the job of both.

Fig 2.6 *General equipment needed for lettercarving: mallets, clamps, a marking gauge and set square, and a stiff brush to keep the carving clean. The mallets shown here are made from lignum vitae. The larger weighs about 1kg (2.2lb), and the smaller 0.5kg (1.1lb).*

USING A MALLET

The wide-ranging applications of mallet work are explored fully in the exercises, but it is useful to outline the basic technique here. The mallet strike starts at the shoulder, with the elbow kept into the body. The arm descends, but slows down *just before* the blow, to allow a relaxed wrist to whip the mallet onto the gouge or chisel handle. This 'whipping' of the wrist gives greater power to the mallet and requires less effort than if the arm was brought down in a rigid manner.

The gouge or chisel is held like a dagger, 'straddling' the blade and handle and extending the

19

thumb along the handle for greater control (see Fig 2.7). It is not necessary to rest the heel of this hand (or the forearm) on the wood, but this is sometimes helpful for steadying the cutting edge when setting exactly to a line.

Fig 2.7   Striking with the mallet. Note the grip on the tool, especially the thumb on the handle which aids control.

SUITABLE WOODS

Almost any close- and even-grained hardwood is suitable for lettercarving. Make sure the wood is properly kiln- or air-dried to guard against splitting or warping. There are a number of factors you should consider when you are selecting your wood.

INSIDE OR OUTSIDE?

If your lettering is destined to live outside, the wood you use will be subject to the elements, including extremes of temperature. Even allowing for preservatives and varnishes, choose a wood which has inherently good weathering properties, such as oak, iroko or sapele.

DIMENSIONS AND PREPARATION

Generally, the thickness of the wood needs to be at least twice the depth to which you intend to cut. This helps to support the work and avoids it looking flimsy and mean. For most incised work, a thickness of around 25mm (1in) is adequate.

If you buy unprepared wood from timber yards, remember to allow enough waste, and check the wood thoroughly for defects and end shakes (splits). Most places will prepare the wood for you, though there may be a fee. Do remember that wood bought at 'nominal' size is *as sawn from the tree*. It will finish (planed up), somewhat thinner. Grain should always be horizontal, as cutting takes place across the grain for the principal components of letters. Sections of limb or trunk that include the bark are popular for signs, giving a 'country look'. If you cut these yourself, be aware of the danger of the wood splitting if the section you have cut includes heartwood and sapwood. If you can, use yew wood for this kind of work, as it is less prone to such splitting than most other woods, and also gives an attractive section. The *wood must be dry* and safe from splitting before you begin to carve. While soaking wet wood in polyethylene glycol (PEG) replaces the water and prevents splitting, I do not recommend its use as it makes the wood very unpleasant to carve.

Wood above certain dimensions needs to be 'glued-up' to the required size (see Fig 2.8). Simple ribbed butt joints are quite adequate, but dowelling or 'biscuiting' adds strength. Make sure the dowels or biscuits are below the level to which you wish to carve (about one-third of the way from the back of the wood is usually about right), and that the joints are as discrete as possible.

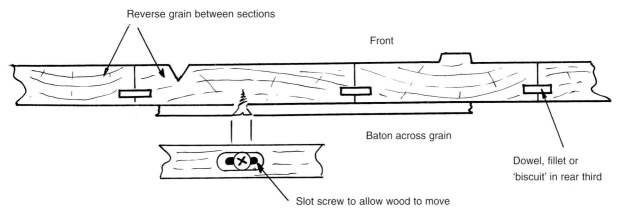

Fig 2.8   Various methods of 'gluing up' (joining together) wood panels for large work.

Large panels need to be lettered in sections. Glue up such panels but leave some joints unglued to allow disassembly into manageable parts. Laying out proceeds with the workpiece in its sash clamps, and the letters are drawn over both glued and unglued joints. The panel is then separated and the letters carved in sections, *skipping the lines which will run over the unglued joints.* Then, beginning at the bottom of the panel, the first free joint is glued up and the lines over it carved, and so on. This way the bulk of the panel passes away from you all the time as it is glued together, limiting any need for a long reach.

FIGURING

Because incised and raised lettering rely on the effects of light and shadow to be effective, figuring in the wood can often get in the way and be detrimental to the effect by distracting the eye. So, for lettering, the blander the wood the better, unless you can find wood that has some 'quiet' workable areas with interesting figuring in other parts that will add to the overall appearance but not interfere with the lettering.

DENSITY

This refers to how open or tight the wood fibres are, rather than how heavy the wood is, although the one does influence the other. Density affects the grain strength and hence the carver's ability to cut weak letter components into it without them breaking off (see Fig 2.9).

Fig 2.9   Tight-grained mahogany (above), and more open-grained oak (below). Generally speaking, the higher the density, the more detail the wood will take.

Low-density woods (most softwoods, such as pine) do not, as a result, carve well. Higher density red and yellow pines, along with cedar, can be carved, but the results are still not as good as those achieved with hardwoods. High-density woods such as pear and other fruitwoods are best suited to fine, intricate letter styles and smaller work. For very small work, you need to use a very high-density wood such as box.

Medium-density woods are those I recommend for the majority of lettering work. Try lime or English oak. This latter has always been a favourite choice for incised and raised lettering. Elm is less suitable for general lettercarving as it has very awkward grain. This makes it unsuitable for carving small raised letters.

THE WORKSURFACE AND HOLDING WORK

Whether your worksurface is a bench or strong table, it needs to be at a convenient working height to prevent backache. The best height is where the bench top comes to a little below your elbow when you are standing. You also need room to put your tools down in a convenient place, and to be able to fix work securely to the worksurface. The bench must be stable and have no 'bounce' (surface springiness that absorbs the energy from the mallet, hence reducing the efficiency of your blows).

Most woodcarvers letter on the horizontal surface of their usual bench. As body weight needs to be put *behind* the cutting edge, gravity is enlisted to assist in this by your being *over* the work. For this reason it is always more difficult to work on a vertical frame, although sometimes there is no choice (for example when lettering a vertical panel *in situ*). Narrow boards are best lettered on a surface tilted about 30° (although you will need an adjacent flat surface to place your tools). Large panels are best lettered in sections to prevent tiring overreach (see page 21).

It is vital that the work be held firmly and not move as carving proceeds. Any movement can ruin an exact cut, and worse, be dangerous. At the same time, though, you usually need to be able to adjust the work from time to time for ease of access. There are numerous ways of fixing work so that it is firm but adjustable: clamps, a frame of wood screwed down around the work, possibly including knock-out wedges, or **snibs** and **dogs** (see Figs 2.10 and 2.11). (Snibs are pieces of wood which rest on the workpiece but are screwed to the bench top. Dogs are large metal staples hammered between a waste part of the workpiece and the bench top.)

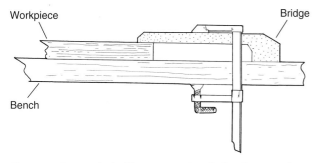

Fig 2.10 One method of fixing a panel to the bench so as to keep the clamps clear using a bridge of wood.

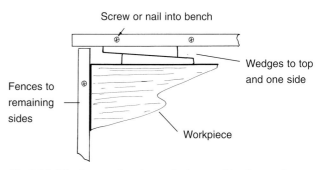

Fig 2.11 The fence and wedge method, as used in the exercises.

LIGHTING

Good lighting is vital, for the health of your eyes and the quality of your work. Try to mirror the light in which the finished letters will appear, if at all possible. Some cross light, such as from an adjustable bench-standing anglepoise or similar lamp, will help to throw the shadows created by the lettering. When you have finished your lettering (incised or raised), change the lighting by, for example, taking the work outside. This will show up any defects hidden by artificial lighting which might need touching up.

SAFETY

It is essential to follow safe working practices. The following basic guidelines must always be followed:

- Always make sure the workpiece is held securely.

- Always place your tools down carefully, and do not allow their edges to project over the edge of the bench.

- Always keep your carving tools razor sharp. Blunt tools require more force to cut with, making them more dangerous, not less.

- Always keep your hands and fingers *behind* the cutting edge. *Never* direct the tool towards any part of your body. Always keep both your hands on the tool, unless you are using a mallet.

- Never try to catch a falling carving tool – let them drop, as trying to catch them can result in serious injury to your hand. Always wear strong footwear to protect your feet against the same threat.

- Always use a carver's brush to remove dust and woodchips. Never blow them away, as this risks getting dust in your eyes.

CHAPTER 3

THE PROCESS OF LETTERCARVING

AIMS

- To make some broad preliminary observations on how lettering is 'made'.
- To see lettercarving as a sequence of stages, each building on the last.
- To note the importance of rhythm and efficiency in lettercarving, and ways in which these are achieved.

There is a sequence of steps in carving a lettered board or panel. The sequence shown in the summary chart below is not immutable, and will vary between workers and the work, but it has a logic which you will find contributes to efficient working and a successful result.

STAGES OF LETTERCARVING

PRELIMINARY STAGE

1 Rough sketches, on paper, to scale.
2 Firming up.
3 Final drawing, on paper, full size.

PREPARATORY STAGE

4 Preparing the wood.
5 Transferring, or laying out the text, on to the wood.

CARVING STAGE

6 Securing the workpiece.
7 Carving the letters.

FINISHING STAGE

8 Cleaning up and finishing the surface.

In lettercarving it is quite often the case that the hidden preliminary design stages take longer, and in many ways are more important, than the carving itself. As you will see this is also very important to bear in mind when costing your work.

This section is intended to give you a good overview of the basic stages of lettercarving, and covers all those areas you should be aware of before you commence the incised lettering exercises. The finer points (though by no means any less important) of the design and layout stages, such as considerations of family resemblance, 'colour' and optical adjustment, along with the benefits of your own research and the design of your own letterforms, are all covered in Chapter 9. By this time you will have completed all the exercises and be thoroughly competent in the two forms of lettercarving, ready to consider the vital stage of design and aesthetics in detail.

ROUGH SKETCHES TO WORKING DRAWINGS

This is where lettercarving usually starts. Unless the design is very simple, or you feel very confident, then you should not miss out this stage!

Rough sketches are quick to do and will save a lot of time and frustration in the long run. Think of the first rough sketches as an exploration, in which you try to fix what's in your mind's eye on to paper (see Fig 3.1).

Concentrate on making quick, small sketches. There is no need to draw cap and base lines – just line up the letters and words by eye into neat rows. Only the outline of the letters is needed. You can leave out the serifs at this stage.

If you are carving a lot of the same size and style of alphabet, then making a set of stencils or templates can save a lot of time. These can be cut out of cardboard, soft thin tin, or aluminium, using carving tools (don't forget to re-sharpen them!) (See Fig 3.2).

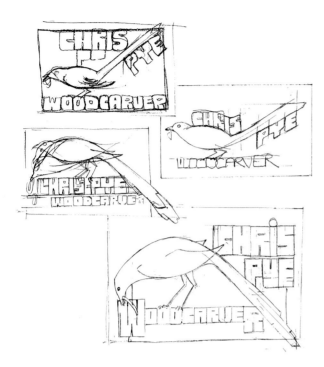

Fig 3.1   Rough sketches showing the development of the idea for the display sign, the final working drawing of which is illustrated on page 26.

Fig 3.2   Letter templates in aluminum.

Sketch down the idea and then try to improve upon it. Use a soft pencil which can be easily erased, or alternatively use chalk on wood or a blackboard at this early stage.

Use the rough sketch stage to:

- Try out, and firm up, your ideas.

- Experiment with different letter styles and sizes.

- Adjust the spacing between letters, words and lines.

- Check the overall arrangement for sense.

Rough sketches are particularly helpful if you make them to *scale*. If you know the panel or board size, draw some frames to these proportions for sketching in. (If you have the panel ready-made then be sure to check first for confusing figuring in the wood which may affect the layout and needs to be taken into account. Bear in mind where the final work is to be sited, its lighting and the angle at which it will be viewed.)

One way to begin is to count up the letters, add a letter for each space, divide the total between the number of lines you have in mind and see what happens. Once you have a few sketches started, you will have something concrete with which to work.

Experiment by moving the words around, and try different arrangements and sizes for sense, emphasis and appearance. Emphasis on certain words can be added as a result of their positioning, or by making them different sizes, weights or styles (such as italicizing) (see Fig 3.3). Think of emphasis as you would when speaking, and you will understand the need to be *selective* for emphasis to work well.

The end result will be a good rough draft, which may include a few of the intended letters drawn full size, over to one side. The first draft should show your intentions clearly enough to:

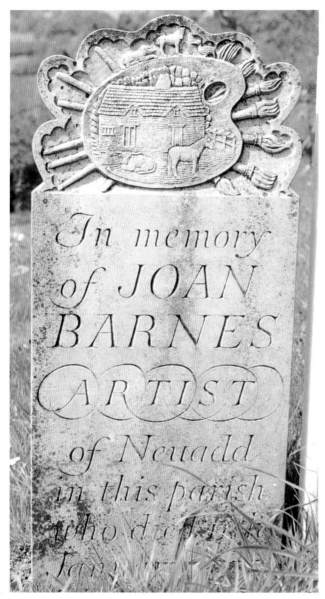

Fig 3.3   A gravestone showing how emphasis comes from different sizes and styles of lettering, as well as their arrangement.

- Proceed to working drawings.

- Be used in discussion with a client if this is required.

- Cost the work.

It is unwise to go as far as preparing a final working drawing without such preliminary layout and cost agreements.

FIRMING UP

When you have a good idea of the way you want to tackle the lettering, move from small, scaled sketches to ones in which the letters are drawn full size on to paper. From your preliminary rough drawings you should be able to work out the letter heights and the distance between lines of text.

Draw cap and base lines in Biro on the paper, but transfer your preliminary sketches to the paper in soft pencil. This way you can rub out and adjust letterforms, while maintaining guide lines. At this stage some 'cutting and pasting' as a means of adjusting the letter spacing, can be a great help.

You can work on the lines in any order, but it is a good idea to work on the longest line, or the one likely to cause most trouble, first. This will give you a sense of spacing for the remainder (see Fig 3.4). To get a better feel for the letter weight, the letters can be shaded to emphasize their forms against the white of the paper.

Fig 3.4   Letters carved above the door of a small church in Abensberg, Bavaria. The spacing of letters relative to the length of lines is very important. You can see here that there is a conflict between the lengths of words and the available space, which to an extent spoils the effect of the lettering.

As your layout reaches a firm arrangement, ask yourself the following questions:

- Is the lettering too tight or too loose, and of an even colour throughout?

- Are there large gaps, or tracks, or empty spaces apparent within the lettering structure?

- Are the line breaks sensible and meaningful?

- Are the letterforms consistent, and are there adjustments to be made to make them appear pleasing to the eye, such as the spacing between them?

- Are the words spelled correctly?

Although the final result of this stage may look rather tatty, you should have answered all these questions and as a result feel in control and happy with what you are undertaking.

FINAL WORKING DRAWING

Firmed-up sketches, as described so far, *may* be good enough to carve from, and if you decide they are, check that the lines are drawn precisely enough (see Fig 3.5). It is not uncommon to find blurred lines in students' drawings that are the result of heavy working-over with the pencil. Remember that a chisel will cut a precise edge and your final drawing must place this edge exactly.

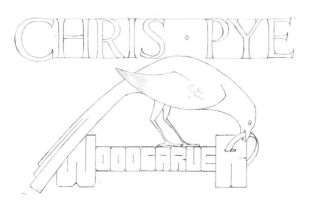

*Fig 3.5 The final working drawing for the display sign. The initial **C** has been made larger to reduce the sense of space on the left. The finished sign is illustrated on page v.*

It is far better to make another, final set of full-size working drawings. You might like to include some shading to show how the V section creates light and shadow. The arrangement should now be thoroughly

worked out and all the spatial and form problems of the letters solved.

Always remember that is is easy to alter lines on paper. Don't proceed unless you are completely satisfied. Hoping everything will 'work out' on the wood is a perilous course to take, because it very rarely does!

Your working drawing may have been given to you by a client. Look at the drawing *as a carver*, to see if there are changes you need to suggest to carve the letters well (see page 6). You may be asked to prepare a sample letter or two (such as the incised letter **A** shown in Fig 3.6). Clients are usually quite willing to discuss their requirements and listen to your views, just as you should always listen to the client. After all, it's in the interest of everyone to get the best result.

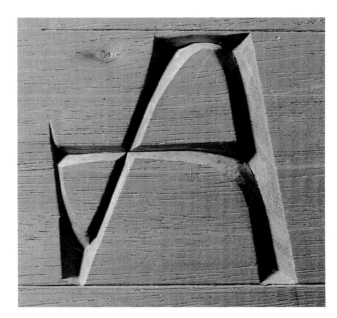

Fig 3.6 Carving a sample of an unusual letter style will establish the best way to tackle the carving.

TRANSFERRING THE DRAWINGS

In spite of all the effort you have put into producing it, regard your working drawing as a guide only, and not as a definitive pattern. If the drawing is meticulously followed as it is transferred to the wood, the final result will usually look a bit stiff and contrived. You may also have to consider grain and figuring, and make slight changes – after all, wood and paper do look different.

Setting out your design on to the wood gives you a last opportunity to adjust and check its position or shape. Always remember, once letters are cut, the layout (and any regrets) will be permanent!

Position the cap and base lines on the wood first, with centre lines if needed, and mark the points where each line of letters starts.

The two commonest ways of transferring a working drawing to the wood are described below.

CARBON PAPER

Although seen as the quick and obvious method, I do not personally recommend it. The wood is not visible, nor are the cap and base lines. There is always some discrepancy between the original and the carbon lines, so letterforms may vary and the letters may not always be positioned correctly, undoing your previous efforts. Errors will be compounded if you trace the lettering from an original first, so there is further work to be done tidying up. In addition, the ink left on the wood surface will smudge and dirty the wood.

LETTER TO LETTER

This is my preferred method. It avoids the pitfalls of carbon paper while still being quite quick, and keeps control over the layout.

Fix a line of lettering accurately to the board *above the cap line* with masking tape, leaving a little space. It may be necessary to cut or fold the working drawing itself (or a photocopy of it) into lines of text.

You need a fine line on the wood to work to. A fine Biro is better for this than a pencil, where the hand resting on the wood as you carve tends to blur the pencil lines, and even rub them out. Thin Biro ink dries, remains cleaner, and has the added advantage that boundary and other lines can be marked on in different colours.

Measure across from wood to paper accurately with a set square and draw all the verticals between the cap

and base lines (see Fig 3.7). On a large panel it may be necessary to use a try square (of the kind used by draughtsmen) or clamp a strip of wood from which to run a plastic drawing square. The spacing of the letters is now established.

Fig 3.7 *Transferring the drawing to the wood. Begin by drawing the verticals between the cap and base lines.*

Fill in the horizontals, obliques and curves using a ruler and compass if necessary (see Fig 3.8). It is not necessary to draw in serifs and small details; these can be directly carved and shaped with the tools by eye.

Fig 3.8 *Filling in the horizontals, obliques and curves.*

27

CARVING

Carving the letters transforms what began as a flat, two-dimensional drawing into three dimensions, bringing the effects of light and shadow into play. Remember to always see the layout on the wood as a guide rather than a rigid pattern that you must slavishly follow.

Arrange the lighting and set out your tools. There is a sequence to carving letters, and this varies for incised and raised letters respectively. For *incised lettering* the pattern is normally like this:

1   Vertical straights.

2   Diagonal straights.

3   Horizontal straights.

4   Corners.

5   Curves.

6   Serifs.

For *raised lettering* the pattern is normally like this:

1   Approximate outlining of letters.

2   Lowering and levelling the ground.

3   Setting in the letters and finishing off.

The order of work may vary a little, depending on the letter style. You may, for example, add the serifs to the straights before passing on to the curves, but the lists show the usual pattern.

The order of work for incised lettering is very specific and is designed to maximize efficiency. Actual carving, whether lettering or otherwise, is not taking place when the tools are lying on the bench – or even when they are in mid-air between the bench and the work. In order to speed up the work, the carver minimizes 'down time' by using each tool for as long as possible. Different sections of a letter (e.g. straight parts) are cut with *different tools* and using a different approach to other sections (e.g. curved parts). The carver learns to recognize what tool is needed and maximize its use, before moving on to the next section and hence the next appropriate tool.

Carving in this ordered way requires practice, but it economizes on effort and time (which has financial implications). It also gives rise to a rhythm in the work: the carver gets into what is best described as a 'flow' or 'momentum'. The cuts, through repetition, take on authority and precision; the amount of effort required diminishes, and the resulting work has a freshness and crispness.

If you lack confidence, or are starting a large amount of lettering, or perhaps having an 'off' day, you will tend to follow the master drawing closely to begin with. As I have already mentioned, the danger with this is that the result can look over-planned, and even self-conscious.

One way to avoid this in a group of lines is to start the carving somewhere in the middle, not at the beginning. Viewers always take most note of *initial* words and letters. When your return to carve these you will have relaxed and got into the rhythm of the work. As a result, the opening letters will appear fresh and the 'stiffer' letters will merge into the middle of the text and be less noticeable.

Make it an inflexible rule to finish each cut *cleanly* before passing on to the next. Don't leave a trail of ragged cuts or unfinished shapes with promises to go back and touch them all up – the reality is that you won't. It is normal practice to carve one line of lettering at a time. Be sure to check over *each line* critically before moving on to the next.

FINISHING

When all the carving is complete, change the lighting, take the workpiece outside, even turn it upside down – anything to freshen a jaded eye. If possible, leave the work a day or two before coming back to make a final inspection. Check over for torn grain and untidy cuts, but avoid 'fiddling' and overworking the letters.

To remove layout lines, you can use a block wrapped with fine sandpaper (minimum 150 grit), or a flat scraper. There is a danger that, if you are over-zealous in removing surface wood, the actual positions of the letter edges will be altered. What was the side wall

Fig 3.9 These signs for a country park were first painted, ignoring any layout lines that had been drawn previously, then sanded with a fine belt sander, and finished.

of the trench becomes the edge. This is a good reason for keeping the walls as flat and clean as possible.

After cleaning up the surface in this way you will need to check over the shapes once again, and possibly adjust some of the edges by eye.

'Finishing' might also involve painting the letters, or varnishing or oiling the work to protect and enhance it (see Fig 3.9). Don't rush this stage – you will have already spent a long time on the carving. Always experiment on a separate piece of wood with a few carved letters to test effects you are unsure of.

COSTING

Most people, including clients, have no idea how long it takes to produce a finished piece of lettercarving. The whole process *may* be very quick, with familiar work, competence and confidence, but often it is not, and there are many hidden costs (see Fig 3.10).

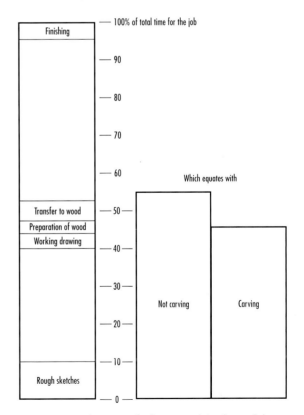

Fig 3.10 A rough timing of a lettering job in the workshop gave this distribution of time. As is clearly shown here, it is common to spend far more time on design than on carving.

29

It is not enough simply to charge for the act of cutting letters. You may need to allow the same length of time for planning, laying out a working drawing stage and transferring to the wood, as for the actual carving – sometimes two or three times as long, depending on the work. This will have to be judged, and only experience can help here.

Lettering by hand is therefore fairly expensive compared to simple painted letters. It is one reason why automatic copying (routing) machines, which need minimal skill, have tended to take the place of hand lettering with carving tools.

Customers are always happier when they know where their money is going and what they are getting for it. This may mean explaining what is involved in the process from rough sketches to finished wood, pointing out the joys of owning something made by a skilled hand and so on. You are also able to be flexible in the choice of styles, sizes and colours, and can mention that a carved sign, for example, will last far longer than a painted-only sign.

COMMON MISTAKES

More than almost any other form of carving, it is difficult, if not impossible, to correct a lettercarving mistake (see Fig 3.11).

Usually, it is not problems with the actual carving that cause a sample of lettering to fail, but the layout (refer back to Fig 3.4 on page 25). So, time spent on the preliminary design and layout stages is always well spent.

Always double check your spelling. For reasons I'm too embarrassed to go into, I now have a habit of checking the spelling of words backwards. It is so easy to see what you want to see, and not what is in front of you (see the name stamp project on page 213).

The hard cure for the fear which many students have of making mistakes is practice, which develops confidence. Tensing up is a good way to push a possible mistake into actually happening, so a relaxed, concentrated attitude from the outset is best. While your confidence is improved but still growing, come to the final edge and shape of a letter in a *gradual* way, rather than taking off too much in one flamboyant, and in essence *over*-confident, cut.

There *is* a degree of adjustment possible in lettercarving. Sometimes a mistake in one part can be incorporated by changing the style slightly. Many incised letters which were intended to be lightweight have ended up rather heavier as a result, and many a raised letter lighter!

Inserting pieces of wood or planing back a particular part of the board and recarving are unsatisfactory solutions to mistakes. Both expedients remain visible, a source of dissatisfaction to the carver, and a poor advertisement. Sometimes you may just have to grit your teeth and start again.

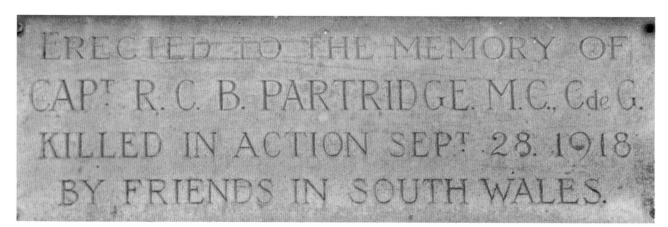

Fig 3.11 Mistakes can take the form of double meanings, as in this engraved copper memorial plaque over a lychgate!

Opposite: 'Smale Fowles' by Gillian Maddison.

PART TWO
INCISED LETTERING

CHAPTER 4

ABOUT INCISED LETTERING

AIMS

This chapter is a catch-all for important general information about incised lettercarving. Some of it you will need to know before you start, the remainder will be useful when you begin your own lettering projects.

'STAB' AND 'STOP' CUTS

A **stab cut** occurs when the cutting edge of a carving tool is pushed, or thumped with a mallet, into the wood. Sometimes just the corner of the tool is used. The effect is simple and precise, and no wood is removed. Stab cuts may be used to create an effect in their own right (see 'Stabbing the root line', page 34).

A **stop cut** is one placed deliberately to prevent the wood fibres from tearing into areas where you don't want them to. Stop cuts disappear in the final carving when they are incorporated into other cuts (see Fig 4.1).

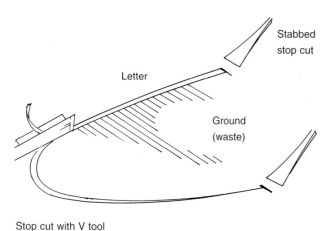

Stop cut with V tool

Fig 4.1   Stop cuts produced by the V tool and the corners of fishtail chisels.

In lettering, stop cuts normally involve stabbing with the corner of a skew or fishtail chisel (see Fig 4.2).

You will need both stop and stab cuts in every style of incised lettering, and these extremely useful techniques are described in the exercises in the next chapter.

Fig 4.2   Making a stop cut with the corner of the skew chisel prevents the grain of the wood breaking off beyond the serif.

DEPTH AND ANGLE OF CUTS

Most incised lettering is cut with two side walls meeting at a centre line, forming an inner V angle at the bottom of the resultant trench.

Trenches of any width are usually incised at an angle of about 60°, which gives the best overall light and shadow effect. A deviation from this of up to plus or minus 10° will be hardly noticeable, but you should always aim to be as consistent as possible. If the two cuts making the V trench are made at exactly the same angle to the wood (say 60°), then the resulting angle at the

e the same (60°). The *depth* to which
in the wood depends on the angle at
ls are offered.

4.3. If a trench of the same width is cut
igher cutting angle (more than 70° to the
contrast of light and shadow on each
ill be greater. This is advantageous when
t is dull, but with a higher cutting angle
e difficult to cut the root of the inner
pecially in the serifs.

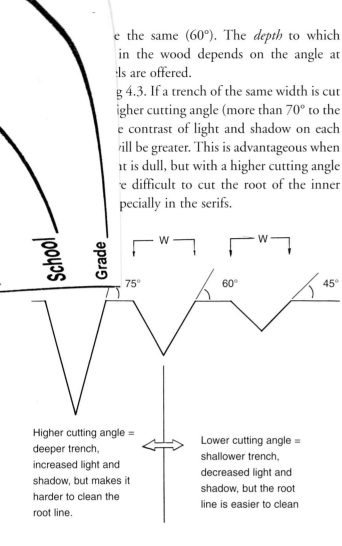

Higher cutting angle =
deeper trench,
increased light and
shadow, but makes it
harder to clean the
root line.

Lower cutting angle =
shallower trench,
decreased light and
shadow, but the root
line is easier to clean

Fig 4.3 *Comparing depths of cut for the same width of trench, cut first with a high cutting angle, then with a low cutting angle. The commonest cutting angle of 60° is shown in the centre.*

If a trench of the same width is cut *shallower*, with a lower cutting angle (less than 50° to the wood), then the contrast of light and shadow on each side will be weak, and the appearance of the letters somewhat flat. A more obtuse angle matters less if the letters are to be painted or otherwise made to contrast with the background, and is preferable if the letters are to be gilded.

A method of estimating the cutting angle is to be found in Chapter 5, Exercise ■4 (see page 44). Experience will give you a sense of what the angle feels like and enable you to go straight to it.

INTERNAL SYMMETRY

Beginners to lettercarving, whether right or left handed, will handle each direction of cut differently. It is important to overcome this bias and cut the angles of the side walls as equally as possible, so that the root lies in the centre. All the parts of the letter will then have the required appearance of symmetry (see Fig 4.4).

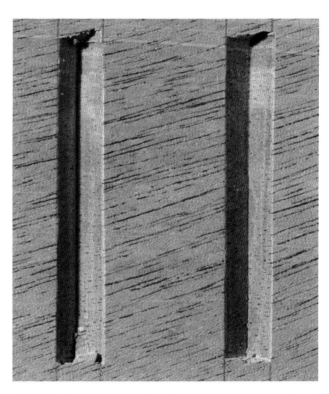

Fig 4.4 *Here you can see why it is important to cut the angles of the side walls as equally as possible. On the left, an asymmetric trench, on the right, a symmetrical trench.*

You *may* choose to deliberately place the root line of the internal angle to one side rather than in the middle, by cutting at two different angles. Some carvers do this to create an artificial shadow effect. Some do it in the lobes of letters, making the outer face of a lobe more prominent with a lower angle. The point is to be able to do this deliberately and consistently, rather than by default. However, I am never happy with these effects as I feel they compete with the natural shadow effects caused by the surrounding light, and do not personally recommend them.

STABBING THE ROOT LINE

Normal practice is to incise a trench so that the two cut faces come together neatly and crisply at the bottom. It's as simple as that – light and shadow will do the rest. However, it may be desirable to stab the deepest point – the root – using whatever chisel or gouge matches the curve exactly. This stabbing of the internal angle extends right into the serif and feathers out at the edges of the letter.

There are two occasions when stabbing the root may be of benefit:

1   When the lighting *in situ* is dull: stabbing tightens up the effect of what light there is, so that the lettering is read as if there were more light than is actually present.

2   When the letters are to be painted: the stab cut helps to keep the bottom angle crisp and prevent pooling of paint or gilder's size.

If wrongly applied, such stabbing can make letters look heavy and roughly worked, even unpleasant. Be selective when you stab the root like this, and use the effect as an exception rather than a rule (see Fig 4.5).

Fig 4.5   *The junctions on the left come together neatly, while those on the right have been stabbed.*

ALTERNATIVES TO THE V SECTION

The V section is the most common and useful of cross-sections for incised lettering, but there are other options. Not all styles of lettering and incising suit one another (for example the roman styles look bad in U section) so discretion and judgment are needed (see Fig 4.6).

Fig 4.6   *Incised trenches with different cross-sections. From left to right: flat-bottomed, U-section and textured sides.*

FLAT-BOTTOMED SECTION

This is a sort of inverted raised lettering, and can be carved following the instructions for inner counters on page 139.

The letters are formed by a channel which has slightly sloping sides to catch light in the same way as those of normal raised lettering. If the sides are square then the letters look rather flat. Don't make the depth too deep – something around half the width of the part of the letter you are carving is normally enough. Square-sectioned trenches suit modern Bauhaus styles, which are sans serif and block-like in form.

U SECTION

A U-shaped section to the letter gives a much softer appearance, as there is no definite point where light is separated from shadow. It is trickier to carve than the normal V section and works better with rounded modern letterforms. Ends are a problem and some adjustment is necessary if there are serifs.

Don't make the channel too deep – no more than the width of the part of the letter you are carving at that point. Deep gouges, (from no. 9–11) are best for this. React quickly to the grain direction if it picks up on one side, and reverse the direction of cut, leaning a little into the roughened face to clean it up.

TEXTURED SIDES

A rough-hewn, forgiving approach can be had by removing most of the wood from the trenches in the way described in the exercises, but finishing off the V section by cutting down the sides with deep gouges. The angle at the bottom can be dressed with a V tool or veiner (small no. 11), or simply stabbed in.

The normal smooth walls are exchanged for rhythmic striations. The effect works best on large letters and is most visually appealing when viewed from a distance.

ALTERNATIVES TO INCISING

OUTLINING

This could be called an intaglio style, as no background wood is removed (see Fig 4.7). The letters are outlined only, by a narrow, tight trench. The centre of each letter remains as the original surface. If the letters are small, stabbing the lines may be all that is needed.

The effect is a lightweight script, useful when there is width but no depth of wood to work with, making deeper incising impossible. I use it for initialling my carved work.

The effect is achieved using the appropriate sizes and shape of gouge. A V tool may also be used, perhaps one with the more acute 45° angle, but remember that the root of a cut with this tool is rounded, not sharp. A knife and the corner of a skew chisel can also be helpful.

Fig 4.7   *Simple outlined lettering (left), and the same with the background frosted (right).*

You can choose to tilt the cuts outlining the letters with an equal bevel on either side of the cut, or with more bevel to the letters, or the opposite face. I prefer to angle (i.e. bevel) the sides of the letters, and have the opposite face a little off vertical, throwing the light more on to the letter than the surroundings.

Here, a V tool or the edges of appropriate chisels are used to form the letter itself (to outline the 'open' letter). The incisions can be a tight, shallow V section, or simply stab marks. The effect is designed to be viewed close up.

STAMPED LETTERING

Outlined letters can be filled in with some form of punch such as a **froster** or **frosting tool**, giving a contrasting surface texture to the surrounding wood. Alternatively, the letters can be left hollow and the surrounding area textured with tool marks, or **frosted** (see Fig 4.7). The froster is discussed on page 117 and its use demonstrated in Chapter 8, exercise **R** 14.

Frosting requires a sufficiently strong mass of wood on which to work, and, as with outline lettering, its light, shaded effect depends on the initial crisp outline for success. The effect will not work in isolation, but only on outlined letters.

Fig 4.8 'Marketplace', carved in maple by Douglas Williams, is an excellent example of successfully carved large letters.

WORKING WITH LARGE LETTERING

I have used a letter height of about 50mm (2in) in the practice chapters (Chapter 5 and Chapter 8). This is a good size to practise with and is subsequently useful for creating signs. You may of course want to carve a letter that is very much larger: perhaps twice, or four times the size, for a sign designed to be seen at a considerable distance (see Fig 4.8). Although the layout is essentially the same (there are differences – see page 171 in Chapter 9), letters of this size do create certain practical problems.

Geometrically, incising at a cutting angle of 60° gives you a trench root depth of a little less than nine-tenths of the letter width at the surface. A rough and easy guide is to assume that a 60° angle of cut gives you *about the same depth of letter as width.* So, if the main vertical stem of a letter is 25mm (1in) wide you would be cutting to a similar depth. A good rule of thumb is to have around the same thickness again of wood *beneath* the incised letters, so in this example you would be looking to work in wood about 50mm (2in) thick.

It is easy to see how, as letters get larger, both the labour costs (there is a lot more wood to be removed) and the material costs (thicker wood) increase considerably. In order to contain such cost increases as much as possible you could decide to:

- **Use thinner wood.**
  Thin wood can make the result look either lightweight, in the sense that letters need 'anchoring', or simply mean. The larger the lettering, the more supportive should the background appear. A frame around the work may help to overcome any sense of thinness.

- **Reduce the cutting angle.**
  A cutting angle of *less* than 45° will look a bit lifeless and flat (see page 32). However, cutting at 45° means that the depth is only half the width of the letter, so much less material is needed. Painting the letters will offset this loss of depth.

A compromise on the angle, and another on the thickness, is the best solution if cost is a problem, with the final letters being painted for contrast.

When it comes to removing the bulk of the wood, you may not have appropriately large tools to work in the normal manner. The following approach may help:

1 Draw a centre line through each letter stem extending beyond the ends of the letter, from which to line up the root.

2 Use a large V tool to remove wood from the centre. You can use a router here but you need to be very careful to keep within the waste wood and not damage what will become the walls of the V trench.

3 Chop out the waste down the side of the letter and into the V using gouges, keeping the trench profile in mind all the time. When working with hardwood or large letters, a lot of the effort can be saved by using the mallet for the roughing out.

4 Clean up the faces with the flattest gouges, finishing with chisels, and scrapers if necessary. Try and get the side walls of the trench as clean and symmetrical as possible, if not completely flat.

5 Use a V tool to finish off the angle at the base of the groove.

CHAPTER 5

INCISED LETTERING EXERCISES

AIMS

- To give a progressive schedule of incising practice in order to develop incising skills.

- To look at the construction of a particular letter style in detail.

- To acquire understanding and practical techniques that can be transferred to other letter styles.

INTRODUCTION

If you have not incised letters before, this is where you begin! Even if you are already familiar with incising techniques, you should still find the following exercises useful and improving, and even if you are quite expert, you will hopefully come across some hints and tips that will be of benefit.

The essence of practice is in repetition, which allows you to rehearse for the real thing, and helps to develop the necessary manual skills. My experience is that some students start conscientiously enough with the exercises, but after a while fall into a pattern of 'end-gaining'. They accelerate through the work to reach the end as quickly as possible, and this applies equally to the individual exercises and the whole plan of work. Unfortunately, this usually results in their selling themselves short. They end up feeling less competent than they should, carving letters less well than they might, and taking longer to get to a professional level than if they had proceeded more slowly and methodically.

If you recognize this tendency to end-gain in yourself, I strongly urge you to slow down and not rush

through these exercises. The mind and body-memory best absorb small amounts of information, repeated often and connected to other bits of information, with time for assimilation.

When you can successfully carve the letter style shown in the exercises, you will find that you have acquired manual skills which are transferable, or easily adapted, to any other style of lettercarving.

Modern roman is also a very useful style in its own right, with wide applications. It leads on easily to an understanding of the structure of, and the way to cut, Trajan roman and many other lettering styles. As an added bonus, you will find these lettercarving skills will greatly benefit your other carving as well.

EXERCISE PLAN

So as to cater for all abilities, the exercises begin with simple tool strokes and cuts, and these then build into the parts of letters, such as stems and serifs, which are then combined to make finished letters. As the whole lettering process has been broken down in this way, you will usually need to be familiar with what has gone before to make complete sense of what you are doing – so start at the beginning! Your carving skill will dictate how quickly you progress, and it does even experienced carvers no harm to practise and perceive the progression towards successful lettering that these exercises represent.

Letterforms can be divided into four distinct families, and these are shown in Table 2. The exercises work through the families in this order, with each technique building upon the last.

When it comes to actual carving, most students progress well on the straights, but find the curves more difficult to master. More practice is usually needed for these, but, once mastered, students normally find curves far more interesting and enjoyable to carve.

During the exercises, you need only copy exactly the letters I have provided. However, to *really understand* the letters, you need to fully appreciate their design and layout, which is discussed and illustrated fully in Chapter 6. My experience has been that students make the best progress by initially carving letters 'verbatim' using my working drawings, and then going on to examine the individual characteristics of each letter in more detail. In other words, do not try to take everything in all at once, but *do* use the information in Chapter 6 in conjunction with the information provided in the exercises when you feel confident enough to do so.

Where applicable, each exercise includes all the elements outlined in Table 3. A complete list of the carving tools you will require for the incised exercises is shown in Fig 5.1. As you will see, many of the tools in the list are also used in raised lettering.

LETTER FAMILIES	
FAMILY	**LETTERS**
Straight vertical & horizontal components only	E, F, H, I, L, T
Straight components with diagonals	A, K, M, N, V, W, X, Y, Z
Curved components only	C, O, S
Combination of straight and curved components	B, D, G, J, P, Q, U

Table 2

STRUCTURE OF THE EXERCISES	
Context	How the exercise fits into the pattern of lettercarving as a whole
Cross references	Useful points of reference throughout the rest of the book, as applicable
Tools	Specific tool list for the exercise
Method technique	Step-by-step guide to the
Aims and problems	What you should achieve, the type of difficulties you may encounter, and how to overcome them
Variations	Suggestions on how to expand the exercise by using different tools etc., thereby increasing your confidence and versatility.

Table 3

TOOL LIST FOR THE INCISED LETTERING EXERCISES	
FOR THE STRAIGHT COMPONENTS	
• 45mm (1 ³⁄₄in)	straight chisel
• 40mm (1 ⁵⁄₈in)	straight chisel
• 35mm (1 ³⁄₈in)	straight chisel
• 30mm (1 ¹⁄₄in)	straight chisel
• 25mm (1 in)	straight chisel
• 20mm (³⁄₄in)	straight chisel
• 15mm (⁵⁄₈in)	straight chisel

This choice of straight (or alongee) chisels is based on cutting the straight elements of 50mm (2in) letters most efficiently. If you do not have all these sizes, you may need to make one tool to do the work of two, and merge the cuts carefully.

FOR THE CURVED COMPONENTS	
• no. 5 x 16mm (1 ⁵⁄₈in)	straight gouge
• no. 6 x 10mm (³⁄₈in)	straight gouge
• no. 6 x 13mm (¹⁄₂in)	straight gouge
• no. 6 x 20mm (³⁄₄in)	straight gouge

FOR THE SERIFS	
• 13mm (¹⁄₂in)	fishtail chisel
• 13mm (¹⁄₂in)	skew chisel
• no. 4 x 16mm (⁵⁄₈in)	fishtail gouge

Fig 5.1

DRAWING OUT THE LETTERFORMS

For the exercises, simply copy and work from the drawings provided, but bear in mind the following features of the modern roman style (refer to Fig 5.2).

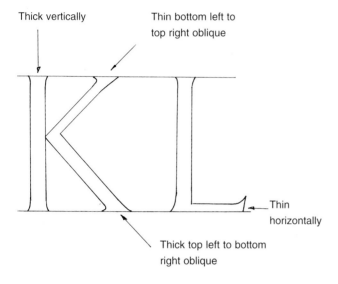

Fig 5.2   Features of modern roman lettering.

- Modern roman letters are made up of thick and thin 'strokes'.

- The thick strokes are twice the width of the thin strokes.

- The thick strokes are about one-eighth of the letter height.

- With a few exceptions, the thick strokes are vertical, or lie sloping diagonally from top left to bottom right.

- The curves are made up of thick and thin parts, aligned as the straight strokes, with the thickest part on the vertical axis.

- Different letters have different widths: some are very thin (**I**, **J**); some very wide (**W**, **M**); some square (**O**, **T**); some less than square (**E**, **B**).

- Stress in *vertical*.

- All stems and arms are straight with parallel sides, not 'waisted' or wavy. This makes the style quick and easy to cut. Waisting as an option is discussed with the other modifications on page 107.

- The curves are also made up of thick and thin parts, aligned as the straight strokes, with the thickest part on the vertical axis.

There are exceptions to these rules, most notably **N** and **Z**, so look out for these as well.

When you want to make practical use of what you have learned, you will need to study Chapter 9 to put the individual letters in context.

What follows will allow you to master the technique of cutting the letters. Shapes which might be a little unrefined at first are easily refined once you get the hang of the method.

EXERCISES

Read through each exercise before beginning it. Have your selected wood (see page 20) prepared and firmly clamped or fixed to a stable bench, with the grain running horizontally (i.e. from left to right) (see Fig 5.3). Check the exercise for wood requirements, and

Fig 5.3   Set up and ready to begin!

always try to have too much wood on hand rather than too little! All the exercises assume right hand dominance. If you are left handed, simply reverse the handing given in the instructions.

STRAIGHT LETTERS

∎1 VERTICAL STABBING WITH MALLET AND CHISEL

CONTEXT

A mallet is needed when incising into tough, hard, wood and wherever the letter size makes hand pushing hard work. Cuts may need some cleaning or truing up by hand after the mallet has taken on the bulk of the task. Here we will produce an 'upright' stabbing cut such as that required for the vertical stems of letters, which prevents grain breaking out in subsequent cuts.

To avoid awkward contortions, you need to be able to swap hands and strike the chisel or gouge with the mallet using the left or the right hand. This is so important that I have made reversing hands a separate exercise (Exercise ∎2, page 41).

CROSS REFERENCES

- Using a mallet (page 19).
- Holding the chisel (page 16).
- Stop cuts (page 32).

TOOLS

- 32mm (1¼in) chisel.
- 1kg (2lb) mallet.

METHOD

1   There is no need to draw anything on to the wood for this exercise. Work anywhere on the surface of the wood that you find comfortable to reach.

2   Grasp the chisel with the left hand across its shoulder and with the thumb extended along the handle.

3   Hold the mallet with the right hand.

4   Position yourself in front of the workpiece and relax both arms and hands. Keep both elbows in towards the body.

5   Place the chisel as if you were carving a vertical letter stem – the cutting edge will be side-on to you. Hold the chisel steady and perpendicular to the wood.

6   Rest the centre of the mallet head on the end of the chisel handle without disturbing it.

7   Raise the mallet about 10cm (4in) and strike the end of the chisel lightly.

8   Without moving the chisel, raise the mallet again, to about head height, and strike firmly downwards. Try to 'think' the blow straight through the vertical chisel and into the wood, and strike cleanly so that the chisel handle is deflected neither to one side or the other (see Fig 5.4).

Fig 5.4   Positioning for a simple stab cut. You can see a successfully completed cut in front of the chisel face.

9   Remove the embedded chisel by levering the handle back and forth *across the width*. Never rock an embedded chisel edge from side to side, as this may snap off some of the edge (see Fig 5.5).

Fig 5.6   Practise until you can create a series of neat stab cuts like these.

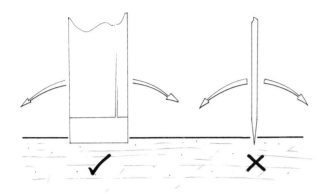

Fig 5.5   If you rock an embedded tool across *its edge there is a real possibility of snapping it. Always lever the handle across the width of the chisel.*

10 You have now made a vertical stab cut. Repeat the two-part strike with the chisel placed a little to one side of the first stab cut. Try not to hold your breath or tense up.

The first little tap bites the chisel edge into the fibres of the wood and locks it in position against any possible movement as the strike proper is prepared. Although not always essential, this two-part strike is a habit to be recommended.

AIMS AND PROBLEMS

You may find striking easy because you are used to hammering or using a mallet, but make sure you can do 10 clean strikes, side by side without deviating the chisel handle, before moving on to the next exercise. The resulting stab mark in the wood should be of uniform width along its length and not thinner at one end.

This simple exercise will help you to develop your hand and eye, and forms the basis of what follows, so if you are not used to such mallet work, you need to do a lot of it – literally hundreds of repetitions, until the action feels comfortable (see Fig 5.6).

VARIATIONS

- Use different sizes of chisel. You will find that the smaller the chisel, the further it is struck into the wood with the same force, so you will need to adjust the mallet blow accordingly. Try using a smaller mallet as well, if you have one.

- Orientate the chisel edges in varying directions, trying to lay several cuts down neatly side by side, as shown in Fig 5.6.

- Create some patterns on the surface of the wood: zig-zags, squares and hatching. Aim to place the corners and lines exactly where you want them.

∎2   VERTICAL STABBING WITH MALLET AND CHISEL, REVERSED HANDS

CONTEXT

After the initial stabbing stop cuts, the sides of the letter are removed, making the characteristic V trench. While all the initial vertical stab cuts can be (and usually are) made without reversing hands, the subsequent angled cuts forming the actual trench must be directed first from one side and then from the other. If the hands are not reversed for this, there will be a strong, easy strike with the mallet from one direction, but a weak strike across the body from the opposite direction. Awkward and unequal striking like this makes it difficult to achieve an equal angle on each side of the trench, and to site the bottom of the V cut cleanly in the centre.

If you have not done it before, reversing hands will feel awkward at first, but it is more efficient, less tiring and gives a more even result in the long run. So do persevere.

Rather than waiting until you need to perform angled stabbing, where reversing is a requirement, get into the habit now by practising it on this simpler, vertical work where it is only an option.

If you are unused to using a mallet you may find that *both* hands feel awkward at first. In some ways this is fortunate, as the facility to use both hands will develop more evenly.

CROSS REFERENCES AND TOOLS

- As Exercise ■1.

METHOD

1   Proceed as with Exercise ■1, but with chisel and mallet hands reversed. You will need to pay more attention to keeping the mallet arm relaxed, and work from the shoulder rather than the elbow.

2   To begin with, make many smaller taps with the head of the mallet, allowing it to drop in a loose, natural way on to the chisel handle. This will develop your eye for a strike from this side. As you begin to feel confident you can put more and more power into the blow. If you begin to miss, ease off and go back to concentrating on your aim.

AIMS AND PROBLEMS

These are the same as those in Exercise ■1, with the addition that you will need to do far more work on your 'weak' side. It is probably impossible to bring your weak hand up to the strength and co-ordination of your

dominant one, but you should be able to develop sufficient co-ordination and strength for incising letters from both sides equally. You need only a desire to achieve this and enough time working at it. The crucial point is: don't just 'hope that it will come', you *must* keep practising.

VARIATIONS

These are also the same as Exercise ■1, but it will also help enormously if you consciously start to improve the co-ordination and strength on your weaker striking side in other ways. Make a point of using your weaker hand for any co-ordinated activity where you would normally use your dominant hand, even if it is only to pick up your cup of tea.

■3   VERTICAL STABBING WITH MALLET, TO A LINE

CONTEXT

The stab cut practised in the previous two exercises is normally placed in the centre of a straight letter element, such as an upright stem. A centre line is not normally drawn in, and the cutting edge is placed by eye. However, it is a good exercise to start by setting the cutting edge on a line to test accuracy, and then setting in the edge neatly between lines to see if that accuracy can be maintained.

CROSS REFERENCES

- As Exercise ■1.

TOOLS

- Set square and pencil.

METHOD

Essentially, this exercise is the same as the two previous ones, but concentrates on accurately following lines.

Fig 5.7   Stabbing accurately to a line.

Fig 5.8   Position the near corner halfway between the lines and lower the edge to bisect the space.

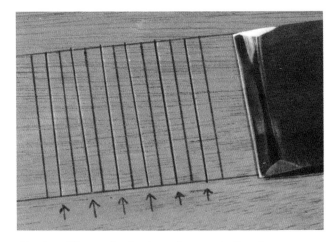

Fig 5.9   The completed stab cuts between the lines. Inspect your results critically to see if there is room for improvement.

1   Draw parallel cap and base lines the same distance apart as the width of the chisel.

2   Towards the near edge of your piece of wood, draw about 10 parallel lines a little longer than the chisel you are using, and about 6mm (¹/₄in) apart.

3   Place the edge of the chisel accurately on the first line, strike, and remove the tool, as before. Work along the row of vertical lines in this way (see Fig 5.7).

4   Draw another series of lines, and repeat this exercise with reversed hands.

5   Draw another series of parallel lines, and this time place the chisel edge exactly *between* the lines. The best way is to place one corner of the chisel edge half-way between the lines first, and then position the other corner so that the cutting edge lies exactly in the middle of and parallel to the two lines (see Fig 5.8). You will need to look to either side of your chisel hand to position the blade, so that when it comes to striking the chisel, make sure the handle is still upright.

6   Strike the handle with the mallet in the usual way, remove the chisel, and repeat along the row of lines (see Fig 5.9).

7   Draw yet another series of lines and repeat this exercise with reversed hands.

AIMS AND PROBLEMS

Stabbing between the lines is more tricky as the centre of the two lines has to be judged by eye. Ideally you should do this with just the hand holding the chisel, but if you find yourself a little shaky, rest the forearm of your chisel hand on the wood. If that is not enough, use the first couple of fingers of the mallet hand, without putting the mallet down, to guide the setting of the chisel.

The resulting stab cuts should lie in the middle of, and parallel to, the drawn lines, and be of an even thickness along their length. Aim for 10 neat cuts like this.

VARIATIONS

Try repeating the exercise with lines drawn horizontally and obliquely, and use different sizes of chisel, including a fishtail chisel if you have one.

◼4 ANGLED CUTTING WITH MALLET

CONTEXT

This exercise shows you how to make opposing angled cuts with the chisel to remove a V trench. An initial stop cut (as in the previous two exercises) comes first, to prevent wood splintering out of control.

You need to be able to assess the angle and hit the chisel with the mallet consistently. It is worth practising an angled strike on its own first to gain confidence, before adding this angled cut to a previously made stop cut to remove wood. Hence, the 'cuts' in this exercise don't actually 'go' anywhere.

TOOLS

- As Exercise ◼1.

METHOD

1 Work as if you are dealing with the vertical stems of letters. The edge of the chisel will be side-on to you, the mallet in your right hand.

2 Refer to Fig 5.10. Start with the chisel dead upright, at 90° to the wood.

3 Lean the chisel to the right (into the mallet) so that the angle to the wood is halved (i.e. 45°).

4 Slowly return the handle, and halve the distance back to the upright position. If you are accurate, this will give you an angle of 67° or so between the chisel and the wood.

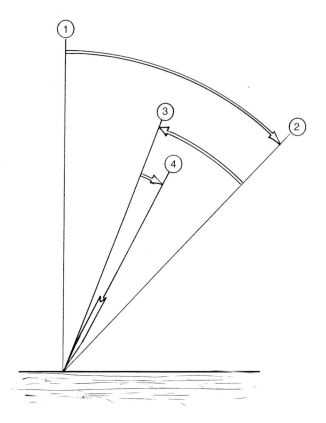

Fig 5.10 Achieving a 60° angle to the wood. (1) start vertically; (2) halve this to 45°; (3) halve this again, and then move the tool down a little more (4).

5 You require the chisel to be angled at about 60°, so lower the handle again *just a little* and you will be there. Make a light tap as previously, followed by a proper mallet strike. Just let the chisel thump into the wood. You soon will see why a stop cut is needed.

6 Remove the chisel correctly (see Exercise ◼1, page 41) and repeat.

AIMS AND PROBLEMS

You will soon get used to what a 60° cutting angle looks like and will be able to angle the chisel correctly almost straight away. If you want to test the angle, make up a standing template of 60° and compare it against your 'manually-calculated' angle, arrived at by the method described above (see Fig 5.11).

Fig 5.11 A template can help to begin with if you are still not sure what the angle feels like.

It is better for the cutting angle to be slightly too shallow than too steep. If the letters are too shallow they can be deepened, but not the other way round.

Do remember that *consistency* is the most important thing, rather than an exact angle. Although in practice, as long as the letter components (say the vertical stems) remain the same width, and the centre line of the trench is in the middle, some variation of the angle is not noticeable, don't let this be an excuse for inconsistency. Try to get the 60° angle the same each time by approaching it in exactly the same way. Too much variation in angle will show up as uneven depth and shadowing in the letters.

The initial mallet tap to snick the chisel edge into the grain and anchor it is even more important when cutting at an angle than when cutting vertically. There is always a tendency for the chisel to come off line when the mallet is raised, especially at an angle, and the first light tap prevents this.

VARIATIONS

Try holding the chisel at angles between 70–50° to get a sense of different angles which you will need in the future, and use different widths of chisel, as in Exercise ∎1.

∎5 ANGLED CUTTING WITH MALLET, REVERSED HANDS

CONTEXT

As I have already explained, striking from both sides by reversing hands is far better than cross-body contortions. This is especially the case when working at an angle (see Fig 5.12). Some people find a reverse angle-cut easier to hit than a reverse vertical, because the handle leans into the mallet with the angled cut.

Fig 5.12 If you don't swap hands when you make angle cuts for the trench walls, you cannot avoid working awkwardly across your body, as you can see here. If nothing else, you will find it hard to see what you are doing.

TOOLS

- As Exercise ∎1.

METHOD

1 Proceed exactly as in the previous exercise but with the hands reversed.

2 You may find that, to begin with, you will be concentrating so much on the strike that you will lose the angle. Normally it is quite difficult to achieve the required co-ordination straight away. Don't worry; try to relax and enjoy the challenge – the important thing is to keep going.

3 As reversing hands can be quite tiring, I suggest you switch between this exercise and the previous one, as was suggested between Exercises ∎1 and ∎2. The brain is quite good at mirror-imaging and will pick up the similar co-ordination needs from both sides. So, practise say 10 mallet strikes from the left, then 10 from the right.

Keep practising until you get the hang of working from both sides, then set yourself a target of 10 consistent strikes with the hands in the 'reversed' position.

AIMS AND PROBLEMS

You should now have the skills required to remove a trench of wood and incise a straight 'element', such as the stem of a letter, and this is the next step, demonstrated in Exercises ∎6 and ∎7. Be sure you are comfortable with vertical stabbing and angled cutting, using both hands, before you move on to the next exercise.

VARIATIONS

This exercise can be varied in the same way as Exercise ∎3. You may also find it useful to refer to the variation notes in Exercise ∎2.

∎6 VERTICAL TRENCH WITH MALLET

CONTEXT

Using the mallet to cut trenches saves an enormous amount of time. In fact, some woods may be so hard, or the letters so large, that mallet work is nigh-on compulsory.

A principal part of most modern roman letterforms with straight elements is a vertical stem, as, for example in the letters **B, D, E, F, N** and so on. The vertical trench needed to form this stem is the easiest to cut, as it goes across the grain. Once the vertical trench is mastered, you can move on to oblique and horizontal trenches. Such trenches are major 'building blocks' in many other alphabet styles.

The stem trench is incised with three cuts: a stop cut to the centre (see Exercises ∎1, ∎2 and ∎3), and an angled cut from either side (see Exercises ∎4 and ∎5).

CROSS REFERENCES

- As Exercise ∎1.

TOOLS

- Set square, ruler.

METHOD

1 With the grain of the wood horizontal to you, use the set square to draw a series of parallel, vertical, lines about 6mm (¼in) apart and the length of the chisel, spreading them about 13mm (½in) apart. Leave a gap between the lines and the edge of the wood. These lines represent the uprights of a letter.

2 Refer to Fig 5.13. For the stop cut, hold the chisel in your left hand and set it vertically and exactly between the first pair of lines. Strike it cleanly with the mallet as described previously, to give a strong impression in the wood.

3 Remove the chisel correctly and place it on the right hand line, angled at about 60° to the wood. Visualize a point immediately below the centre line at which you are aiming.

4 Strike with the mallet to cut down towards this point below the centre line, without changing the angle. You will see how the pressure from the bevel into the wood pushes fibres into the stop cut.

5 Remove the chisel, reverse hands and line up the cutting edge on the left hand line at the same angle.

6 Use the mallet to make a second cut from the opposite direction towards an imaginary point below the centre line.

7 At this point a V-shaped chip of wood the length of the chisel should come away. However, if the side cuts haven't driven the cutting edge in deeply enough you may need to repeat the angled blows with the mallet merging the cuts. There is usually no need to repeat the stop cut.

8 Move on to the next pair of lines and repeat the stop and angled cuts to produce a second trench (see Fig 5.14).

Fig 5.13 Making the centre stop cut, following by the two angle cuts which release the chip and shape the trench. This simple technique is a crucial one, and must be mastered.

Fig 5.14 You should end up with a series of vertical practice trenches like these. Make sure they are all of an equal width.

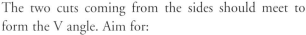

The two cuts coming from the sides should meet to form the V angle. Aim for:

- Clean cuts with sides as flat as possible.

- A clean intersection at the bottom of the cuts without stab marks – a dead-straight edge to the tool assists greatly in achieving this.

- The root line parallel to the edges. Each side should be equal, and the trench have a sense of symmetry.

- Trenches of consistent depth and width.

Assess each trench after cutting it to see if you have a tendency to cut one side at a higher angle than the other. Adjust your technique as necessary for the next attempt, and keep the trenches you make for the next exercise.

AIMS AND PROBLEMS

Cutting a neat trench with the mallet needs care to get it right, and you will see how initial practice with the component cuts in the previous exercises enables you to concentrate on forming the trench, rather than, say, hitting the end of the chisel handle (see Fig 5.15).

Fig 5.15 Combining what you have learned so far to cut a neat trench with the aid of the mallet: the stop cut, followed by the two angled cuts, reversing hands for the second of these.

The mallet often produces work which needs some tidying up by hand, and this is the subject of the next exercise. For now it is best to resist the temptation to dispense with the mallet, and seek to improve your skill with it. If the walls of the trench show mallet marks or the bottom is not quite sharp and clean, but the walls are equal and the centre line parallel, then call this a successful trench, to be touched up in the following exercise.

VARIATIONS

In practice, a lettercarver will start with the mallet at one end of a row of uprights and make all the centre stab cuts before returning to the beginning to make the angled cuts, and then change tools. This is a good way to achieve consistent results, so draw another row of parallel lines but make all the centre stab cuts together, starting at one end. Then make the right-hand angle cuts, then the left hand. Then go along the row cleaning up with the mallet. Repeat the exercise with different sizes of chisel, widths of lines, and different angles (and therefore depths).

■7 VERTICAL TRENCH, TIDYING BY HAND

CONTEXT

Some cleaning up is sometimes required after the mallet work, especially if several strikes were needed. The letter sides may not be absolutely flat, or there may be unacceptably visible mallet lines. The centre line may be offset, or the root of the trench a bit rough.

Tidying up these defects is best left until all the mallet work for a particular run of troughs is finished. The same chisel is then used by hand, before being swapped for another for the next run of mallet work.

With hard woods and large lettering, this sort of cleaning up can be quite tiring and there is a limit to how much wood can be pared away comfortably. So always use the mallet to finish as neatly as possible. For small lettering, the mallet may not be needed at all, and you can push in stop cuts and remove the troughs by hand, working in the way described here.

CROSS REFERENCES

• Holding carving tools (page 16).

TOOLS

• As Exercise ■1.

METHOD

1   Use the troughs made in the previous exercise, or create some new ones with the mallet. Use only those troughs that you think are in a good enough initial condition to be successfully cleaned up by hand.

2   Hold the chisel in the pen and dagger grip, with your dominant (right) hand on blade.

3   To bring sufficient pressure to bear on the chisel, you must bring your body into play. Cross your body with the hand gripping the handle (left) and nestle this hand into the opposite (right) shoulder. Pressure from your body weight is applied, from the shoulder, by leaning into the work. The blade hand guides the cut into the wood (see Fig 5.16).

Fig 5.16 Cleaning up the trench by hand. The root often needs attention at this stage.

4 Begin by stabbing down a line exactly in the centre, which will serve as the final meeting point of the sides – the root.

5 Without changing hand position, use your weight behind the tool to pare down the right hand wall of the trench at the correct 60° angle. Meet the stop cut neatly at the bottom. You will have to adjust your body to the side a little for this.

6 To pare the opposite trench wall you must switch shoulders and bring the hand holding the handle to the left shoulder, *without changing hands on the chisel*. This allows you to maintain a clear view of the work and prevents an awkward body position.

7 Pare the second wall at the correct angle and form a neat V angle at the base of the trench. The wall you choose to pare, or the order in which the walls are cleaned up, depends on what needs to be done. You may be successful with one stroke, or need to take several light cuts to clean up the valley-like trench.

Remember you are aiming to get the sides as flat and cleanly cut as possible, meeting neatly at the bottom without stab marks. Each side should be a mirror image of the other, with the surface edges parallel with the root line. Try to get all the troughs the same depth, by ensuring you cut at a consistent angle and width of line.

Work your way along the troughs cleaning up as many as possible. Don't take too long or fiddle – incising looks better and fresher when it is done by means of a few precise strokes rather than numerous 'tinkering' ones. When you run out of troughs, make some more with the mallet as in the last exercise.

AIMS AND PROBLEMS

If you run into an area of awkward grain, try taking a slightly narrower chisel and paring down the wall with a sideways movement, giving a slicing cut.

When the letter (and therefore the chisel), is very large, cleaning up as described here can be quite hard work. Substituting a narrower chisel and cleaning with a slicing action can be helpful, but take care to merge the

cuts together. In this case, leave the original surface edge as cut by the original, larger, chisel. This will give the neatest line and appearance to the trench.

Aim to finish off 10 good vertical trenches. These will be needed for the next exercise.

18 SERIFS (I)

CONTEXT

Adding serifs to a vertical trench such as that made in the last exercise will produce your first complete modern roman letter: **I**. This is the simplest letter to cut, and its form is partly present in several other straight letters, such as **E** and **L**, as well as those which combine curves, such as **B** and **R**.

There are several important practical points about serifs that you need to know before you begin. Normally, all the straight letter parts are cut first, and the serifs added at a subsequent stage. 'Added' is not quite the right word; serifs must look like an integral part of the letterform and never like an afterthought.

Serifs are *deeper* in their centre than the trench from which they arise. They resemble an inverted pyramid with the deepest point where the face edges come together. For this reason, serifs are best cut with fishtail tools: stop cuts are made first, to control the wood grain within the serif, then a triangular chip of wood is removed with two side cuts and another across the end. In all three angled cuts, the tool corner is pushed deeper into the centre than is possible with the normal 90° corner of parallel-sided tools.

The end wall of a serif slopes into the centre of the inverted pyramid. If you were to cut a vertical stem, say, to its full width – from cap to base line – you would cut into this end wall. When letters are laid out between cap and base lines, the chisel that is used to remove the vertical trench *must be narrower to allow for the serifs at each end* (see Fig 5.17). From this you will gather that the cap and base lines between which you have been incising vertical trenches have served the purpose of the exercise but, in a layout which included serifs, would not have allowed for them.

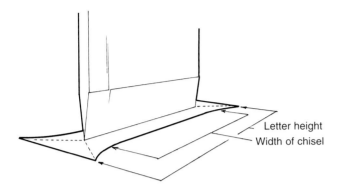

Fig 5.17 A narrower chisel than the letter height is needed to avoid cutting into the end wall of the serifs.

In order to add serifs to the trenches you have cut so far, you will need to draw another set of cap and base lines beyond those originally drawn in Exercise ■7. *The gap required to allow for a serif between the end of a vertical trench and the cap and base lines is usually a little less than the trench width* (see Fig 5.18). When cutting letters with serifs, the width of chisel required must take into account the end wall of the serifs.

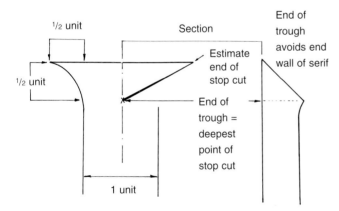

Fig 5.18 Front and side views of the serif in the letter I, showing how to estimate the stop cuts, which go from the root of the serif to the surface at their extremities.

A roman serif has a bracket on either side, not more than half the width of the trench from which it arises. In other words, the serif corners on the cap and base lines of a letter such as **I** will be about twice the width of the trench apart.

Whatever their shape, serifs must look the *same shape* between letters, and lie along, or orientate to, the cap or base lines.

You will find that removing the heel corners for both fishtail gouge and chisel is particularly helpful here for allowing access into the narrower corners of the serifs without fouling the wood on either side (see page 115, Fig 7.11).

CROSS REFERENCES

- Serifs (page 13).

- Pen and dagger grip (page 17).
  Remember to put your shoulder (and weight) behind the cut rather than working from the elbows with arms extended.

TOOLS

- 32mm (1¼in) chisel.
- No. 4 x 16mm (⅝in) fishtail gouge.
- 13mm (½in) fishtail chisel.
  You can use a skew chisel in place of a fishtail, but I recommend the latter, with a 30° skew, using the long point.

METHOD

1 You will need to carve series of neat trenches lying between two parallel lines, as finished in the last exercise. Draw in two more lines, outside and parallel to the first, leaving gaps at either end of about the width of the trench. If you are using the fishtail chisel, the gap should be about 3mm (1/8in). Draw the trench edges up to the cap and base lines as they would be in a proper letter layout.

To begin with, if you are having difficulty visualizing their shape, draw the serifs in, using Fig 5.18 as a guide. In practice the serifs are never drawn in but estimated and cut by eye, which is what you should aim to do and in the following I have assumed the outline of the serifs is not drawn.

51

Fig 5.19 *Stab the first stop cut with the corner of the fishtail chisel.*

Fig 5.20 *Then make the second stop cut.*

Fig 5.21 *Make the first side cut with the fishtail gouge.*

2   Try and visualize the inverted pyramid shape you intend to cut. Starting with the cap serifs, make two stop cuts with the fishtail chisel, first to the right then the left, before shaping the serif proper. In dense wood these can be made with a mallet, but here you can do it by hand. Estimate the line of the cut from the centre of the trench at its end, to a point where the right extremity of the serif will lie. Hold the fishtail chisel in the pen and dagger grip and place it along your estimated line, so that one corner is at the serif centre.

The corner of the fishtail descends to the deepest part of the serif, in the centre. The cutting edge rises out of the wood towards the corner of the serif, stopping at its end when it meets the cap line (see Fig 5.19).

3   Start by pushing the corner of the fishtail vertically down into the centre, keeping the other corner free of the wood. You will find you have to pull back the tool handle to the left.

4   Leaving the corner in the centre and without releasing the blade from the wood, swing the handle up and across so that the cutting edge slices along your imagined line to the outer point of the serif. Stop there and lift out the tool.

5   Repeat the stab cut on the opposite side. It doesn't actually matter which side of the serif you choose first, but try to work in a rhythmical manner (see Fig 5.20).

6   Swap to the fishtail gouge, holding it once more in the pen and dagger grip. Even though the cut starts low, the tool handle rises, and I prefer this grip over the low-angle grip (see page 16). As with the stab cuts, it doesn't matter which side you cut first. We will start with the right again. Begin with the handle low. Place the lower corner of the fishtail in the trench with the mouth of the gouge to the right. Bring the lower corner to the end of the trench in the centre line and rest the cutting edge on the edge of the trench, mouth down. This is the starting position (see Fig 5.21).

The cut you need to make into the right side of the serif has a two-fold movement: first, the corner must be pushed down and forward slightly into the deepest part of the serif to meet the point of the stop cut you made with the chisel. Second, the handle must be raised and rotated so that the cutting edge creates the shape of the serif, with the sides of the trench continuing into the serif walls up to the cap line.

Cut the right side of the serif in this way up to the cap line. Although the gouge is not flat, it should be possible to merge the side of the trench into the serif. This cut also replaces the original straight stop cut with a curving serif wall. Then cut the side of the serif on the opposite side (see Fig 5.22). The end wall of the serif also lies at an angle, and is cut using the fishtail chisel.

7   Hold the chisel in the pen and dagger grip and rest your forearm on the wood – the cut will be made from the right. You will have to swing your body to the right side to make the cut comfortably. Place one corner of the chisel on the point where the outside edge of the serif meets the cap line. The corner of the tool must follow one line while the cutting edge travels along another.

The corner must be pushed down and forward slightly into the deepest part of the serif, following what will be the junction of the serif's end and side walls. When the corner reaches the centre, stop. The corner acts as a pivot for the next movement. The handle must now be pushed over so that the slicing cutting edge follows the cap line to the opposite corner of the serif.

8   Make this cut to the right. Be decisive. If you push the corner down the junction to the centre of the serif, and the edge along the cap line, the end wall will naturally arise at the correct angle, but keep on the angle you are holding the tool (see Fig 5.23).

9   A chip will be ejected, and you will be able to see how well you have done (see Fig 5.24). It is quite normal to find there is a little tidying up to do in the deep centre of the serif. This can be done with the chisel, rather than reverting to the gouge. Be careful not to deepen the serif too much – you need enough to create a shadow, but not so much that cleaning up becomes a problem.

Fig 5.22 Then make the second side cut.

Fig 5.23 Begin the end wall cut with the fishtail chisel.

Fig 5.24 Here you can see the end wall cut has released a correctly-shaped chip.

10 Now cut the base-line serif in a similar way. You will need to position your body well to the side to make the cuts with the gouge comfortably and to avoid directing the tool towards yourself. This is preferable to turning the work upside down, but you can adjust the work if you prefer and pretend the base is the cap line. The other cuts (stab and end wall) can be made square-on, but with the movements reorientated.

AIMS AND PROBLEMS

The finished serif should merge with the main trench and have neat junctions between side and end walls. The centre point should be precise. Neither the junctions, centre or root of the trench should be stabbed, and all the walls should be cleanly cut. When you have cut the cap and base serif to the trench, pause and congratulate yourself – you've just cut your first letter!

One of the first problems in cutting the serifs is in aligning all the junctions and arriving at neat lines and a centre point. The corners need to be placed, and the cutting edges run, in a fairly exact way. This involves tool control, which must be learnt. You also need a sense of the *shape* you are aiming at, which can also be learnt. The way to learn, believe it or not, is to cut lots of serifs! So repeat this exercise over and over again, cutting new trenches if you run out.

Be decisive in your cuts. Try not to pick at the wood, but create the serif in as few strokes of the cutting edge as possible. The trick lies in doing the same cut each time, and proceeding methodically.

In this exercise I assumed there would be no problem with grain when you cut the end wall. In reality, you may have found the wood tearing if you followed my directions, because you were going against the grain. The fibres run horizontally in most lettering – generally along the direction of the end wall cut. The actual direction of this cut in any instance will depend on the lie of the fibres in the wood at that point. You need to look at the grain and decide in which direction to offer the chisel in order to cut *with* it (see Fig 5.25). If you get it wrong and the grain tears, react

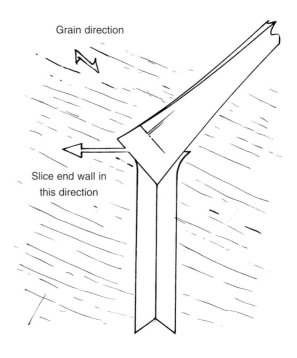

Fig 5.25 *The direction of the grain at the end wall affects which side you need to approach it with the fishtail chisel.*

immediately and cut from the opposite direction. *Never persist in the original direction!* You may find you are switching from right to left as you pass from serif to serif, swapping hands depending on the grain direction. Serifs in other directions are easier in this respect, because the cutting is *across* the fibres.

It is not unusual for newcomers to excavate quite a deep serif, and have difficulties in getting it clean. As a guide, serifs should be less than half the depth of the letter again.

You *can* make stop cuts using the fishtail gouge. I tend not to because I cut *all* the stop cuts at the same time, including those at the junctions of letter parts, for which the fishtail gouge would not be suitable.

Aim to carve a good individual serif to the criteria given above. Then match it with a second. Aim to make a series of 10 serifs, top and bottom, with as similar an appearance as possible.

VARIATIONS

Serifs don't have to be flat along the top; they may be hollowed. To do this, use the fishtail gouge instead of a chisel, but in exactly the same way. Be careful of the grain at the edge, reversing the direction of cut as necessary. You may have to finish off from the centre of the 'hollow'. Try cutting 10 hollow serifs in this way (see Fig 5.26).

Fig 5.26 Hollowed (left) and straight (right) serif ends.

Try a variety of serif shapes and sizes, for example: wider or narrower; arising from deeper in the stem; or a serif that is more hooked.

Try cutting a 'sans serif' end to a trench. The end wall of the trench still slopes at an angle down to the root. There is the same danger of cutting into this end wall as there would be if a serif were present. Select an appropriate width of chisel to cut the trench, and take your line from the centre of the serif to the corner where the trench will meet the cap or base line. Cut, as before, to this shape, only do *not* sink the centre point. The trench ends in a simple end wall without deepening (see Fig 5.27).

Fig 5.27 A sans serif trench end.

∎9 HORIZONTAL TRENCHES

CONTEXT

As I have mentioned, lettering is normally carved with the wood grain running horizontally. This allows the major cuts (vertical) to lie *across* the grain and gives the neatest, quickest, result. However, orientated this way, any horizontal cuts lie *along* the grain. Instead of being cleanly cut first time, the fibres tend to tear along the walls of the trench and, in an attempt to clean up, beginners often end up making the trench wider and deeper than they wanted. In modern roman, horizontal trenches are thin strokes with little spare wood, so the effect of such errors can be disastrous.

Although the method is very similar to the straight troughs cut in Exercises ∎6 and ∎7, at some points a somewhat different approach is needed.

TOOLS

- As Exercise ∎1.

METHOD

1   The wood must have the grain horizontal (left to right). Draw two vertical lines the width of the chisel apart and square to the edge of the wood.

2   Between these lines draw a series of parallel lines, which will be the incised trenches. Make them 6mm (1/4in) apart and with a gap in between each pair of about 10mm (3/8in).

3   Set the edge of the chisel in the centre of the first set of lines and tap it with the mallet to make the centre stab cut as we have done before. You will observe two things. First, the chisel enters the wood much more easily than when it was stabbed across the grain, because the shape *prises apart* fibres rather than cutting them. This means that you need to be light with the mallet, and on small letter parts you

Fig 5.28 Using the vertical trench technique for horizontal trenches does not work. The cutting edge tends to pass between the wood fibres lying in the same direction, lifting and tearing them.

Fig 5.29 The solution is to make a stop cut to prevent the horizontal grain tearing.

Fig 5.30 Close-up of the junction of a T, showing torn grain not visible at normal viewing distance.

can use hand pressure only. Second, the wedge of the chisel bevel pushes the fibres apart and the cut extends as a split a little beyond the vertical boundary lines. The effect of this sideways pressure has therefore to be carefully controlled.

4   As an experiment, make two angled cuts as you did for the vertical trenches – it is not necessary to change hands with a horizontal cut. You will see that the fibres tear along the sides, but the waste wood remains attached at each end, and doesn't jump free. It is also likely that the fibres tore beyond the vertical boundary lines. An unsatis-factory result (see Fig 5.28).

5   Leave this failed trench and go to the next one. This time tap the corner of the chisel lightly into each end of what will be the trench *before* making the centre stab cut, creating a stop cut at each end to prevent the fibres tearing beyond the vertical lines (see Fig 5.29). Visualize the trench and make sure you do not cut below its depth – remember, always cut shallower rather than deeper.

6   Make the central stab cut as before. Then make the two angled cuts from about 1mm (³/₆₄in) within the guiding horizontal lines. This will give you the opportunity to clean up the letter walls. You should find the central waste piece of the trench comes away. If it remains clinging by a few fibres at the ends or along the walls, nick these with the corner or edge of the chisel so that the waste is freed.

7   Try and clean up the walls by paring up to the horizontal lines using the pen and dagger grip. Come to a neat centre line in the trench root. Taking thin cuts with the same chisel is often enough for dense woods. If the wood fibres are still tearing (more common with open-grain woods – see Fig 5.30) then a different approach is needed. Make another trench, and use a slightly narrower chisel to slice down at an angle along the walls to the root, as described in Exercise ■7 (see page 49). The slicing cut is possible because the chisel is narrower, and you should be able to finish the

horizontal trench neatly with clean, flat sides and a controlled depth (see Fig 5.31).

9   Repeat the exercise with the other sets of parallel horizontal lines.

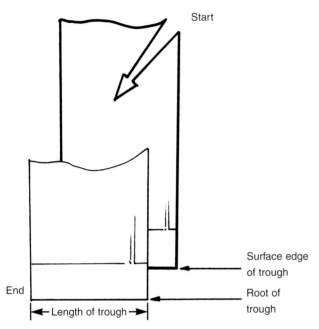

Fig 5.31 A slicing cut is needed to clean across the grain in horizontal trenches.

AIMS AND PROBLEMS

In practice the horizontal parts of letters are attached to other vertical parts. So, for example, when cutting the letter **H** there would be no need for end stop cuts to the cross bar, as the ends pass into the wide vertical trench, and there is also room for the slicing cut. Here it would be a matter of controlling the depth by carefully paring back to the correct width. Other letters have similar room for the tools to be used in this way (except for **T**) and these are worked in Exercise ■11 on page 59.

It is not always necessary to switch to a narrower chisel. When incising a series of letters you would put in the end stop cuts together and switch to a narrower chisel for all those horizontal parts that needed it.

Incise 10 horizontal trenches. Don't worry about the very ends – these will be seriffed, or would normally run into a vertical trench. The walls should be flat and neat without torn grain; the root should be in the centre, parallel to the sides and clean.

VARIATIONS

Cut different sizes of trench: wider and narrower, and to different lengths. Try out different woods to see how the tearing of the grain is affected by their differing densities.

■10 SERIFS (II)

CONTEXT

This exercise concentrates on putting serifs on the ends of horizontal trenches. The method is similar to that for cap and base line serifs. As in Exercise ■9 (see page 55), you need extra length to cut the serif. As I have explained, all serifs have sloping end walls, and it is important not to cut into these when removing the trench.

TOOLS

• As Exercise ■8 (see page 50).

METHOD

1   You will need the series of horizontal trenches from the last exercise, again 6mm (¹/₄in) wide. Add a further vertical line 4mm (¹/₈in) further out on each side. These lines will be where the ends of the serifs lie.

2   Fig 5.32 shows what you are aiming for. Hold the fishtail chisel in the pen and dagger grip for the initial stop cuts. You will need to swing your body round to the side to feel unhindered and comfortable as you cut. Start on the right or the left, as you prefer.

3   Imagine the lines from the centre of the serif to the outermost corners. It doesn't matter which line you start with.

Fig 5.32 Serifs added to a horizontal trench.

4   Plunge the corner of the chisel into the centre of the serif and slice the cutting edge down and along the imagined line to the far corner – just as you did before with cap and base serifs. Repeat to the other corner.

5   Change to the fishtail gouge and cut the two sides of the serif, as in Exercise ∎8. The principal difference here is that the cuts will be *against* the grain. With sharp tools and tight grain there should be no problem, and the cuts should be clean. However, you may find the grain tearing up, and if so, go as far as you can and stop there for a moment.

6   Now revert to the chisel and remove the end wall of the serif, maintaining the same angle as the side walls of the trench.

7   If you had a problem with the grain tearing, once you have removed the end wall chip, go back to the gouge and make a cleaning cut in the *opposite* direction, so that the corner of the gouge starts at the outermost corner of the serif, and descends along the junction line to the deepest point. Allow the cutting edge to shape the serif. This way you will be cutting cleanly with the grain.

Cut serifs to each side of the horizontal trench. Try and control the shape and size and incise them with as few tool strokes as possible.

AIMS AND PROBLEMS

Unlike serifs on cap and base lines, there is more variety in serifs orientated in other directions in modern roman. For example, all the right hand serifs of the letter **E** have different shapes, although the basic inverted pyramid with a deep centre still applies.

During the layout stage on wood, while you would not normally draw in the cap and base serifs to the vertical stems, you might want to indicate the orientation of the end of serifs in other directions as you mark off the limits of the component lines. In this exercise however, you have made just the basic cuts. Individual letters and serif shapes will be dealt with in the next exercise.

With the exception of **T** and **Z**, all horizontal serifs occur to the right of the letters, and carvers tend to be better at one side than the other. Serif-like shapes occur in other letter styles, so it is well to be proficient in all directions when it comes to serif cutting.

Cut 10 serifs to both sides, making them the same shape. The walls should be cleanly cut without torn grain and the centre point precise. Junctions should not be stabbed.

VARIATIONS

Try carving different sizes of serif, and experiment by using the fishtail gouge throughout, in order to end up with hollow-ended serifs.

■11 LETTERS H, T, F, L & E

CONTEXT

You should now be able to carve inside vertical and horizontal trenches, as well as cap, base and vertical serifs. These elements can now be assembled into your first batch of complete letters. What has been covered so far should enable you to carve (in addition to **I**) six modern roman letters. You should now find the learning process speeding up as you acquire the basic techniques, and as a result new letters can be mastered more quickly.

The one new thing to learn here is how to make the junction between vertical and horizontal components. This is best dealt with as they are practised.

Draw out the letters to size following each drawing, one at a time, repeating each letter until you feel confident.

TOOLS

- 40mm, 30mm, 25mm, 20mm, (1⅝in, 1¼in, 1in, ¾in) chisels.

- 13mm (½in) fishtail chisel.

- No. 4 x 16mm (⅝in) fishtail gouge.

METHOD

H

1 Refer to Fig 5.33. Cut the two vertical trenches first. The 40mm (1⅝in) chisel I recommend for this letter size allows a gap at each end for cap and base serifs. If you are incising to a different size you must remember this and choose your chisel accordingly.

2 Add the crossbar using the 30mm (1⅛in) chisel, starting with the central stop cut. The width of the chisel should pass into the trench at either side. Then make two angled cuts, leaving a little waste to pare back cleanly to the line. As the horizontal bar is half the width of the vertical one, its root should emerge half way down the vertical wall (see Fig 5.34).

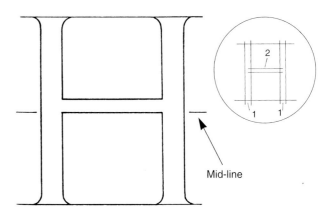

Mid-line

Fig 5.33 H: construction.

Fig 5.34 Detail of the junction of the vertical stem and the crossbar.

3 Add cap and base serifs with flat end walls.

T

1 Refer to Fig 5.35. Cut the vertical trench first using the 40mm (1⅝in) chisel. This time the gap at the top is for the crossbar rather than a serif.

2 Cut the top bar with the 30mm (1⅛in) chisel, allowing for the serif. Start with a small stop cut at each end directed into the serif corners. You can use the corner of the regular chisel for this or use the fishtail.

3 Use the fishtail to form the junction between the vertical and horizontal parts, before using it to make the stop cuts for the base serif. The top wall of the horizontal bar runs down to the root of the vertical stem – like the end wall of a serif – and this

59

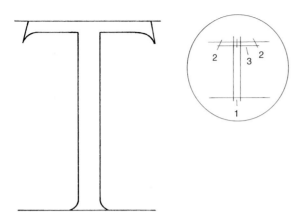

Fig 5.35 T: construction.

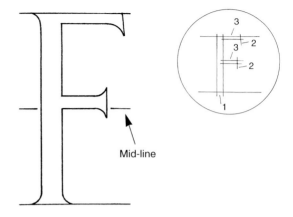

Fig 5.37 F: construction.

needs to be maintained. Start with a centre stop cut into the section of vertical waste, running up to the horizontal bar. Finish off the vertical trench up to the bar with correctly angled cuts, merging with the existing walls. Clean down the top wall of the crossbar with the corner of the chisel to form the junction.

4 Cut the base serif.

5 Now carve the cap serifs. The bottom half of each serif is cut in the usual way, but aiming for their particular shape. Draw the serif in if you are unsure. To cut the slope of the end wall, angle the chisel outwards. The top half of the serif is cut in the same way as the sans serif described in Exercise ■10 on page 57. The finished letter is shown in Fig. 5.36.

F

1 Refer to Fig 5.37. Cut the vertical stem first with the 40mm (1⁵⁄₈in) chisel, stopping short at each end.

2 Make stop cuts with the fishtail chisel for *all* the serifs, including those on the horizontal arms. Bear in mind their differing shapes, and that the cap serif on the vertical stem extends to the left only.

3 Cut the horizontal top arm with the 20mm (³⁄₄in) chisel.

4 Cut the sides to all the serifs, *except* that of the lower arm. Remember to merge them with the walls.

5 Use the fishtail chisel to form the end walls of the serifs, the junction of the top arm and vertical stem, and the lower arm and serif. The brackets of the lower arm serif are quite pronounced, and can be cut with the fishtail chisel. The finished letter is shown, along with **E**, in Fig 5.38.

Fig 5.36 T: finished letter.

Fig 5.38 E and F: finished letters.

60

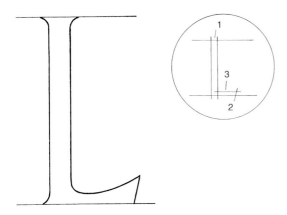

Fig 5.39 L: construction.

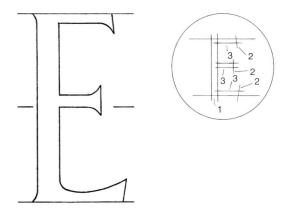

Fig 5.40 E: construction.

L

1 Refer to Fig 5.39. Cut the vertical stem with the 40mm (1⅝in) chisel.

2 Apply stop cuts to the serifs and lower junction.

3 Cut the horizontal bar with the 20mm (¾in) chisel.

4 Finish with the fishtail chisel. This method closely resembles an inverted **F**. However, there are two further refinements: one to the free horizontal serif, the other to the junction.

5 The upper side of the base serif should be swept back into the horizontal leg. This is best done with the fishtail gouge when the serif is shaped, but may be refined with the fishtail chisel when the end wall is cut. You can leave off the lower side of this serif, or dip it slightly. It should resemble the serifs on **E** and **T**.

6 The fishtail gouge can be used to round the junction so that the leg merges into the stem. It is easier (and follows the grain) to work from the leg, handling the gouge as if you were cutting a serif. The line of the open counter should flow smoothly from serif to stem, a common refinement seen throughout the modern roman alphabet. See letters **A–Z**, page 95.

E

Refer to Fig 5.40. This letter is a combination of **F** and **L**, and the cutting order should be: vertical stem; stop cuts to serifs; horizontals (but not the middle arm); serif brackets; end walls and middle arm. Finally, check the lower serif, and round off the inner junction between the upright and the leg. Take particular care at the top junction, which should look like that shown in Fig 5.41.

Fig 5.41 Detail of the top junction.

61

AIMS AND PROBLEMS

With a little practise you should find these letters fairly straightforward. Aim to cut several of each of the letters until you feel confident. I suggest you time a letter and see if you can be quicker the next time, but *don't* rush to beat the clock! Make each cut precise and telling.

VARIATIONS

Experiment with different letter sizes. If your chisels are too narrow for large letters, you will have to merge the cuts carefully. See how the details of individual letters (see Chapter 6) can be applied to your incising work, and, similarly, look at modifications that can be made to these letters, which are also discussed in Chapter 6, page 106.

■12 OBLIQUE TRENCHES

CONTEXT

Obliques occur in several letters and should cause no problems if you can incise vertical and horizontal trenches. This section also looks more at adding oblique serifs to troughs.

TOOLS

- 40mm (1⁵/₈in) chisel.
- Mallet.
- Ruler and protractor.

METHOD

1   Draw two horizontal lines 38mm (1¹/₂in) apart. As elsewhere, these are not actual cap and base lines because waste needs to be left for the serifs.

2   Refer to Fig 5.42. Draw three groups of parallel, paired oblique lines at an angle of about 70° to the horizontal, as follows:

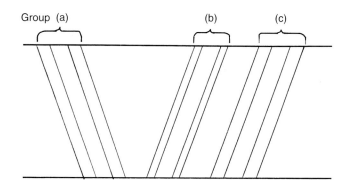

Fig 5.42 Layout for the angled cuts: wide trenches tilting left and right, and a narrow trench tilting right.

(a)   A group 6mm (¹/₄in) apart with gaps of 10mm (³/₈in) between, tilted to the *left* – these represent the wide, oblique elements of a letter.

(b)   A group 6mm (¹/₄in) apart with gaps of 10mm (³/₈in) between, tilted to the *right*. The only *wide* stroke tilted right in roman is in **Z**; all others are thin.

(c)   A group of obliques tilted to the *right*, 3mm (¹/₈in) apart, to represent the thin elements of letters such as **A**, **K**, **M**, **W** and **K**. The 40mm (1⁵/₈in) chisel should fit neatly between cap and base lines at this angle.

3   Use the mallet to stab a central stop cut followed by two angled cuts in the normal manner for each trench, cleaning up if necessary (see Fig 5.43). Change hands with the mallet as required as cuts come from the left or right.

Fig 5.43 An angled trench, ready for serifs.

4 When you have a series of neat trenches, draw in true cap and base lines 3mm (¹/sin) outside of your working lines. If it helps, draw in the serifs. The rule still applies that these extend by half the trench width on either side, but you will see how one side is extended and the other 'hooked'.

5 Follow the previous procedures for cutting serifs, starting with the stop cuts from the centre of the serif to the outer corners (see Fig 5.44).

6 Follow these with two cuts of the fishtail gouge to make the sides: one sweeping the oblique wall into the extended point, the other cranking tightly to form the hook (see Fig 5.45).

7 Finally, finish off the end wall with the fishtail chisel (see Fig 5.46). The finished serif is shown in Fig 5.47.

AIMS AND PROBLEMS

As you cut the oblique trenches you will have seen how the grain is pushed out at each end by the wedge-effect of the bevel. This *may* lead to problems at junctions, as the apexes of the inner counters of letters (such as **A**), can be 'jumped' out. The next exercise will focus on this.

The extended side of the serif is cut *against* the grain. With sharp tools and tight grain this should be no problem and the serif should appear clean. However, if grain does pick up, reverse the direction of cut – in the same way as you may need to for the end wall cut.

The hooked side of the serif lies more *across* the grain, making it rarely a problem. The hook may merge with the oblique or join it at more of an angle. Cut a series of 10 obliques, with serifs.

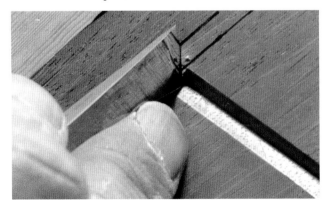

Fig 5.44 Cutting angled serifs. Begin with the stop cuts.

VARIATIONS

Use the fishtail gouge rather than the chisel to form hollow ends to the serifs, and try different sizes of obliques, varying the angle to see what effect the grain has upon them.

Fig 5.45 Making the angled cuts to the walls with the fishtail gouge.

Fig 5.46 Making the final cut across the end wall with the fishtail chisel.

Fig 5.47 The finished serif.

■13 JOINING OBLIQUES

LETTERS A, M, N, V, W, K, Z, X & Y

CONTEXT

The junction formed when oblique lines meet takes several forms. **A**, **M**, **N**, **V** and **W** orientate across the grain, whereas **K** and **Z** orientate along the grain and require more care.

To a greater or lesser degree, there is always a problem with shortness of grain (wood fibres) at the junction of all these letters, and a careful approach needs to be taken, otherwise (for example with **A**), the result may be anything from the crumbling of the inner apex to, at worst, the jumping out of the whole inner counter (see Fig 5.48).

The problem lies in the wedge-like effect of the bevel, which exerts a sideways pressure on the short grain, which, if unsupported, will fracture. This approach therefore avoids heavy handedness at all costs!

This exercise concentrates on the junctions, using **A** to illustrate the method. **A** is followed by the other letters with a similar function. The exercise then covers the remaining letters: **X** and **Y**, the junctions of which are relatively straightforward.

Other than **A**, the incising of whole letters is not covered in detail, as the overall approach has already been described in previous exercises. As usual, take your letterforms supplied with each description.

TOOLS

- 45mm, 40mm, 30mm, 25mm, 20mm (1³/₄in, 1⁵/₈in, 1³/₈in, 1¹/₄in, 1in, ³/₄in) chisels. Use size appropriate.

- 13mm (¹/₂in) fishtail chisel.

- No. 4 x 16mm (⁵/₈in) fishtail gouge.

- Mallet.

METHOD

A

1 With the wood grain horizontal, draw the letter **A** between cap and base lines (see Fig 5.49).

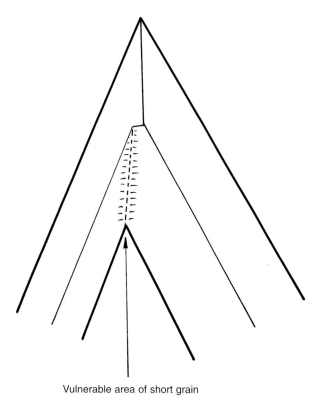

Fig 5.48 The junction of angled trenches includes short grain at the top of the inner counter. This area can be jumped out if you are not careful.

Vulnerable area of short grain

Fig 5.49 A: construction.

2   The size of chisel you need for obliques must take into account the serif (similar to other straight cuts) and the junction. Choose a width that falls short of the two points, as shown in Fig 5.50). If you are following Fig 5.49 and making your letters 50mm (2in), then you will require a 40mm (1⁵/8in) wide chisel.

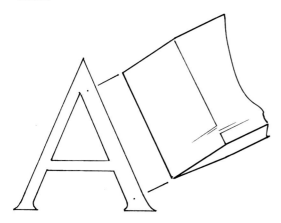

Fig 5.50 The required chisel width for an oblique trench is estimated between the points indicated here. Choosing this width avoids the end wall of the serif at one end, and short grain at the junction at the other.

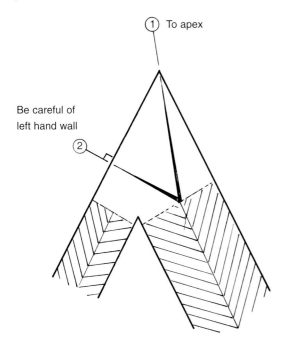

Fig 5.51 Make two stop cuts from the root of the wide trench. (1) runs to the apex, (2) to the wood surface at right angles to the left hand trench.

3   Stab in both centre stop cuts to the two oblique limbs. The left is a lighter cut than the right because it is thinner. Place the chisel carefully to avoid both the serif and junction area, and cut both oblique trenches in the normal way.

4   Now, using the same chisel or the fishtail, make two further stab cuts from the root at the top of the wide (right) trench, one to the wood surface at the apex of the letter, and another to the wood surface at right angles to the left trench (see Fig 5.51). These should both be light cuts to avoid 'trauma' to the short grain in the inner counter (see Fig 5.52).

Fig 5.52 To cut the apex, begin with the stop cuts.

5   Now cut the apex, working the walls from right to *left*, swapping mallet hands as required.

6   Carefully cut the outside wall on the right oblique trench first, from root to apex (see Fig 5.53).

Fig 5.53 Then make the first angled cut from root to apex.

Fig 5.54 *The second angled cut runs from the root to beyond the weak area, to the surface of the wood.*

Fig 5.55 *The third angled cut slices down to the root of the left oblique, again beyond the weak area, safely isolating it.*

Fig 5.56 *The fourth angled cut finishes the left wall down to the root.*

7   Then trim in the right inner wall beyond the short grain tip of the inner counter (see Fig 5.54).

8   Finish the other side of the tip of the inner counter (see Fig 5.55).

9   Finish with the outside wall on the left side of the letter, from root to apex (see Fig 5.56). You may need to trim up by hand with slicing cuts, but you should be able to finish the junction with the large chisel which you used to cut the obliques in the first place (see Figs 5.57 and 5.58).

10 Now add the serifs and crossbar in the normal manner and the letter is finished (see Fig 5.59).

Fig 5.57 *Finish off the apex with the corner of the large chisel.*

Fig 5.58 *The finished junction.*

Fig 5.59 Completed letter A.

AIMS AND PROBLEMS

Aim to swap hands while using the same chisel. You *can* swap to the lighter fishtail chisel, with or without the mallet, if you wish, and follow the same sequence of cuts, tackling the walls from the right. The trick is to shape the apex of the inner counter before the wood becomes weak through shortening of grain.

M, N, V, W

Refer to Figs 5.60–63. The procedure for these letters is very similar to that for **A**, but the drawn angle will be different in some cases. For those junctions which are 'upside down' there is no need to contort your body, as you will find cuts can be made comfortably from the new (reversed) direction.

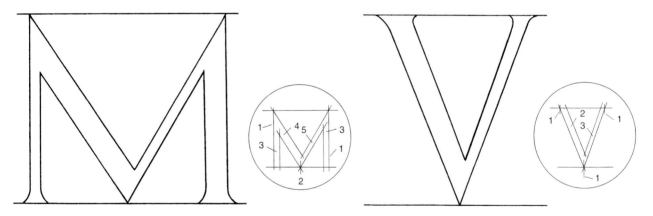

Fig 5.60 M: construction.

Fig 5.62 V: construction.

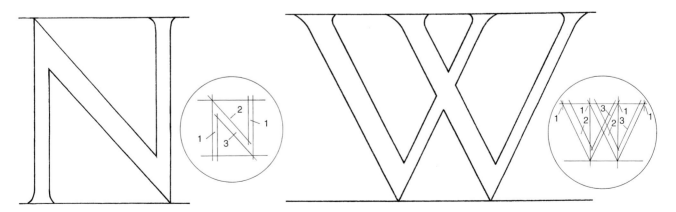

Fig 5.61 N: construction.

Fig 5.63 W: construction.

For the angled cuts, *always start with the outer wall of the thick oblique* and work across to the other side. Where there is more than one junction, you will probably find you get a more consistent appearance if you cut them in parallel, rather than in series. The finished letters are shown in Figs 5.64 and 5.65.

Fig 5.64 Finished letters M and N.

Fig 5.65 Finished letters V and W.

K

Refer to Fig 5.66. **K** differs from the previous oblique letters in that whereas with **A** the apex has nothing above it – so if you made the letter a fraction taller by raising the apex the effect would only be an increase in height – **K** has a vertical immediately next to the apex, and it is a common error to run the apex into the vertical trough.

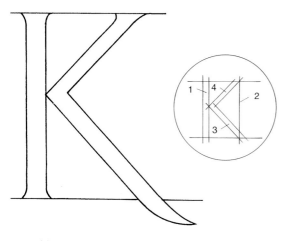

Fig 5.66 K: construction.

The junction should *arrive* at the upright but not *invade* it (see Fig 5.67). This requires a particularly sensitive approach, as the grain is weak at this point, as it is in the junction counter.

The leg of **K** is best formed to resemble that of **R**. In both cases the leg can end on the base line in a serif, or in a curved tail.

Fig 5.67 Close-up of the junction of K. It is vital that the apex does not invade the upright by breaking through the short grain.

Z

Refer to Fig 5.68. **Z** has horizontal grain into the junction, which means taking the more cautious approach with the horizontal trenches. In addition, beginners tend to concentrate on cleaning up the horizontals at the same time as forming the junctions, which can cause the horizontals to deepen at the junction ends, so be careful here.

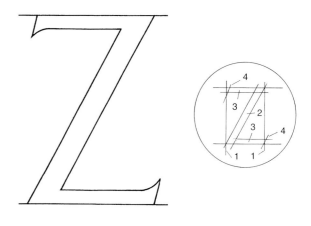

Fig 5.68 Z: construction.

X

Refer to Fig 5.69. First cut the thick oblique fully, and then impose the thin one, with a light initial stop cut. If you do not have the correct width of chisel for the trenches, make sure you merge the cuts to leave the lines of the obliques neat and uniform.

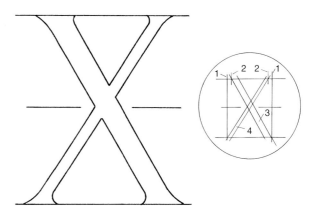

Fig 5.69 X: construction.

69

Y

Refer to Fig 5.70. Cut the short vertical, and then cut the left thick oblique from it – as if one vertical line had been bent. Then bring in the thin oblique from the right. The lower edge of the trench meets the obtuse angle of the upright.

The three finished letters **X**, **Y** and **Z** are shown in Fig 5.71.

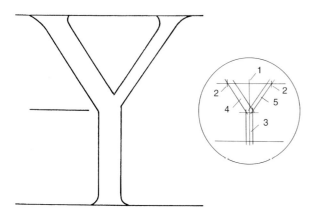

Fig 5.70 Y: construction.

VARIATIONS

Experiment with different letter sizes until you are confident. You should now be able to form junctions at any angle – try and prove it!

You have now completed all 16 roman letters with straight components only. The next set of exercises takes us on to the more challenging curved shapes required to carve the remaining letters.

CURVED LETTERS

The curved trenches of letters are incised in a similar way to straight trenches: a centre stab cut is made first, followed by angled cuts from each side. However, there is a difference in the selection of gouges and in the way they are manipulated and it is this which often throws newcomers.

Some letterers – who are usually not carvers in the first instance – adopt a 'nibble and merge' approach to curves: the nearest cross-section (sweep) of gouge for a particular curve is selected and many cuts are then made from the side, working around the form. One can work

Fig 5.71 Finished letters X, Y and Z.

this way, but it is not the best approach. It tends to use more tools than is necessary, take far longer, and leave scalloped walls and rough lines at the trench root.

Clean, precise, flowing cuts are needed for good lettering work, and the method which follows is the best I have found for creating them. The gouges are selected through an understanding of how they make their cuts and handle in an economic way, so that, for example, one tool does the work of several.

The first exercises make some fundamental observations about gouges through practice cuts. These are then built up into a sample letter: **O**, which is then followed by the two other curved letters: **C** and **S**.

14 VERTICAL STABBING WITH MALLET AND GOUGE (I)

CONTEXT

This is a quick and simple exercise, demonstrating an important geometric principle of gouges.

TOOLS

- No. 6 x 20mm (³/₄in) gouge.
- Mallet.

METHOD

1   Hold the gouge *vertically* in your left hand with the cutting edge resting on the wood and pointing towards the right.

2   Tap in the stab cut with the mallet.

3   Remove the gouge by pulling the handle *along* the edge, towards one corner. As with straight chisels, this is the safest way to pull out an embedded cutting edge – rocking the tool *across* the edge is liable to damage it.

4   Make a second cut to the right of the first, this time tilting the gouge 45° to the right. Make a second stab cut, and compare the two cuts (see Fig 5.72).

Fig 5.72 You can see that the angled cut on the right is 'quicker' (its radius has been reduced) than the one on the left.

AIMS AND PROBLEMS

Because the cross-section, or sweep, of a gouge is based on a circle, when the blade is offered at an angle into the surface plane of the wood, the result is more of an ellipse. If you have trouble visualizing this, imagine the gouge to be part of a cylinder, then sliced across at an angle (see Fig 5.73).

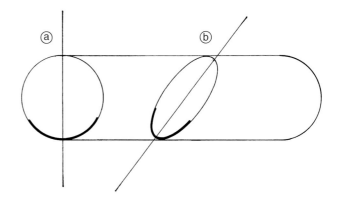

Fig 5.73 The blade of a gouge is actually a segment of a cylinder. Entering vertically into the wood is like cutting the cylinder straight across, and gives the sweep of the gouge (a). Entering at an angle slices the cylinder, and produces an oval profile (b), effectively deepening the sweep.

In practice, the original sweep of the gouge becomes 'quicker' – its radius is reduced – and this makes it a deeper gouge. The upshot of this is that if the gouge you used to make the vertical stab cuts to the centres of curved components is used at an angle, it will cut a *tighter* circle. The outer curves of letters, from which angle cuts are made inwardly, are actually *larger* than the centre-stabbed circles and really need a flatter gouge (i.e. one with a flatter sweep).

Bear this fact in mind as you work through the following exercises. Hopefully, the implications will help you develop a strategy for picking the right gouge for a particular curve.

VARIATIONS

Try this with different gouges before moving on to the next exercise.

▌15 VERTICAL STABBING WITH MALLET AND GOUGE (II)

CONTEXT

Curves are a little more complicated than cutting straight trenches, and many students view them with trepidation. The selection of the right gouge for the curve is actually straightforward, once the principles of how the tools cut are grasped. The manipulation of gouges is completely different to that of chisels: it is not just a matter of pushing in and 'nibbling' – controlled, flowing, clean cuts are required. In many ways the technique is like the 'setting in' of an edge in relief carving, which is one of the reasons why lettering really helps the development of other carving skills. This exercise will further help you to master the required techniques.

TOOLS

- No. 6 x 20mm (³/₄in) straight gouge.
- Mallet.

METHOD

As all *true* gouges have sweeps which are arcs of a circle, being able to use this feature is a vital part of carving successful curves. In this exercise you are going to create a circle with stab cuts using the gouge, *anticlockwise*. The corner which moves around the circle first is called the **leading corner**, and the following corner is called the **trailing corner**.

1   Hold the gouge vertically in the left hand with the cutting edge resting on the wood and the inside pointing towards the left.

2   Tap the gouge with the mallet to make a light stab cut (see Fig 5.74).

Fig 5.74 Start with a vertical stab cut.

3   Tilt the gouge towards yourself a little to free the top corner (see Fig 5.75). Ease the gouge along its cut so that the leading corner clears the wood and

Fig 5.75 Lift the leading edge above the surface of the wood.

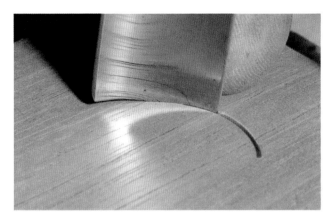

Fig 5.76 Push the gouge along, allowing the initial stab cut to guide the travel of the blade.

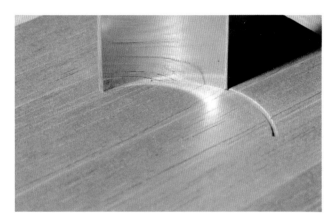

Fig 5.77 Place another stab cut.

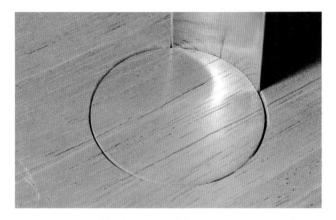

Fig 5.78 Eventually, the gouge will have cut a complete circle.

passes about half a gouge width further along to the left. The initial stab cut acts as a jig, guiding the metal as it slides along. You will need to rotate your wrist to accommodate the motion (see Fig 5.76).

4   Return the gouge to a vertical position and tap it with the mallet making another stop cut (see Fig 5.77).

5   Now repeat the process: lift the leading corner, ease it forward along the cut, bring it upright and stab again.

6   Eventually the gouge will work its way round to complete a perfect circle (see Fig 5.78). Don't force the gouge. Allow it to cut its own path and have faith that it will eventually arrive where it began!

7   Try the process again, this time striking harder with the mallet. Notice how the gouge sinks in deeper. Try running the gouge up to three quarters of its width along the cut before striking.

AIMS AND PROBLEMS

I remember the first time I ever created a circle with a gouge, and the child-like satisfaction I got from the fact that it worked! You will see that, as with the vertical stabbing of straights, there is no need to reverse the chisel (gouge) and mallet hands, but there will be when it comes to angled cuts.

You may experience difficulties if the leading corner is not allowed to clear the wood each time the gouge is repositioned, in which case it will chew up the fibres – you need to allow the trailing corner and the edge in the cut to guide the direction of the tool, and align it correctly.

It is a very useful fact that gouges will 'jig' in this fashion to create centre stop cuts to curved elements, and I suggest you play with this idea using the variations below. This is not the end of the story, however, as will be shown in the next exercise!

VARIATIONS

Start the circle from another point, and try different sizes of circle using different gouges. Then try cutting the circles both clockwise and anticlockwise. Once you are happy with these techniques, mix the gouges and try joining cuts neatly to form ovals, ellipses or wavy lines.

▌16 VERTICAL STABBING WITH MALLET AND GOUGE (III)

CONTEXT

A simple circle is not the only shape possible with the gouge rotating. Two features of the gouge will be apparent in this simple, but very important exercise, which can be added to what you have learned already.

TOOLS

• No. 6 x 20mm (³/₄in) gouge.

METHOD

1 Incise a light circle in the wood as in the previous exercise.

2 Place the gouge on the circle line, back in the starting position, and tap in a little deeper, ready to go round again.

3 This time, as you lift the leading corner, instead of following the drawn circle, twist the gouge so that it slides into a position *within* the line. The leading corner, as the edge passes along by about a third, will now lie a little within the circle. Keep the leading corner up, and tap in with the mallet (see Fig 5.79).

Fig 5.79 Start winding in the cut rather than following the circle.

4 You can now continue in similar fashion to spiral the cut towards the centre, but, since the sweep of the gouge is fixed, as the curve of the spiral gets tighter you cannot stab in by returning the gouge to the upright position. You need to use the leading corner more and more, keeping the tool angled back as you move it forward a little at a time and rotate the gouge (see Fig 5.80). The tighter the curve you wish to negotiate, the more you have to use only the corner of the gouge, proceeding in little jumps as it acts like the keel of a boat. You may need to use fingers from your mallet hand to adjust the tool position.

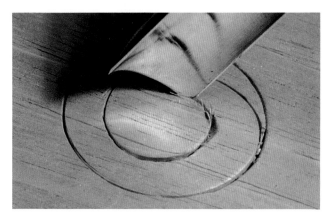

Fig 5.80 By pulling back the handle, and skating more on the trailing corner, you can easily cut a spiral into the centre of the original circle.

5 Wind the cut round towards the centre. Before you get there, you will see that, although you are using all the leading corner and little edge (leaning the tool back and just stabbing down with the corner in little steps), there is a limit to how far you can force the tool to cut a tighter circle before it chews up the wood.

6 Return the tool to the starting position on the original incised circle, and instead of cutting a tighter circle with the gouge, try to slide the gouge along so that you reposition it *outside* the line, and try to cut an expanding spiral (see Fig 5.81). Lift the leading corner as you move the edge forward as before, but rotate the handle a little in the opposite direction. You will find the result disappointing, because this action is practically impossible using a gouge. The implications of this are discussed below.

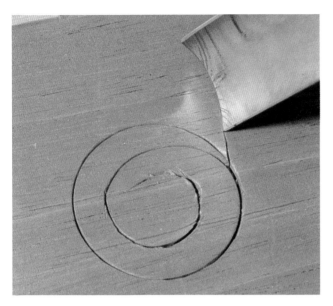

Fig 5.81 You will find it is virtually impossible to guide the gouge into a widening circle.

AIMS AND PROBLEMS

This exercise shows how gouges can easily be wound into tighter curves, but not into flatter ones. Cutting into tighter curves with the gouge is the way to form central stop cuts. Even if these cuts look a little 'chopped', any roughness will disappear entirely as the angle cuts remove wood and form the trench proper.

In addition to being able to make stop cuts to curves, there are several principles to be drawn from this and the preceding two exercises. Bearing in mind that we are using gouges in a particular way and context, we can put the results of Exercises ■14–■16 together.

- Exercise ■14 showed that the sweep (curve) of a gouge is only evident as such when presented *square on* to the surface of the wood.

- Exercise ■14 also showed that when the blade is presented to the wood *at an angle*, the cut is effectively a *deeper* one than the given sweep would seem to imply.

- Exercise ■15 showed how gouges will readily cut circles when presented square on to the wood.

- Exercise ■16 demonstrated how cutting *tighter* circles is possible through the natural sweep of a gouge, but not *wider* ones.

- Exercise ■16 also illustrated the fact that gouges are not limited to the one cut, but any one gouge can be made to do the work of several.

This is very important information, and to see what it adds up to, take the letter **O**, which is the first curved letter you will cut, in Exercise ■19.

O has a simple symmetrical shape in the modern roman style. The outside line is compass struck, but it can represent the curve of any letter. Because the letter must obey the 'horizontal: thin; vertical: thick' rule, the inner curve changes shape and the letter is deeper at the sides than at the top and bottom. The stab cut needed in the centre must also change curvature as the line goes round the circle. So, lots of different curves – how to choose the gouges?

There are two principles that apply to all incised curves:

1. For vertical stabbing cuts, down the centre of curves, you can use either: a gouge with a matching sweep; or a gouge with a slightly *flatter* sweep, manipulated around the curve, but *not* a gouge with a quicker sweep.

2. For the angled cuts, outside and inside, you can use either: a gouge with a sweep slightly *flatter* than the curve of the line from which you are entering the wood (so that when tilted to the appropriate angle to the wood it matches the curve of the line); or a gouge which can be manipulated into tighter curves where necessary (but not flatter curves, where it would scallop the surface).

With the letter **O** you can use the gouge selected for the *outside* angle cut to stab the centre line all round, and cut the inside angled curves top and bottom. This is because the outside line has the largest diameter, and you can manipulate the gouge you use here into all the other *tighter* curves. By altering the angle of presentation, the effective sweep of the gouge is altered. What you will *not* be able to do is use this gouge to cut the inside angled walls where they lie more vertical, or are upright. This is because they are *flatter* than the sweep of the gouge. As you will see, the letter **O** can be incised with only two gouges, even though the curves within it are compound.

Using these principles you can judge the gouges you need just from the layout of the letter. You can match size and style of letter to the tools in hand, or know which additional tool you are likely to need.

All this will become even more evident when put into practice. Before we tackle the actual letter, the method of manipulating the gouges around curves needs to be mastered, and this is the subject of the next two exercises.

One last point relating to this exercise: you should have noticed that when the corner of the tool is the principle cutter it will easily sink into the wood when tapped *along* the grain, but less so when tapped *across* it. It is important to remember this when cutting thin and thick curves (of differing depths) and you will need to vary the strength of mallet tap.

VARIATIONS

Repeat the winding-in exercise with all your gouges and see what you can make them do, and then mix the gouges and proceed clockwise and anti-clockwise to create more complicated swirls and patterns. Finally, see how pulling back the handle to expose more corner to the wood affects the tightness of cut.

∎17 CRESCENTS (I)

CONTEXT

This exercise concentrates on the angle cuts which form a curving trench, and shows you the basic cutting method, which is built up over the next few exercises. It is important to be confident that you have grasped the basic principles before moving on.

TOOLS

- No. 6 x 20mm gouge.

METHOD

1   Make a vertical stab cut into the wood with the gouge, going across grain, with the mouth of the gouge to the left. Remove the gouge properly. Note that this stab cut must end up a uniform depth with vertical presentation.

2   Present the gouge at a 60° angle about 6mm (¹/₄in) away to the right, with its mouth towards the stop cut.

3   Lightly strike in the angle cut with a mallet and you will see the crescent form (see Fig 5.82).

Fig 5.82 The angled cut following the vertical stab cut produces a crescent, clearly shown here.

As the gouge goes in at an angle, the centre part of the edge goes deeper into the wood than the edges. But, because the depth of the stop cut is uniform and shallow, the two cuts can only meet at the edges, not in the middle – any wood that comes out will be torn off ('jumped') by the wedge of the bevel (see Fig 5.83). So this is as far as you can go with the mallet, and the crescent must be cleaned up by hand, first from a vertical and then from an angled, direction, as follows:

1   Take the gouge in the pen and dagger grip. You *must* have: your thumb resting on the side, or a little in the hollow of the blade nearest you; your index finger on the other side of the blade to the thumb, so that the blade is gripped between; your

Fig 5.83 The angled cut cannot meet both the centre root of the crescent and the corners at the same time, so waste is left in the middle, which will have to be cleaned up by hand.

Fig 5.84 Here you can see the starting position, with the corner of the gouge positioned at the near corner of the crescent (above). The gouge is then rotated, and the handle lowered, to lead the gouge corner along the root of the crescent to clean it (below).

middle finger supporting the bevel from behind and resting on the wood; and your ring and little fingers bracing the middle fingers from behind, and also resting on the wood.

2   You will find that the 'dagger' hand naturally tends to bring the handle over towards the body as you lift the far corner clear of the wood. This is the action you want: it is the near corner and the proximate part of the blade which will do most of the work in this and all curved cutting (see Fig 5.84).

3   Make sure that, when bringing over the handle, the blade pivots on the thumb. This is extremely important, and crucial to this method of incising. Make sure also that you bring your shoulder into the tool handle, so that your body weight is behind the cut.

4   Position the gouge exactly into the vertical stop cut.

5   Bring the handle towards you to lift the far corner clear of the wood, pivoting on your thumb. From this position, you should be able to push the sharp corner down to the bottom of the crescent, going a little deeper in the middle and rising out at the far end. The tool must be rotated a little to follow the curve of the vertical wall you are creating. Take only a light cut to begin with.

6   You will almost certainly need another angled cut, deepening it into the final root of the curve. Position the gouge at the correct angle exactly over the place from which you started the angle cut, and slide it down the wall to the rough part at the bottom of the cut. Repeat the slicing cut with the corner to meet the bottom of the vertical cut. Again, take it lightly to begin with (see Fig 5.85).

7   If the chip does not come away, repeat the vertical and angle cuts until it does. You must judge the depth to which you push the corner: aim for both walls to meet at a neat root, with the depth varying along the length of the crescent. Don't go too deep – no more than the width of the crescent. Keep these crescents for Exercise ■18.

Cutting crescents in the opposite direction requires some change of finger position on the blade hand, but all the other positions remain the same.

Begin by making the stab cut as before with the mouth of the gouge to the right. Then, with the mallet in your left hand, make the angle cut. The trench will then need cleaning up, cutting vertically and then at an angle as before. The finger positions will change as follows.

FOR THE VERTICAL CUT

Hold the gouge exactly as you did for the previous crescent, with the middle finger behind the bevel. Now rotate the tool through 180° so the mouth faces towards the hand. The middle finger should now be in the hollow of the gouge ('in cannel'). All the other fingers and thumb remain the same (see Fig 5.86). You can also lean the gouge to the right and use it in an upside-down position, this will be needed for the next exercise where you will learn how to cut the inside of crescents.

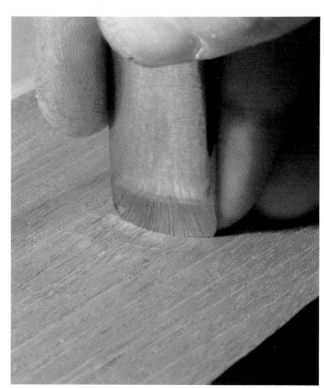

Fig 5.85 Close-up of cleaning the crescent root, starting by deepening the vertical wall. You can see that it is the corner of the tool which does the work, producing a clean crescent with a vertical inner wall, like that shown here.

Fig 5.86 Position of the fingers for vertical cuts in the opposite direction. Note the middle finger is resting on the wood, acting as a fence.

FOR THE ANGLED CUT

If you leave your middle finger in the hollow of the blade as you lean it to the left, you cannot see what you are doing. Take it out of the hollow to join the two fingers resting on the wood. Bring the nail of your middle finger a little around the back of the blade to support the bevel. The nail and knuckle of the middle finger now join the thumb in acting as a fulcrum on which to pivot the cut. Your thumb and index fingers should still straddle the sides of the blade (see Fig 5.87).

Clean up the crescent in the same way as before, using the tool in these new finger positions, and bringing your body behind the cut. Again be careful of the depth. Keep these crescents for Exercise ∎18.

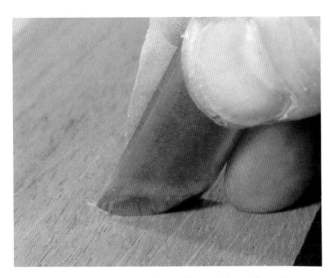

Fig 5.87 The position of the fingers for angled cuts from the opposite direction.

AIMS AND PROBLEMS

The crescents in both directions should be neat along their surface edges, ideally with the walls flat. However, if they end up a little concave, this is fine. The root should be a tidy join with no evidence of stab cuts.

Cuts like these with the gouge are *compound* actions: one hand rotates the handle and adjusts the angle of presentation as the blade pivots on the thumb, while the fingers of the other hand sensitively control the cut of sharp corner and edge; their direction and depth.

At first, the finger positions may feel a little awkward. The whole movement, where both hands work together in one fluid movement, takes a little getting used to, but it will be obvious when you are manipulating the tool correctly. The only way to achieve this is of course to keep repeating this simple exercise! I suggest you cut at least 10 crescents.

When you do a lot of curved cuts in this way, you may find your thumb and the knuckle of your middle finger on which the blade pivots get sore, or that your fingers cramp or tire quickly. You will find that these parts soon toughen up, and your fingers and thumb will strengthen with practice. Cramping is caused by tensing the fingers, so *do* relax. If you find a sore thumb a problem however, a plaster will help to cushion and protect.

VARIATIONS

Cut crescents in both directions; with different gouges; to different sizes; and in different directions to the grain.

∎18 CRESCENTS (II)

CONTEXT

This exercise concentrates on cutting the *inside* curve of the crescents cut in the previous exercise, using a gouge 'upside down' for an angled cut.

Between the points of the crescent, the inside curve is flatter than the outside. Add to this the fact that gouges cut a deeper hollow when used at an angle, and you will see we need a significantly flatter gouge than the one used for the outside curve.

TOOLS

- No. 5 x 16mm (⅝in) straight gouge.

METHOD

1   Start with a crescent (as cut in the last exercise) which has its hollow to the right if you are right dominant; otherwise to the left. This is the easiest type to master.

2 Look at the crescent: it consists of an outside angled wall and an inside vertical wall over the root. The root itself starts at one corner (on the surface), descends to a low point in the centre, and rises again to the surface at the far corner. When cutting the inside curve you need to bear in mind the shape of the root as much as its surface edge.

3 Hold the gouge in the pen and dagger grip, its sweep orientated as the crescent, and place it approximately over the vertical wall (which drops to the root of the curve), with its near corner exactly on the lower point of the crescent.

4 Tilt the handle of gouge to the right (to give the correct cutting angle), and towards you a little to lift its leading corner – it is the corner and near cutting edge of the blade which will do the work here.

5 Now pivot the gouge on your thumb while pushing it forward a little so that it slices the shape of the inner curve. Take a small cut to begin with, then stronger cuts as you become more confident.

6 For the full cut, the near corner of the tool must descend into the crescent and follow the root line – at the same time as its cutting edge incises the surface line – rising out at the far point (see Fig 5.88).

7 If the wood is very hard, you may need to deftly remove some of the waste of the crescent with a mallet before proceeding to the full cut, as described in Stage 6, above.

Repeat the exercise on as many crescents as possible until you feel comfortable with the technique. Then move on to work with the crescents facing in the opposite direction (to the left).

For these, the approach is exactly the same as above, but with the finger positions altered into the tool grip described in Exercise ∎17 on page 76. Again, continue cutting these inner sides to crescents until you are confident with the technique, and then combine the last two exercises, and incise some full crescents (i.e. angle cuts to both sides). A summary of the method for this is:

Fig 5.88 *Cutting the inner wall of the crescent. Slicing begins with the corner of the gouge following the root, and exiting at the other corner.*

1   Make a stab cut to the centre using the mallet.

2   With the same gouge, make the outside angle cut using the mallet.

3   With the same gouge, clean up the outside angle cut by hand.

4   Swap to the flatter gouge to make the inner angle cut by hand (use the mallet if necessary to begin with).

5   Clean up as necessary with either gouge.

It may be that, in order to get a clean root, you need to swap between gouges a few times. Final touches may need the merest stroke with the cutting edge to release wood fibres. Try and visualize your cuts and make them as few and telling as possible – the more swapping and fiddling about you do, the slower the work and more laboured the final appearance.

AIMS AND PROBLEMS

The inside wall should be as flat as possible from surface to root as it curves round the crescent; it may have a slight 'belly' from the hollow of the gouge, but this is acceptable. The root line and surface edges should be clean and flowing, and the points of the crescent neat.

The knack is to *keep an eye on both the root and the surface edge as you work*, and manipulating the corner and near edge of the gouge to make a smooth cut. This applies to the shaping of both the inside and outside walls of crescents.

Most students find one orientation of the gouge – and therefore the carving in one direction of the inner crescent wall – easier than the other. However, persevere: adjusting your fingers on the tool grip and the position of your body will quickly become natural to you, providing you put in the practice! Aim to finish off 10 decent crescents with inside cuts, and then incise several complete crescents.

VARIATIONS

Finish off all the crescents you cut in the previous exercise, and then cut some full crescents while varying the size and the orientation: hollow to the left, to the right, above and below.

∎19 CIRCLES

CONTEXT

This important exercise extends crescents into fuller curves, and then into circles, working first on the outer angle cut, then on the inner. With crescents, it is easy to see, and hence to work with, the *change* of depth with width. However, you also need to be able to keep to the *same* depth of cut, consistently, while the width of the trench stays the same.

TOOLS

- No. 6 x 20mm ($^3/_4$in), No. 5 x 16mm ($^5/_8$in) gouges.
- Compass.

METHOD

1   You used the no. 6 gouge to stab circles previously. Use the compass to draw a circle to fit its sweep. Then draw a second circle about 3mm ($^1/_8$in) *inside* the first circle. Then draw a third circle the same distance *inside* the second. The centre line follows the root of the trench to be cut, and the other two lines form the outer and inner surface edges of the trench.

2   Stab round the middle circle vertically with the gouge, turning the tool to follow the line while lifting the leading corner. In a letter, this would be the stop cut which follows round the root line.

3   Hold the same gouge in the pen and dagger grip and take out a small crescent cut from the outside of the stab cut to the right. This crescent should extend to the outer line, with its depth about the same as the width between the lines. It is in effect the 'embryonic' outside wall.

4   To extend the crescent in an anticlockwise direction, keep the angle and place the cutting edge in the root so that the bevel rests on the start of the outside wall.

5   Lift the far corner of the gouge so that about one third of the cutting edge is clear of the wood, while keeping the bevel against the outside wall.

6   Push the gouge forward with your thumb and rotate the handle so that the edge slices a continuation of the crescent cut.

7   You will find that the amount of forward movement you can make will depend a lot on the hardness of the wood. Go as far as you can, then finish off the cut by slicing the cutting edge down to the root. Maintain the cutting angle and follow the outer line.

8   Start again by placing the gouge in this new cut and extend the crescent a little further round in the same way, using the outside line as your guide. The trick is to slice with the gouge as you push it forward with your thumb, controlling the direction with the dagger hand (see Fig 5.89).

Fig 5.89 Extending a crescent into a circle.

9   Keep going like this, and you will turn what started as a crescent into a circular trench. It is possible, with a medium soft wood such as lime, to run the outer angle cut all the way round in one go.

10   You may need to deepen the stab cut to release the chip. Leave cleaning up proper until the inside angle cut has been made.

11   Use the flatter gouge in the same manner to form the inside angle cut, working your way anticlockwise round the circle. It is often more difficult to keep the angle consistent while getting a smooth slice – the blade and handle must wind round quite dramatically to make good use of the corner.

12   Finally, clean up the root, if necessary returning to the first gouge.

AIMS AND PROBLEMS

The result should be a neat circle of uniform width and depth with a centre root, flat walls and tidy edges.

As with the last exercises, there is a knack to this technique which comes fairly quickly with practice. Beginners tend to stab the root heavily and go deeper than they should. Relax, and go lightly with the corner of the tool in the root, especially when cleaning up. Don't make the trench too wide to begin with.

Repeat the exercise until you find you can get a good-looking circle, and do attempt the following variations, as they will be very helpful for incising diverse curved letterforms.

VARIATIONS

Cut the circle in the opposite (clockwise) direction, and when you feel confident, some wider trenches. In practice the waste is removed from large and deep curves with a mallet, (see Exercise ∎20) and you can experiment with this here. Finally, try different sizes of circle, working out which size of gouge is appropriate for each.

∎20 LETTER O

CONTEXT

The circle you incised in the previous exercise had the same width of trench all the way round, and in this it differed from the previous crescents you carved, which were of varying trench widths. The letter **O** in modern roman is something of a hybrid between the two: the outside line is circular and compass-struck but, in order to obey the 'horizontal: thin; vertical: thick' rule, the inside line varies smoothly in its distance from the outer circle. As the trench gets wider, it also gets deeper, and vice versa.

In the finished letter, the maximum thickness of the trench is midway between cap and base lines, and the thinnest points are at the exact top and bottom. This is because the stress is vertical. If you look at Fig 5.90 you will see the inside vertical walls are flatter to accommodate this change, and to achieve this you will need to use a flatter gouge.

TOOLS

- No. 6 x 20mm (³/₄in), No. 5 x 16mm (⁵/₈in) gouges.

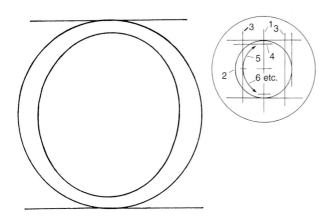

Fig 5.90 *O: construction.*

METHOD

1 Construct the letterform as shown in Fig 5.89. Try to estimate the centre line by eye rather than drawing it.

2 Use the no. 6 x 20mm (³/₄in) gouge and mallet to stab all round the centre line. Start in the widest part with a strong vertical stab, but remember that the stab cut must become shallower in the thinner parts. As the cut is vertical, there is no need to change hands (see Fig 5.91).

Fig 5.91 *Begin with the centre stop cuts.*

3 Use the mallet to cut away waste into the trench around the outside of the letter, *keeping within the line*. Keep a careful eye on the depth, and lean the gouge out at the appropriate angle (60°). You may have to stab vertically again in the wider parts to relieve the chips of wood and lower the root (see Fig 5.92).

Fig 5.92 *Make angled cuts to the outside.*

Fig 5.93 *Use the same gouge for the top and bottom inside angle cuts.*

Fig 5.94 *Then swap to a flatter gouge for the middle section.*

Fig 5.95 *Clean up the outside wall down to the root. You may have to work on the inner walls as well at this stage.*

4   Because gouges can be made to make deeper curves, you can cut the inner walls at the top and bottom of the letter with the same gouge. Remove waste carefully and extend the inner walls to either side, where they will eventually merge with the flatter inner walls (see Fig 5.93).

5   Switch to the flatter gouge and make an inside angle cut to the flatter inside curve on one side. The gouge will, of course, be 'upside down', to match the inner wall of the letter. Keep within the drawn lines and do not try to cut down to the root, as you are only removing waste at this stage (see Fig 5.94).

6   Swap mallet hands and remove a symmetrical angled cut on the opposite side.

7   At this stage the letter will look a bit of a mess. Don't panic! The next step is to clean up and shape the outer and inner walls in the manner of the last exercise, when you cut circles. The difference is in having to take the varying depth into account, which is like the crescent cutting in Exercises ∎17 and ∎18.

8   Begin with the outside and the deeper gouge. Start at the widest part (on the right), and work upwards and anticlockwise from here to the thin part. Then move to the bottom half of this side, and finally transfer to the left half of the letterform and follow the same sequence: middle, bottom, top (see Fig 5.95).

9   Sweep the cutting edges of the gouges accurately around the curves, keeping the leading corner clear of the wood, swapping finger positions and adjusting your body to each cut. Use the same gouge for as long as possible before moving on to the next. Make sure that the two walls meet neatly without stab cuts or torn fibres in the root of the trench (see Fig 5.96).

Fig 5.96 The finished letter.

AIMS AND PROBLEMS

You have now cut your first curved letter – congratulations! All other curved letters are variations on this theme, differing either in size of curve, or in the specific shape that you have to work to.

The final letter should be crisp-looking with smoothly flowing edges, flat walls and a neat central root. As mentioned before, a *slight* bellying on the inside walls, or concavity to the outside walls is acceptable, as it will not really be noticeable.

If your letter **O** falls short of this description, then the answer is to carve others until they begin to look right. It usually takes more practice to cut curves than straights but, once mastered, I think you will enjoy carving them more.

I normally proceed in the order given in Stage 7 on page 83, dealing with the outside first, then the inside, then the final cleaning up. You may choose to keep the mallet and cut away some of the inside waste with the two gouges first before cleaning up, or to cut the outer curves in a different order. It doesn't particularly matter – what does is being methodical and as efficient as possible.

Aim to cut enough **O**s until you feel comfortable and in control; I suggest 10. A real test of control is to cut two letter **O**s next to each other as if they were a part of a word. You will need to draw them accurately first, so look up details of **O** in the individual letters section that follows the exercises.

VARIATIONS

Carve different sizes of **O**, using different gouges.

■21 LETTERS C & S

CONTEXT

The letter **C** is relatively straightforward, with only the top arm, which flattens a little, and the serif, needing special attention.

The letter **S** is easier than it looks! In this letterform there is a short flat central section; although hardly noticeable, it is carved first and greatly helps the subsequent carving of the curves. **S** has two different curves, both smaller than those you have tackled so far. If you can incise this letter, all other small, lobed letterforms can be cut as well.

TOOLS

- No. 5 x 16mm ($^5/_8$in), no. 6 x 20mm ($^3/_4$in), 13mm ($^1/_2$in), and 10mm ($^3/_8$in) gouges.

- 13mm ($^1/_2$in) fishtail chisel.

- No. 4 x 16mm ($^5/_8$in) fishtail gouge. A skew chisel may be needed in the root of the serif.

METHOD

C
Refer to Fig 5.97. Most of this letter can be treated like **O**.

1 Stab the centre line using the mallet and the no. 6 x 20mm ($^3/_4$in) gouge.

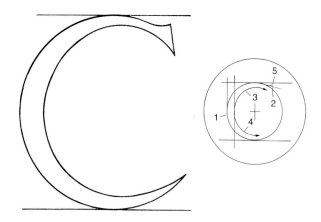

Fig 5.97 C: construction.

Fig 5.98 Make the end wall cut.

Fig 5.99 Finish the top wall of the serif. Cutting the serif can often be done without stop cuts.

2 Make the angle cut to the outside using the mallet and the no. 6 x 20mm (³/4in) gouge.

3 Make a flat angle cut to the more vertical inside part, using the mallet and the no. 5 x 16mm (⁵/8in) gouge.

4 Make the remaining inner angle cuts with the mallet and the no. 6 x 20mm (³/4in) gouge.

5 Clean up by hand, sweeping the curves.

6 For the lower arm, bring the end to a point, in the same way as you have previously cut crescents.

7 For the upper arm, begin, as with the lower arm, by running the curve into a crescent, the point of which coincides with the lower corner of the serif. The way I have drawn C in Fig 5.97, the sense of flattening occurs mainly on the outer part of the arm – the inner counter remains curved. If you want to flatten the inner counter more, then switch to a flatter gouge.

8 Next, tackle the serif in the usual way. Use the fishtail chisel to make stop cuts. The lower bracket is already formed, so use the chisel to make the end wall cut to the serif, and shape the upper bracket. It is at this point that you can make a long merging cut to the upper bracket that gives a flatter more open appearance to the letter (see Figs 5.98 and 5.99).

The finished letter is shown in Fig 5.100.

Fig 5.100 Finished letter C.

S

1   Refer to Fig 5.101. Start by removing an oblique straight trench from the centre part of the **S** with the fishtail chisel. Make sure that the straight cuts do not extend into the territory of the curved cuts.

2   From the oblique trench, cut the upper and lower curves following the same pattern as you did with the **C**. You will be using different sizes of tool, but the technique is the same, and in some ways it is easier because the bends are smaller (though you still need to use your body to avoid stress to your elbows).

3   Make sure that the curves merge with the straight section so that the straight is hardly obvious at all. You may need to return to the straight chisel for this.

4   For the upper serif, run the inner counter line into the end at the lower point of the serif first, and then shape the top part of the serif in a similar manner to the **C**. Use the fishtail gouge for the curved top bracket, and the chisel for the end wall.

5   For the lower serif, run the inner counter line to the upper corner of the serif. Make stop cuts into the corners of the serif and use the fishtail gouge to pick up the lower edge of the curved trench and sweep it elegantly into the serif. Use the fishtail chisel for the end wall. The finished letter is shown in Fig 5.102.

AIMS

If you have mastered the techniques covered so far, these letters should present no problem. Both letters should have flowing lines, clean, flat walls and neat central roots with no stab marks.

The letter **S** may be cut without the straight oblique section. Begin with the curved stab cuts and take out the upper and lower trenches. You will be left with a central part which can be tidied up with the corner and near edge of the fishtail chisel.

Aim to cut several letters until they come quickly and smoothly. You could time yourself – but don't sacrifice quality! As with **O**, a real test is to incise two of the same letters side by side.

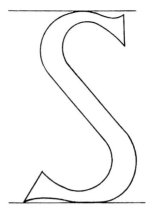 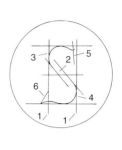

Fig 5.101 S: construction.

Fig 5.102 Finished letter: S.

VARIATIONS

Carve different sizes of letter, selecting different gouges. Feel free to experiment with the shapes and explore the technique. Look up the shapes of these letters in Chapter 6 for further details.

STRAIGHT/CURVED COMBINATIONS

∎22 LETTERS J, Q, D, U, G, P, R & B

CONTEXT

Having cut straight-only, and curved-only letters, putting the parts together is relatively simple – it is the junctions between them which need special care.

As with the previous letter sequences, I have based the sequence of letters on their ease of working and they should be practised in that order.

It is only necessary to run through these remaining letters briefly, indicating important points, such as the formation of junctions.

TOOLS

- Select from those used so far in the practical exercises for each letter.

METHOD

J

1　Refer to Fig 5.103. Incise the vertical trench.

2　Cut the top serif and the small half serif (to the base line).

3　Cut the tail as a crescent. Incise the inner edge from the straight, to end at a point, rather than the other way round, and merge the lines. Bring the outer line of the curve to meet the half serif at the base line (see Fig 5.104). You will need the fishtail chisel to clean the junction.

Fig 5.104　Detail of J, showing the tail and half serif.

Q

1　Refer to Fig 5.105. Incise a complete letter **O** first.

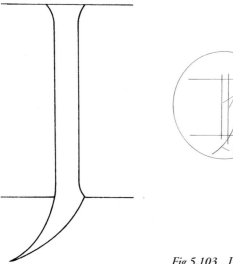

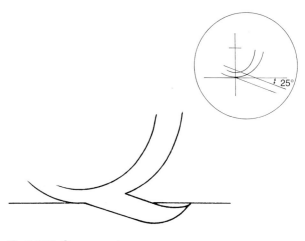

Fig 5.103　J: construction.　　*Fig 5.105　Q: construction.*

2   Remove a short straight trench to start the tail, and end it with a crescent. The danger here is for wood to crumble where the tail meets the main body of the letter; more so if you want the tail to cross into the counter. Wood fractures if the initial, wedge-like stop cut is too heavy, so keep your cuts light.

D

1   Refer to Figs 5.106 and 5.107. Carve the upright trench.

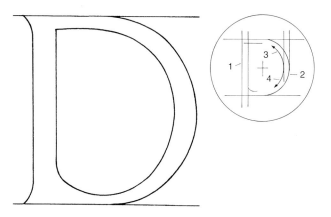

Fig 5.106 D: construction.

Fig 5.107 Finished letter D.

2   Make the top and bottom stop cuts to the serifs.

3   Carve the curved bowl.

4   The junctions are like those for **L** or **F**, carved in Exercise ∎11, but with more subtlety to their shape. The fishtail chisel is the best tool for finishing off the square top junction. The bottom junction is best tackled with the fishtail gouge, running the inner counter line to the vertical and reversing the tool to sweep the outer line into the serif. As with **L**, etc., round over the lower junction last of all.

U

1   Refer to Fig 5.108. Carve the upright trenches first. Make sure the left trench does not invade the curved part of the letter.

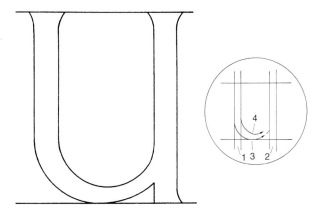

Fig 5.108 U: construction.

2   Make the stop cuts for serifs with the fishtail chisel and finish off the lower left hand corner of the stem on the right – the bracket of the serif is missing here.

3   Bring the curve round to the right hand stem. Be gentle with the stabbing near the junction: this part is very weak, and the little triangle between the bowl and the upright must not be jumped out. Continue the curve as a thin line into the upright, rather than ending at a point (see Fig 5.109).

Fig 5.109 U: detail of the junction.

G

1   Refer to Fig 5.110. Cut the short upright stem first, allowing for the serif as usual.

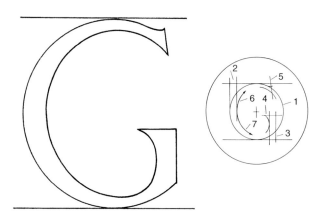

Fig 5.110 G: construction.

2   Make stop cuts to the serif, and also for a half serif on the lower part of the stem. In this, **G** resembles **J**.

3   For the curved bowl, run the top part of the curve into the serif, as for **C**. Run the lower part into the bottom of the stem to meet the serif. On the inside junction, an angle should be evident, rather than a smooth curve.

4   Finish off the serifs, treating the top serif like **C** (see Fig 5.111).

*Fig 5.111 Finished letter **G**.*

P

1   Refer to Fig 5.112. Carve the upright trench.

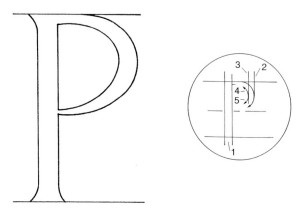

Fig 5.112 P: construction.

2   Carve the stop cuts.

3   For the lobe, allow the bottom part to break neatly into the upright. The top part is like a smaller version of **D** (see Fig 5.113).

Fig 5.113 Finished letter P.

Fig 5.115 Finished letter R.

R

1 Refer to Fig 5.114. Carve the upright trench.

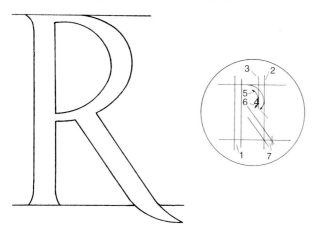

Fig 5.114 R: construction.

2 Carve the straight section of the leg (all straights are carved at the same stage.) Allow a gap between the lobe and the oblique trench, and enough room to join in the curve below.

3 Carve the stop cuts.

4 Then carve the lobe – as for **P**.

5 Carve the serifs.

6 Join in the leg using the fishtail chisel.

7 Then add the tail to the leg, merging in a crescent (see Fig 5.115).

B

1 Refer to Fig 5.116. Carve the upright trench.

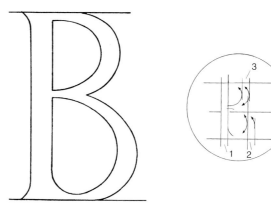

Fig 5.116 B: construction.

2   Make the stop cut for serifs.

3   The different sized bowls of this letter require different gouges. Cut the top bowl first, coming round into the upright at the top, like the **P**, and cutting into it neatly at the bottom. Then cut the lower bowl, bringing it up to the first and merging it in so that the junctions with the stem coincide. Note that this bowl has a slightly flattened upper surface which needs controlled toolwork.

4   Carve the serifs and finish off the junctions at the top (as **P**) and the bottom (as **D**). The finished letter is shown in Fig 5.117).

*Fig 5.117 Finished letter **B**.*

AIMS AND PROBLEMS

You have now cut all the letters of the modern roman alphabet. Of them all you probably found **B**, rather than **S**, the most difficult to shape and carve well. This is no surprise as it is the hardest letter to do, and requires more practice than any of the others. Problems sometimes arise through having to concentrate on more than one thing at a time. For example, it is not uncommon for depth to get out of control while paying attention to the surface edges. As always, you need to repeat the exercise so that familiarity fits all the actions together.

Now you should be able to tackle any other letter style, and be able to form whatever curves, straights, or combinations of these elements you want. For example, roman numerals have no parts or junctions that you are not already familiar with, from working through the alphabet.

You may have found that you prefer to cut the letter parts differently, or in a different order, from that which I have suggested. Feel free to experiment – what I have offered here should be regarded as sound starting guidelines rather than unalterable rules.

As with the other exercises, cut several of each letter, and then cut two of the same letter next to one another. Refer to the following chapter to familiarize yourself with the specific details of individual letters.

VARIATIONS

Try carving different sizes of letter.

▮23 USING THE V TOOL

CONTEXT

I rarely use the V tool for incised lettering, for reasons which should be apparent by the end of this exercise. However, it *does* have a place, and can be useful in styles with flamboyant strokes, that look more like pen or brush lettering. The V tool tends to be of more use in raised lettering and you will find further exercises for that context on page 131. In this exercise I want to give you an idea of what the V tool can and cannot do, so that you can decide when and whether you wish to use it.

TOOLS

- 60° x 16mm (³/₈in) V tool.
- 16mm (³/₈in) skew chisel.
- Pencil.

CROSS REFERENCES

- V tool (page 16).
- Low-angle grip (page 17).

METHOD

1 Start with a clean, flat piece of wood, clamped to the bench.

2 Hold the V tool in the low-angle grip. You need to be competent switching hands to prevent awkward movements. It is best to practise this from the start. The heel of the front hand slides over the wood to fix the angle of cut. Raise or lower the handle to deepen (widen) or lighten the cut. Tension between hands controls forward movement. Follow the tool with your whole body. The corners of the tool should remain above the surface, never cutting into the wood (see Fig 5.118).

3 Make a series of parallel straight cuts away from you, copying each previous cut as closely as possible. Lower the handle of the tool a little after you have commenced each cut, then lower it again as you leave the cut. The corners of the tool should remain above the surface, never cutting into the wood.

4 Now try making deeper and shallower cuts, in all directions, straight and curved, with and across the grain, changing hands according to direction (see Fig 5.119). Try freehand 'drawing' as well.

5 When you have finished, use the point of a skew or fishtail chisel to cut off and tidy the ends of the individual trenches.

6 Use the mallet as well with quick light taps, and when you feel comfortable with the tool, start a spiral from the outside and work the V channel tighter and tighter towards the centre, and see what

Fig 5.118 Running grooves with the V tool. Both hands work together to control and manipulate the cut.

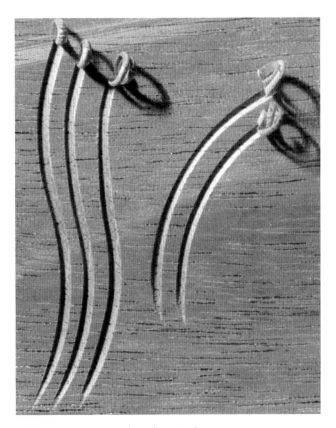

Fig 5.119 Grooves made with a V tool.

happens – Figs 5.120 and 5.121 give a clue to the likely outcome.

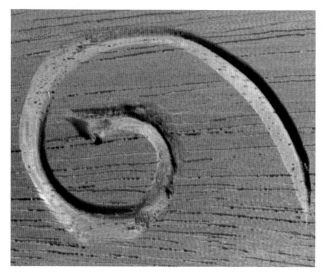

Fig 5.120 A spiral cut made with a V tool.

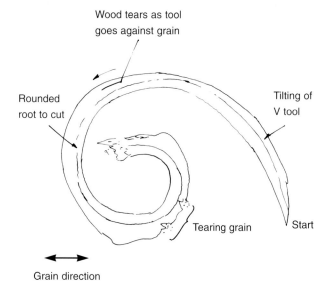

Wood tears as tool
goes against grain

Rounded
root to cut

Tilting of
V tool

Tearing grain

Start

Grain direction

Fig 5.121 Features of the cut, showing some of the problems you may have encountered.

AIMS AND PROBLEMS

I hope you experimented with the V tool, as this is the best way to find out what you can do with it. It is not easy to get flowing cuts to begin with, as both hands must co-ordinate with the eye and the rest of the body. Pivot on the corner bone of the hand which rests on the wood for curves. Cuts to the right are executed when the right hand holds the blade and rests on the wood, and vice versa.

From what happened in the exercise, and looking closely at the V channels and cuts, you can observe the following:

- **The root of the V trench is rounded.**
  As opposed to the sharp angle it would have had if it had been incised with carving tools. The appearance of letterforms will be affected by mixing the two, and if this cannot be avoided, then try and merge the rounded root with the sharp root slowly, rather than abruptly.

- **When one side of the V tool cuts *with* the grain, the other cuts *against* it.**
  With a very sharp V tool and dense wood, tearing grain is rarely a problem. If it starts to happen, try taking more, and lighter cuts, rather than fewer and heavier ones. You may also need to reverse the direction of cut, and lean the tool over slightly to clean up the torn trench wall.

- **As the curve gets tighter, the sides of the V tool judder and snatch the grain.**
  This is what happens with any straight carving tool attempting to negotiate a deep hollow. The greater the depth of cut, the more this effect is likely to happen. Cutting the spiral showed that the V tool is best at *slow* curves, and at tighter curves *only when the cut is shallower*. You may need to switch to carving tools for the tightest letter bends, which the V tool won't cut cleanly.

The limitations this tool has in cutting anything other than slow curves make it a poor choice for most incised lettering.

VARIATIONS

Try sketching and then imitating shorthand writing with the tool. If possible, try different sizes of V tool, and ones with a 45° angle.

CHAPTER 6

CHARACTERISTICS OF INDIVIDUAL LETTERS IN MODERN ROMAN

In this section I want to look at each letter of the modern roman alphabet in turn, making notes on the construction of individual letters, family resemblances (see also page 160) and some of the ways letters can be modified to help deal with optical effects (see also page 169). Following this section is a summary of width sizes, and some simple modifications you can make to this style of alphabet.

In describing the individual letters, I use two new terms. One **unit** is the width of a *thick* stroke, such as a vertical stem, as in letter **I**. One **half unit** is therefore the width of a *thin* stroke, which in modern roman is also half the thick stroke. For example, a horizontal arm, such as in **T** or **F** (see Fig 6.1).

Where I give alternative suggestions for shaping the letters, these are more standard practice than the 'modifications', which appear on page 106.

The numbers in brackets refer to the numbers shown on the drawings.

LETTERS A–Z

A

See Fig 6.2. The point extends slightly over the cap line, about one half unit (**1**). The apex of the junction lies on the vertical mid-line of the letter.

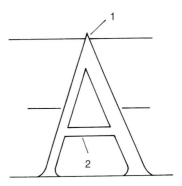

Fig 6.2   Features of the letter A.

The top inner counter tends to close up above the crossbar, which is a thin stroke (**2**). The bar should be placed *lower*, so that the two counters appear to have the same amount of space.

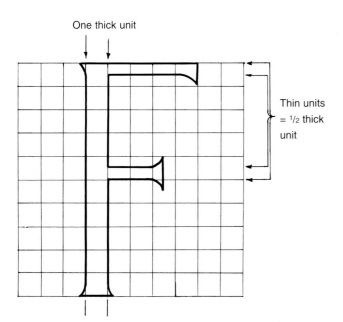

Fig 6.1   Dimensions of letter components and their placing can be discussed in terms of simple units, related to divisions of letter height.

B

See Fig 6.3. Although the 'natural' division of this letter would seem to be symmetrically about the mid-line, this actually makes it appear unstable. The centre join between the lobes is raised about one half unit. Optically, this will look in the mid-position (**1**). This enlarges the lower lobe, with an extra width of about one unit over the upper lobe (**2**). Don't make the lower lobe too wide, or the letter will look fat.

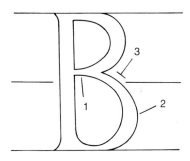

Fig 6.3   Features of the letter B.

The lower lobe is also flattened slightly on its top part, leading the eye to the junction and the top lobe (**3**). The curve of the lobe should still be rising as it meets the stem, and *not* meet it horizontally.

C

See Fig 6.4. This letter should be extended slightly *above* the cap line and below the base line (**1**). Its width is about one unit (i.e. a little narrower than **O**).

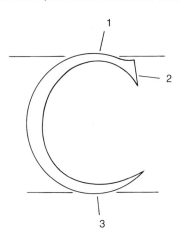

Fig 6.4   Features of the letter C.

C is compass struck in the modern roman style, but is not simply a cut off **O**. The top arm is flattened (i.e. lies more horizontally), and is slightly elongated to open up the counter.

The top serif of **C** angles away from the vertical to open the mouth of the letter, and is stronger than the bottom serif (**2**). It can also be stronger than the top serif in **G**, as the arm of **G** takes up inner space.

The bottom curve of **C** may be slightly heavier than the stress in this style would normally dictate, and tapers to a point, while still following the circle (**3**). Alternatively, it may flatten out slightly, and have a small serif angle away from the vertical, similar, but smaller than, the top serif.

The thickest point of **C** should be slightly thicker than the normal thick width.

D

See Fig 6.5. The width of **D** is a little less than the full circle of **O**, but is definitely *not* a half circle – there needs to be a feeling of roundness and width.

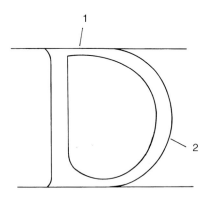

Fig 6.5   Features of the letter D.

The curve of **D** becomes a thin horizontal stroke at the top and bottom, adding space within the letter (**1**). This letter looks good in a family with an angle at the top junction, and a curve at the lower one.

D does not need to extend beyond the cap or base lines, because of the solid way in which it meets them.

The stress in the curve of this letter is vertical (**2**). The thickest point should be made slightly thicker than the normal width.

E

See Fig 6.6. Stability is given to this letter by its different limb lengths. The lower arm is the longest (**1**). This should be merged with the serif, pointing the serif out to open the counter and prevent any sense of the letter being 'closed in'. The upper arm is the next shortest, by about one half unit (not including the serif) (**2**). The serif is either square or, preferably, pointing out to open the counter. If this is the case, point the serif out at a lesser angle than the lower serif. The same applies to **F**. The centre arm is shorter again by a half unit, but should not be made to look stubby (**3**). It is always at right angles to the main stem and its distinct serif ends vertically.

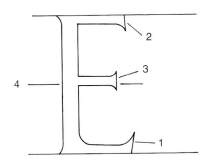

*Fig 6.6   Features of the letter **E**.*

The centre arm should be raised by a half unit above the mid-line, to open the lower counter which tends to look smaller (**4**). Raising the centre arm also adds further stability to the letter.

F

See Fig 6.7. This letter is essentially the upper part of **E**, which it should resemble in terms of arm lengths. The lower arm looks better left at the mid-line, as there is plenty of space below, unless it is next to an **E**, in which case an echo of the **E** form is preferable (**1**), so that the lower arm of **F** is at the same level as the mid-arm of **E**.

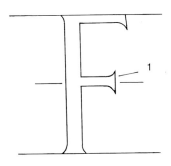

*Fig 6.7   Features of the letter **F**.*

G

See Fig 6.8. This letter should resemble **C** in its flattened top part (with serif), its overall curve, its size and its sense of roundness. The top serif (**1**) should be a little smaller than that of **C**, because the counter is taken up with the vertical arm, and may overhang the stem slightly.

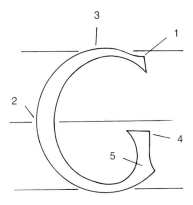

*Fig 6.8   Features of the letter **G**.*

The thickest point of **G** should be slightly thicker than the normal thick stroke (**2**), and the letter should be slightly above the cap line and below the base line (**3**). The stem should end in a horizontal, square serif somewhere between the mid-line and one unit *below* it (**4**). The serif may point inwards only, or be present on both sides of the stem. The stem may be shortened to make the letter appear 'lighter' to suit the overall spacing in a word.

Where the lowest part of the curve rises to meet the stem, it should be allowed to thicken a little before the junction (**5**). The junction of stem and curve may swell as a discrete serif to the far side, or the stem may be allowed to drop below the base line, in a tail – as with **J**.

H

See Fig 6.9. Essentially a wide letter, **H** is made of two **I**s joined with a thin crossbar. Although the letter width is variable, depending on the evenness of space between the surrounding letters, it should not be made too narrow.

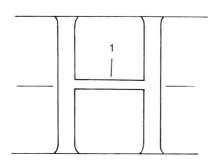

Fig 6.9 *Features of the letter* **H**.

The crossbar should be raised by a half unit above the mid-line, to create an even feel to the spaces in the letter; otherwise the lower counter will look smaller (**1**).

I

See Fig 6.10. **I** is the basic stem unit of modern roman. Although you can find examples of **I** being used to replace **J** in classical inscriptions, this is not a practice I recommend in modern lettering! Sometimes the lower serif of **I** is made slightly heavier than the upper, to stand the letter more firmly on the base line.

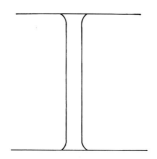

Fig 5.37 *F: construction.*

J

See Fig 6.11. **J** resembles **I** in its upper portion (**1**). The serif should be made more distinct, and extended a little to the left.

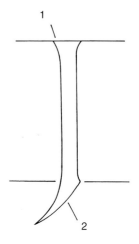

Fig 6.11 *Features of the letter* **J**.

The tail can be drawn out in a curve, on to the base line, or below it, and can resemble the lower arms of **K** and **R** (**2**). A subtle half serif is another alternative, opposing the flow of the tail's curve. The tail should not be curved in on itself, nor made to be too long, as this makes the letter look unbalanced. The tail should be somewhat abrupt, and preserve the straightness of the stem. A **J** with the tail crossing the base line looks more stable than a **J** which perches on it. As a guide, the tail should reach forwards about one unit (i.e. the width of the letter), and go below the line to between one-quarter and one-third the height of the letter.

Another option is to end the tail *above* the base line in a discrete serif, like the lower arm of **C**.

K

See Fig 6.12. Like **B**, there is a natural symmetry around the mid-line of **K** which makes the junction appear too low. The junction should be raised a half unit above the mid-line to balance this effect and make the letter appear more stable (**1**).

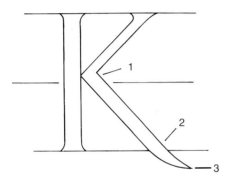

Fig 6.12 Features of the letter K.

The lower end of the (descending) leg meets the base line a thick unit *beyond* a line dropped vertically from where the rising arm meets the cap line (**2**). This enlarged lower part of **K** gives a strong, 'scaffolded' feeling, and prevents the lower counter closing up. The leg should be straight, and can end in a serif or tail (**3**). A 'wavy' leg should be avoided. The tail may extend below the base line, or rest on it, depending on the amount of the space with the next letter in the text. Treat **R** the same way.

L

See Fig 6.13. Essentially this is the lower part of **E**, which it should resemble closely. There is scope for lengthening or shortening the leg to fill in open space against the next letter (**1**). The lower serif should be tilted out, to open up the counter (**2**).

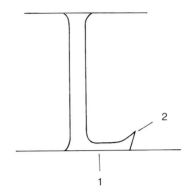

Fig 6.13 Features of the letter L.

M

See Fig 6.14. In modern roman, the outer legs of **M** are left vertical. They may be splayed outwards a little, (about one thick unit), to open up the side counters, but **M** should never be made to look like an inverted **W**.

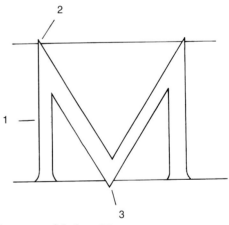

Fig 6.14 Features of the letter M.

The first vertical leg is (exceptionally), thin, in order to give a pleasing pattern of thin, thick, thin, thick to the letter (**1**). The top angles end in points, which are projected a little above the cap line (**2**).

Serifs are commonly added to **M** in modern roman. Rest the serifs on the cap line, and hook them to the outside of the letter only. **A** and **N** should be treated in the same way.

The middle point of **M** may project slightly *below* the base line, or end a thick unit above it (**3**).

N

(See Fig 6.15). According to the rules, all the parts of this letter should be thick, but as this looks heavy and dull, the uprights are, exceptionally, thin, and the two serifs on each leg should be made distinct (**1**).

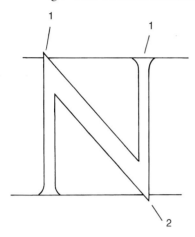

Fig 6.15 Features of the letter N.

In modern roman the angles of **N** end in points – like **A** and **M** – which project slightly above the cap, and below the base lines (**2**).

A top serif is also common, but *never* on the bottom angle. The serif is part of the vertical, not the oblique, component. It rests on the cap line and extends to the left only, following the sense of the diagonal. **A** and **M** should be treated in the same way.

O

See Fig 6.16. **O** is compass struck in modern roman, with the stress vertical, like the other rounded letters. The letter can be made narrower for evenness of colour, but remember to match it with the other rounded forms.

O should be extended slightly above the cap line and below the base line (**1**), and its thickest point made slightly thicker than the normal thick stroke (**2**).

The line of the inner curve must flow continuously as it flattens somewhat through the vertical (**3**).

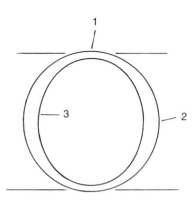

Fig 6.16 Features of the letter O.

P

See Fig 6.17. **P** is not just a cut off **B** or **R**. The bowl of this letter is larger, and needs to appear quite strong. The lower end of the bowl – a thin stroke coming in horizontally – touches the stem at a right angle a little *below* the mid-line, taking away any sense of 'legginess' in the letter. Sometimes a little gap is left.

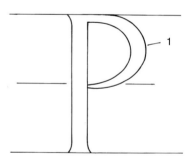

Fig 6.17 Features of the letter P.

The external line may be compass-struck, and the thickest point of the loop made slightly thicker than the normal thick unit (**1**).

Q

See Fig 6.18. This is essentially **O** with a tail. The tail is a strong, graceful wide stroke of variable length (**1**). It should not intrude into the circle itself – this would tend to close down the letter. The tail should be started about one unit to the right of the point where the main circle meets the base line. It then descends at an angle of about 25° to the base line, straight, with a curve on the end, rather like the leg of **K** and **R**. Avoid a 'wavy' tail.

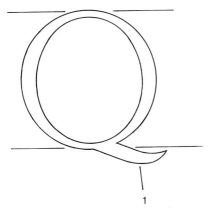

Fig 6.18 Features of the letter Q.

R

See Fig 6.19. The inner curve of the bowl descends to meet the stem at right angles. A corner is formed by the lower end of the loop meeting the top end of the oblique leg. This corner meets the stem at a *point*, rather than cutting it (**1**).

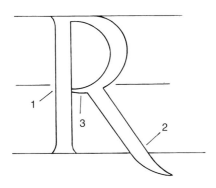

Fig 6.19 Features of the letter R.

Although the leg commonly arises from the lowest point of the loop, where it abuts the stem, another common variation is for the leg to arise about one unit (but no more) along the loop, which avoids cutting short grain. (Treat **K** in the same manner.) The lower end of the leg meets the base line one unit beyond a vertical line dropped from the outside of the bowl. This means the leg lies at an angle of about 45° (**2**). The lower counter of **R** is thus enlarged, and this prevents a closed up, unstable feeling to the letter. The leg should be straight and feel as if it *supports* the letter. It ends in a serif (resembling **A** and **K**), or a tail (resembling **K**). A tail may rest on the line or extend below it. These options will affect the amount of space between **R** and the next letter.

The bowl should be strong and round, like the upper bowl of **B**. The point where the loop meets the stem should be lowered by a half unit, rather than leaving it at the true mid-point (**3**).

S

See Fig 6.20. In the exercises, the central section of **S** was somewhat straight for ease of cutting, although this 'straightness' should hardly be apparent (**1**). A continuous curve is of course an alternative. In this case, make an initial straight central section as before, but smaller (having more a function of a stop cut), which will be ultimately subsumed into the curved trenches.

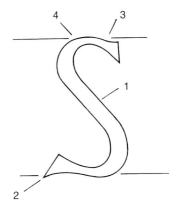

Fig 6.20 Features of the letter S.

If **S** is drawn with an equal, geometrical symmetry, rather than optical symmetry, the centre of gravity will appear rather high, as with **B**. To compensate for this, the lower bowl should be made larger by raising the natural mid-point by about one unit. If **S** is drawn as two half circles, it will appear to fall backwards, to the left. To counter this, the lower end should be brought out to the left by about a unit beyond a vertical line dropped from the edge of the upper bowl. The lower serif should also be strengthened while tilting it to the right (**2**).

The upper counter should be opened by making the end of the arm more horizontal, with a light serif, tilted outwards, rather like **C** (**3**).

S should be extended slightly above the cap line and below the base line to avoid appearing short (**4**).

T

See Fig 6.21. The lower part of **T** is essentially an **I**. The cross arms may be lengthened or shortened to take up space with the adjacent letter, and preserve an even colour.

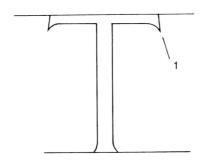

Fig 6.21 Features of the letter T.

Tilting the cross arm serifs opens up the counter a little (**1**). Each of these serifs may arise on the underside only, or, if smaller, extend to the upper side.

U

See Fig 6.22. **U** is best made with a stabilizing stem. The continuous round-bottomed form is lighter in weight (and so may be used to affect colour), but tends to look

unstable. As **U** was not an original roman letter, you are free to choose the round-bottomed form if you prefer, either with two thick uprights, or one thick (normally the left) and one thin upright.

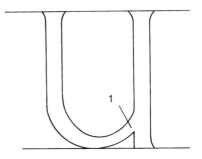

Fig 6.22 Features of the letter U.

The lowest point of the curve will be thin (i.e. a thin unit), slightly thickening again before meeting the stem (**1**). It should not be allowed to peter out to a point. Take care at the junction, as the little triangle of wood that remains below the junction will have short grain and be liable to break away. This is more of a problem with open-grained, less dense woods (such as oak), than with denser ones.

V

See Fig 6.23. **V** is essentially an inverted **A** without the crossbar. It must not be made too narrow and *never* used to replace **U**.

The apex of the junction lies on the vertical mid-line of the letter, and its point may project slightly *below* the base line (**1**).

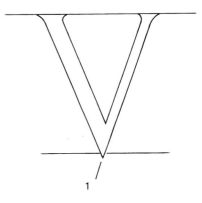

Fig 6.23 Features of the letter V.

W

See Fig 6.24. German, more appropriately, refers to **W** as 'double-V', rather than 'double-U'. The letter should be treated as two Vs, crossing in the middle and retaining all four serifs.

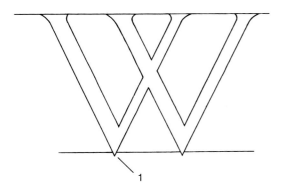

Fig 6.24 Features of the letter W.

Like **M**, **W** is a wide letter, and should not look pinched. It also follows the same pattern of thick and thin strokes.

It is not easy to keep the central serifs separated, especially when the letter needs to be tightened for space. Alternatives are to cut off the left thin oblique where it meets the inner thick one (so losing a serif), or having a central point (so losing both serifs).

The lower points may project slightly *below* the base line (**1**), and any upper mid-point slightly *above* the cap line, to give a sense of ending *on* them.

X

See Fig 6.25. If **X** is drawn with equal symmetry above and below the mid-line, the centre of gravity looks low and the lower counter appears smaller. The junction needs to be raised by about a half unit, which will bring the top corners together a little, and open up the lower counter (**1**).

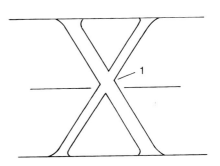

Fig 6.25 Features of the letter X.

Y

See Fig 6.26. The outside lines of the arms meet the stem at the mid-line, forming the same obtuse angle on either side (**1**). The thick stem and arm should be drawn first, and the thin arm then brought in to the junction (**2**).

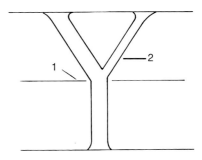

Fig 6.26 Features of the letter Y.

Z

See Fig 6.27. Like **N** this is a letter which breaks the thick/thin rules. The upper arm should be shortened by a half unit to prevent a sense of it overhanging (**1**). The serif may point down at right angles or be tilted out a little (as with **T**) to open the counter.

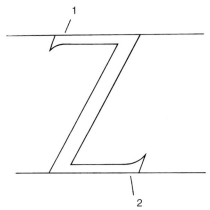

Fig 6.27 Features of the letter Z.

The lower leg can be lengthened by one half unit, with the serif orientated vertically or tilted outwards a little (**2**). There is scope for lengthening both horizontal components to fill in open space against the next letter.

&

See Fig 6.28. The ampersand was first used in the nineteenth century and combines elements of the letters **e** and **t**. In the main, it is a space-saving device to be used with discretion; it can add symmetry to names, for example. The stress is vertical in modern roman.

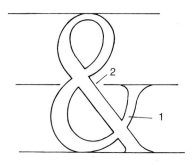

Fig 6.28 Features of the ampersand.

The rising arm remains a little thick as it brushes the base line, diminishing to (and keeping at) a half unit in width as it passes upwards to the serif. Alternatively it may end in a tail (**1**). The descending oblique leg is straight, like the leg of **A** (**2**).

FAMILY RESEMBLANCES

Table 4 gives a checklist of similarities, in addition to the ones we have met already, which arise between letters, or may be included.

SUMMARY OF WIDTHS

The height of a whole letter is fixed as the distance between cap and base line. The width of a letter *stroke* may be reckoned as a proportion of the height. The modern roman alphabet is made up of thick and thin strokes. The thick stroke is fixed as one eighth of the letter height to give a strong looking letter. This may of course be altered: a tenth will give a 'lighter', more elegant look, and this is the ratio of 'traditional' roman. Where a style is termed 'bold' or 'light' it is the thickness of the strokes in relation to the height which is under consideration.

The widths of whole letters vary between letter styles. In both modern and traditional roman, widths are more or less fixed, with the letterer having some scope for altering form within the style, to accommodate spacing with the next letter. Estimating letter widths by units can be useful for calculating word lengths when laying out. One 'classic' way of estimating the widths of letters is to use the ratio of upright stem thickness to letter height. If the distance between cap and base lines is 10 units, the overall letter widths for roman letterstyle can be given proportionally, as shown in Table 5.

Here, the width of the **I** is 1:10 of its height, giving a light, traditional roman letter weight.

If you maintain the proportional widths of whole letters given in the table, but use a ratio of 1:8 (upright stem thickness: letter height), then the letters will appear a little heavier. This is the ratio used in the exercises. The

Checklist of family resemblances	
Square junction at top of letter	B, D, E, F, P, R, T
Curves to the bottom junction which can optionally be hollowed for lightness	B, D
Flatter top horizontal arm	C, G, S
Compass struck	C, D, G, O, Q
Partially compass struck	P, B, R, S
Stressed as **O**	B, C, D, G, P, Q, R, S, U
Enlarged lower part	B, E, H, K, S, X
Free limbs occasionally drawn out	E, F, J, K, L, R, T, Z
Pointed letters which may extend above the cap line	A, M, N
Pointed letters which may extend below the base line	M, N, V, W
Letters which curve over the cap line and below the base line	C, O, G, Q, S

Table 4

Proportional letter widths	
Units	**Letters**
1	I, J
4	E, F, L
5	B, P, S
6	R, K
7	X
8	A, C, D, G, H, N, T, U, V, Y, Z
10	O, Q
13	M, W

Table 5

Letter widths	
Over wide	M, W,
Wide (1:1)	O, Q, C, G, D
Medium (3:4)	A, H, T, N, U, V, X, Y, Z
Narrow (1:2)	B, E, F, K, L, P, R, S
Over narrow	I, J

Table 6

thin strokes remain half the width of the thick strokes.

Another more general way of looking at letter widths is to group modern roman letters into roughly similar widths, as shown in Table 6.

Here, (1:1) means the ratio of height to width – in this case, square (see Fig 6.29).

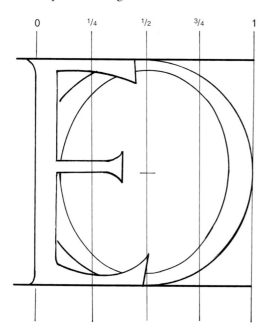

Fig 6.29 Letter widths based on proportions of a square between cap and base lines.

In both instances, these numbers and ratios are *only to be used as a guide* – helpful for calculations and when beginning lettering. Letter width is often decided by their 'feel', which in turn is decided on the basis of the experience of their designer. Work towards being familiar enough with all the letters to draw them to their correct widths (as you perceive this) by eye.

MODIFICATIONS TO MODERN ROMAN

Modern roman has many versions, differing in details such as serifs, proportions and weight of letterforms. Look around and you will see all sorts of variations. You might like to redraw some of the letters from the exercises with these changes in mind, to see how they look, but remember to maintain resemblances between like letters.

Here are a few examples of the way in which **A** may be modified.

- **Squared to the cap line.**
  Instead of a point, **A** can finish with a square end, at the cap line, and without a serif. This square end may be dropped a little on its left corner (see Fig 6.30). To maintain family resemblance you would need to consider the other letters ending in a point: **M, N, V** and **W**. Carve this by making an end wall on the thick stroke, as in the manner of carving a sans serif, but using straight tools and without splaying.

Fig 6.30 Letters such as A can end square to the cap line, rather than finishing with a (slightly extended) point.

- **Serif rather than point at the cap line.**
  Instead of a point, the **A** can end in a serif, not extending beyond the cap line (see Fig 6.31). Make the serif on the thick oblique stroke the same as – or slightly less wide than – that on the lower end, but beaked in the opposite direction. Bring the thin stroke to join it at the normal angle.

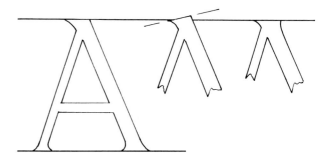

Fig 6.31 Alternatively, A and its family group (see Table 4, page 105) can end with a serif on the cap line.

- **Flourished.**
  The roman alphabet has a particularly crisp, martial feel about it, and really does not look well if

subjected to arabesques, or any sort of ornamentation which detracts from its essential classical form. However, some small flourish or 'tail' is sometimes given to the apex of **A** – this is made on the thick stroke, and the thin stroke is led up to it (see Fig 6.32). A similar flourish would also appear in **N**. A flourish on the left diagonal of **M** is also possible, but looks better if the legs are not splayed. The lower arms of **E**, **J**, **K** and **L** can also echo this flourish.

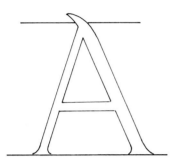

Fig 6.32 A small flourish can be added to A, as shown here, without detriment to the modern roman style.

Waisted.

A letter is 'waisted' when the straight parts, instead of having parallel edges, are a little thinner in the middle, giving the letter a waist (see Fig 6.33). This gives a more graceful, softer more elegant quality, but can easily be overdone. Details of how to waist a letter are given in Chapter 11 in the section dealing with the versal style (see page 178).

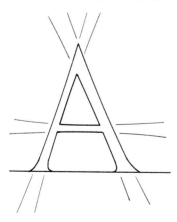

Fig 6.33 Waisting of letters occurs when the parts narrow a little in the middle. Sometimes this is mistakenly called 'entasis', which is the opposite effect and involves thickening *the middle of uprights.*

WORKING WITH ROMAN AND ARABIC NUMERALS

There are two styles of numeral. The first derives from the original Roman method of counting which is still seen in very formal settings, such as civic buildings, but is largely outmoded (see Fig 6.34). The second derives from Arabic, and is the style with which we are familiar on a day-to-day basis.

Fig 6.34 An example of Roman numerals carved in wood, in this case as pierced relief.

ROMAN NUMERALS

Roman numerals are not difficult to carve, as they are made up of combinations of letters:

I = 1	C = 100
V = 5	D = 500
X = 10	M = 1000
L = 50	

Nowadays it is unusual to find Roman numerals used in preference to ordinary numbers. They can be annoying to the majority of readers, who don't understand them, and are therefore never used where plain numbers will do.

The problem is in making sure you assemble them correctly to make the number you want. Numbers are made by grouping together and adding up the units shown above. The principle rule is that *only three units of one type can occur together.*

For example, 1, 2, 3 is I, II, III. According to the rule, no more than three Is may occur together so the next number (4) is made by *subtracting* from the next unit up (5). So 4 is IV. Then comes 5 (V), the next whole unit, and then you start again: VI, VII, VIII (6, 7, 8). 9 is IX, and so on. 1997 is MCMXCVII, made up of M (1000) + CM (900) + XC (90) + VII (7).

ARABIC-BASED NUMERALS

From their origins they have been conscripted into the roman style with which we are familiar. As Arabic script looks very different from roman, some bending of the 'rules' has had to occur to get them to fit, with varying degrees of success. There are several ways of presenting them. The challenge is to find an arrangement that looks a pleasing unit, like a word, rather than a jumble of shapes.

Carving Arabic numerals is straightforward: the numbers are made up of straight and curved sections, as are the letters (see Figs 6.35 and 6.36).

Fig 6.36 Numbers can be incised with exactly the same techniques as letters.

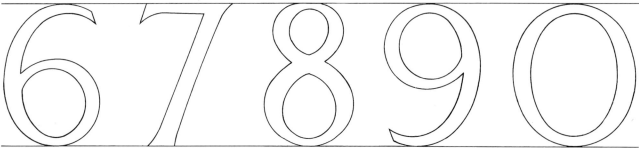

Fig 6.35   The numerals we are most familiar with are Arabic in origin but are given a roman treatment as far as is possible.

Opposite: 'Dave's Original' by Douglas Williams.

PART THREE

RAISED LETTERING

CHAPTER 7

ABOUT RAISED LETTERING

AIMS

- To bring together some of the underlying principles of raised lettering.

- To offer practical guidelines on depth, angle of cut, tools and woods, and advise on common mistakes and problems.

- To suggest some alternative approaches to finishing letters and backgrounds *not* covered in the exercises in Chapter 8.

INTRODUCTION

The practical exercises in the next chapter demonstrate the specific methods and approaches involved in raised lettercarving, while these background notes contribute to the whole picture. Raised lettering has already been discussed in earlier chapters, and you may find it helpful to refresh your memory on the points I have covered thus far.

First, a definition of raised (or relief) lettering was given on page 10. Essentially, raised letters stand proud of the background (or more simply 'ground'), and the lettercarver practises straightforward low relief carving to precise outlines.

The sides of the three-dimensional letters are called 'walls', and there are two crucial junctions, marking changes of plane, formed where the walls meet either the surface (surface edge) or the ground (ground edge) (see Fig 7.1).

Second, the use of raised lettering, its strengths and weaknesses was compared with incised lettering in Table 1 on page 11, and discussed in its own right on page 10.

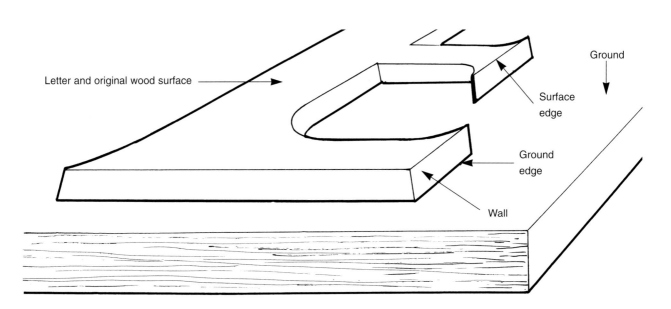

Fig 7.1   Junctions and planes in a raised letter.

Raised lettering is *not* a simple alternative to incised lettering, even though it might seem that way. The process takes longer, for a start, and grain strength has a great impact on the suitability of the letterforms for raised lettering, and their layout.

View raised lettering as an entirely separate option to incised lettering, which has practical advantages when it comes to lighting and context. Raised lettering can produce lovely results, and may lead to a widening interest in relief carving as a whole (see Figs 7.2 and 7.3).

Fig 7.2 *Relief carved letter **B** by Deborah Hurst, adapted from a medieval illuminated letter from the British Museum. It is carved in lime, polychromed and gilded, and measures 20cm (8in) square.*

Fig 7.3 *Screen with raised lettering at the church of Abbey Dore, Herefordshire. This is the work of John Abel (1577–64), king's carpenter.*

GUIDELINES

There are several, common questions about raised lettering which are worth addressing at the start.

HOW DEEP SHOULD THE BACKGROUND BE?

The ground (background) needs to be deep enough to get the necessary contrasting effect, but not so deep as to create unnecessary work for the carver.

There are no fixed rules as to the depth of cut. One of the main deciding factors is *how thin the thinnest parts of the letterform are*. The ground of an even, block-like letterform – where there is very little difference between thick and thin parts – might be reduced to somewhere between a half to two-thirds (no more) of the width of the letter at the surface. It is always a good idea to carve a preliminary sample letter or two, to get a sense of what feels like the right depth for the letterform (see Fig 7.4).

If the ground is reduced around any part of a letter further than the width of that part, then two things

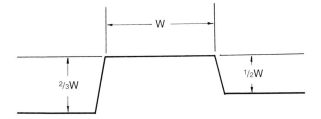

Fig 7.4 *For a block-like letter, the usual depth for the ground is somewhere between a half and two-thirds the width of the letter at the surface. The depth must take into consideration the weakening of parts through short grain.*

happen: first, reading becomes more difficult, because the eye becomes confused between the surface and the side wall. Second, the thin parts become much weaker and more easily broken, both in the carving and *in situ*.

If there is a big difference beween thick and thin parts, then it is the *thinner* parts that need to be taken as the guide. This is why raised letterforms are heavier, and the contrast between thick and thin strokes is less pronounced.

The depth that is necessary for raised lettering is not particularly difficult to carve – even a light relief (say to a depth of one-quarter of the surface width) can give a good effect. The main problem is in outlining the letters neatly and getting clean walls and edges.

There are two dangers for those new to relief carving:

- **Taking the background too deep in the first place.** This makes getting into corners more difficult, and increases the effect of the side walls on the appearance of the letters at the surface. Err towards a lighter depth to begin with – the ground can always be reduced (see page 126). A simple gauge which can be used to judge the depth is shown in Fig 7.5.

Fig 7.5   A simple gauge to check depth can be made with a masonry nail or similar, a close-fitting hole at right angles to a piece of wood and a locking woodscrew.

- **Varying the depth of ground throughout the work.** Different depths make reading more difficult, so keep to the same ground level across the carving. The letters should appear as if they have been placed on, or naturally grown out of, the background.

    The ground needn't be perfectly flat in an engineering sense, but it must *appear* uniformly level. This is helped by taking care that the two edges (surface and ground) lie clear, clean, and as parallel as possible. The ground may be less deep when textured, because texturing makes up for the depth by providing contrast between the letterform and the surroundings.

WHAT ANGLE SHOULD THE WALLS OF THE LETTERS BE?

The walls, or sides, of raised letters can be either **sloped** or **square** to the background, and each approach gives a different effect. Walls are *never* undercut.

Sloped walls are visible from the front, along with the letter shape itself. An angle of about 10° is usual for relief lettering, but this can vary between 5° and 15° (see Fig 7.6).

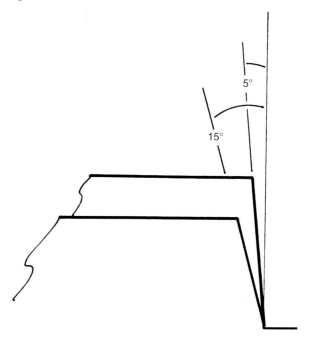

Fig 7.6   The walls of a raised letter may either be square to the ground or sloping – usually between 5 and 15°. The resulting effects are quite different.

Don't measure the angle, simply tilt the carving tool a little bit from vertical. The important thing is to be *consistent*, and maintain *exactly* the same angle throughout. To begin with, err the angle on the bigger side until you get a sense of its appropriateness. It can always be trimmed back later.

The tilted walls of raised letters catch and reflect the light well, and throw the letters more into three dimensions. They also tend to make the letters look larger and heavier. A problem encountered with sloping side walls is that the walls within counters close together as the background is reduced, and can even meet before they reach the ground. This is especially so in the smaller counters such as the bowls of **P** or **R**. These counters can be quickly filled with wall and the ground never reached. The more square the angle, the closer the letters can be placed before the walls impinge on each other (see Fig 7.7).

Deepening ground

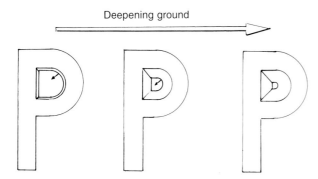

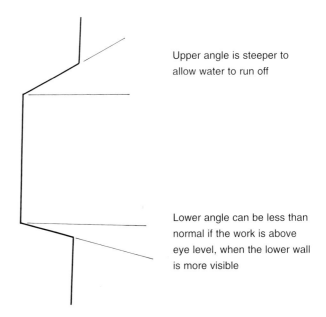

Upper angle is steeper to allow water to run off

Lower angle can be less than normal if the work is above eye level, when the lower wall is more visible

Fig 7.7   If the ground is too deep for the width of letter, the walls can begin to close counters, as you can see here. The narrower the letter parts, the shallower the ground needs to be if the walls aren't going to take over the appearance.

Fig 7.8   The angle of slope can be carved to take into account the environment in which the work is to be placed.

You need to look at the effect – and here carving a sample letter helps – and decide whether it is acceptable. Maintain the logic of the sloping sides: *don't alter the angle to try to separate letters,* or allow the sides to meet.

On the other hand, raised lettering can be arranged tightly to *make* walls come together. With some alphabets, especially the modern block styles, the effect can look attractively pattern-like.

If the final lettercarving is to reside outside, and if the viewing angle allows, then the *upper* surfaces of all the letters can be given a steeper angle to allow water to run off more easily (see Fig 7.8).

The sides of square walls are not visible when the letter is looked at straight on. It is as if the letters have been fretted out and stuck on to the background. If this is the effect you want, then it may be simpler, quicker and neater to actually do this.

Although not as physically strong as when angled sides buttress the letter surface, square-sided letters have a definite, attractive appearance of their own. They are lighter-looking and may appear to float above the ground dramatically, as the brain is confused over ground depth and surface.

IS THE LAYOUT DIFFERENT?

The height and width of a raised letter is measured between *top and bottom surface edges,* whether the sides splay or not. At these points the cap and base lines are drawn in the layout, but it is not necessary to include a margin for slanted walls.

Because raised letters have a wall that is visible beyond the mere outline of the letter, they appear larger than incised letters. This should be borne in mind and the letters spaced a little more widely than usual.

With the above provisos, the letter structure, layout, the sense of colour in spacing, family resemblances and optical effects are the same for raised letters as for incised letters.

Once the letters are drawn on the wood, identify any weak elements – such as short grain – which may suggest potential problems, and put a ring around them to remind you to be careful at these points.

Raised lettering is often accompanied by relief carving, and may have an integral frame. There is scope here for relating the lettering more directly to the carving, as well as bringing parts of a letterform up to, or even breaking through, the frame.

ARE DIFFERENT WOODS NEEDED?

Wood was discussed on page 20. Most woods suitable for relief carving will also be suitable for raised lettering. But in the same way that the openness or tightness of the wood fibres in any particular wood will influence the amount or desirability of carved detail, this factor will affect what raised letter size or style is possible or advisable. You need to balance letter size and openness of grain in the planning stages. It may be that incising is the best choice of approach after all.

Woods with 'open grain' such as oak, elm or sweet chestnut are less liable to support free or thin components orientated across the grain, so these woods are more suitable for larger bolder letters and are also good outdoor woods. For letterforms which include thin and free components, a high density wood is best: maple, cherry, beech, pear and other fruitwoods, Brazilian mahogany and lime are all good choices.

Clean the wood up first and inspect the surface carefully before laying out. Look especially for hairline cracks or shakes which may affect vulnerable parts. Defects such as small knots may be worked into the design, but may prove difficult to carve over cleanly.

HOLDING WORK

Clamps fixing the wood to the bench often get in the way in raised carving. The cutting approach of the tools to the background is more horizontal compared with incised lettering, and the clamps obstruct free movement of the hands and forearms. The background often needs to be removed where the clamps grip, so they have to be repositioned, and the metal of the clamps represents a danger to the cutting edges of the carving tools.

I find a better solution is to screw or tack a low fence around the work, with or without wedges, to hold it in position. Make sure the screws themselves are countersunk well out of the way. If you don't like the idea of screwing directly on to your worksurface, use a plywood board which itself has fences.

There is less direct thumping with the mallet involved in raised lettering, so your worksurface can be a lot lighter than that required for the extensive mallet work in incised lettering.

ARE DIFFERENT TOOLS NEEDED?

You will need the same basic carving tools as you did for incised lettering. They are held and manipulated by the same two grips (see page 17), but have different functions, and these are discussed in the following chapter.

Sharpness is, as ever, extremely important, especially if the ground is to be left straight from the cutting edge and for controlling the appearance of the finished work.

You will also need some new tools. **Grounding tools** (or **grounders**) are necessary to flatten the ground between letters. These take the form of shortbent (spoon) flat gouges. The size you need will depend on the width of the ground between the letters and within the counters that you need to clear, and this can be worked out from the paper layout. You can obviously use a smaller tool in a larger space, but it is harder, if not impossible, the other way round.

You *can* manage with straight tools, but shortbent (spoon) tools make the job a lot easier. The name 'grounder' or 'grounding tool' is often given in old books to shortbent back *chisels* only. However, I have always found the corners of these tools continually dig into the wood, and I believe they take their name more from a time when backgrounds were punched or frosted over, hiding any such marks and tears. My advice is *not* to use shortbent chisels, but stick with the flattest shortbent gouges (see Figs 7.9 and 7.10). Shortbent (spoon) skew chisels, both left and right, are very useful for cleaning up corners, and the V tool will now prove very useful.

The corners of gouges and chisels used to 'set in' or accurately shape the letters, work best with the corners of the heels taken off. The thinner sides of the bevel gets the cutting edge into corners and junctions without bruising the wood (see Fig 7.11).

The tools needed to follow the exercises are listed at the beginning of Chapter 8.

Fig 7.9 *A shortbent gouge (left) takes a clear shaving, whereas the corners of a shortbent chisel tend to dig in, making the gouge a far better tool for the clean levelling of the ground.*

Fig 7.10 *Here you can see how the tight bend of the gouge allows it to get into otherwise inaccessible areas. When buying these tools, the tighter the bend the better for this kind of work.*

Fig 7.11 *Side views of the chisels: normal (left) and with heel corners removed (right). A shallower side to the chisel helps it enter corners without fouling the wood.*

CARVING

There are two approaches to taking away the ground around letters, once the layout on the wood is complete: either the wood is removed around the letters *first*, with an allowance for waste. The walls of the letters are then trimmed up or **set in** to their correct shape. Or, the letters are outlined or set in with V tool, chisels and gouges, and *then* the background is removed.

The problem with setting in first is that when you push a gouge or chisel into the wood, the bevel acts like a wedge, exerting a sideways pressure (see Fig 7.12). This side pressure can unwittingly fracture the grain of weak or unsupported elements, so some degree of 'sneaking up' on the letterform may be necessary where the grain is short. The exercises in the next chapter will demonstrate this.

Some mixing of both the approaches outlined above is usual and often inevitable, depending both on the letterstyle and the inclination of the carver. What normally happens is that the carver will, say, remove wood from around the whole block of lettering, with only minor inroads into the main interspaces, and then pare up, set in the letters and finish off the ground. Patience is needed to clear away the background, especially without the aid of a router, and some students find this stage of the work less immediate than incised carving and a little tedious. A router provides a quick way to remove the bulk of the ground first. Routers are discussed on page 118 and in the project on page 217.

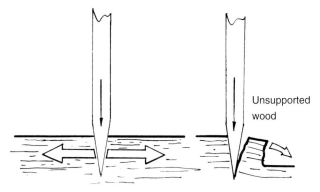

Unsupported wood

Sideways pressure from bevels

Fig 7.12 *Sideways pressure from the bevel of a blade pushed into the wood can break off unsupported, weak parts of letters.*

TWO EDGES

Lettering that is raised above a background must have two edges or corners where there is a forceful change of plane. These edges appear as lines, and it is vital that you give them care and attention. The **surface edge** is where the surface of the wood meets the wall of the letter. This gives the principle appearance of the letter to the eye. The **ground edge** is where the wall meets the ground below. The look will depend on the angle the walls tilt, or whether they are square. The ground edge echoes the surface edge, and really is 'in the background'. Both edge lines will be parallel.

It is essential that the edge lines are crisp and in no way uneven. Any unevenness here will be far more apparent than a slightly uneven ground. Therefore, you need to be sure that:

- The surface edge is cut cleanly, and the lines flow true to the drawn letters to give a crispness to the letterform.

- The junction of the side wall and ground are cut cleanly, without stab marks, as if the letters simply rest on the ground (see Fig 7.13).

Fig 7.13 Try to get the junctions of side walls and ground as neat and clean as possible, without stab marks.

- The ground edge lines follow the flow of the surface lines accurately, whatever the angle. This means keeping the ground the same depth around the walls. Although the depth can be allowed to have some gentle variation elsewhere, it *must* be run uniformly throughout the letter spaces.

- The walls are tidy and consistent. If not, and you subsequently clean the carving with a block of sandpaper, you risk lowering the surface edge into rough walls, affecting the appearance of the letter.

LETTER SHAPING

Raised letters are normally left with the surface flat and smooth. This may be the original surface, as a result of a final light sanding. However, you can also consider either internal or external shaping as alternative methods of finishing (see Fig 7.14).

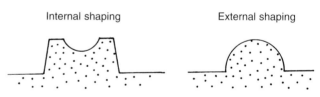

Internal shaping   External shaping

Fig 7.14 Profiled examples of the internal and external shaping of raised letters.

INTERNAL SHAPING

The flat surface of large, robust letters can be decorated with lines (outlines) around their edges, or channels along their centres. Leave a little gap of original wood around the edges of the letters for strength, as there is a risk of corners or edges crumbling. This technique should only be applied to tight-grained wood.

EXTERNAL SHAPING

Letters can be rounded over, or given a chamfered or moulded edge. You will need to use gouges in an 'upside

116

down' position – with their mouths towards the wood – and make mitre-like joints where limbs and stems meet. Backbent gouges will be needed to round over inside curves.

BACKGROUNDS

While the background is best left flat – in the sense of it being a uniform plane, it need not be smooth. If a dead-smooth background is what you require, the best method is to level it well and then use scrapers, before sandpaper. Scrapers are thin pieces of metal, such as bits of old hacksaw blades, with the edges square and sharp. They must be 'ticketed': their edges hooked over with a harder piece of metal, such as the side corner or a chisel.

TOOLED GROUNDS

Leaving prominent carving tool marks over the background (known as **tooling**) can add contrast, especially if the letters themselves are to be left unpainted (see Fig 7.15). It is also a lot quicker than achieving a smooth surface finish. Tooling may be regular and patterned, a mixture of long or short cuts, or random.

Keeping the ground edges clean can be difficult, and may require stabbing stop cuts, or chasing grooves around the letters. The rougher the handworking, the more 'rustic' the finished product tends to look. If overdone, a tooled ground can distract overmuch from the letters themselves.

TEXTURED GROUNDS

When the ground, or indeed any wood surface, is patterned using punches and similar implements, as opposed to carving tools, this is known as **texturing**.

The best and quickest tool for texturing a background is the **froster** or **frosting tool**, which produces a **frosted** ground (see Figs 7.16 and 7.17). The froster is sometimes referred to as a 'matting' tool, and the ground said to be 'matted', probably because the rough, dull appearance contrasts with the polished surface of the letters.

Fig 7.15 The background in Fig 7.13 (page 116) was created using a flat gouge. Here, the same area has been lightly textured using a deeper gouge.

Fig 7.16 The working ends of frosting or matting tools. The two on the right have been made by filing nails with a triangular file.

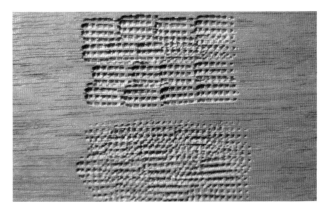

Fig 7.17 The effect of heavy (top) and light (bottom) frosting.

The froster is a many-toothed punch, available in various sizes to cover different shaped surfaces or fit into corners. However, frosters can be easily made from a thick nail – its end or head – or the end of a bolt, by grooving it with a triangular file. There is no need to harden the metal.

The more distant the lettering from the viewer, the larger the letters and the more open the point spacing of the frosting needs to be. So, the closer the lettering is viewed, the finer the point spacing required. Large punch holes in the wood look better at a distance, as they have the effect of blurring together, but are not suitable for work which will be viewed close up.

Aim either at frosting in a completely random fashion, with an overlapping texture, *or* maintaining an appearance of order and logic throughout. Above all, be *consistent* throughout the ground. Frosting the background can be practised by referring to Exercise **R**14 on page 154.

It is regarded as good carving practice that the frosting tool – and for that matter any other punch – should *only* be used on a cleanly finished surface. It should *not* be used in an attempt to disguise a torn surface that has been badly cut or torn – it doesn't!

STAMPED SURFACES

Here, the letters are neatly drawn out and the surrounding surface stamped (frosted or matted) *without actually removing any wood*. It could be argued that the result is a sort of relief – in that the letter is clearly distinguished from its surroundings – but it is not relief in the sense of being 'raised'. Nor is it really carving at all, as no carving tools are used. Nevertheless, it is a very quick technique, and may well be an appropriate option in some circumstances where the lettering must appear very light, such as on furniture (see Fig 7.18).

Fig 7.18 Using a frosting tool to either 'fill in' or outline a letter.

ROUTERS

The electric router, in the context of raised lettering, is a 'wasting' machine (see Fig 7.19). Careful working with the correct sizes of cutters can remove almost all the wood to a perfectly flat ground around the letterforms, with only a small amount of setting in remaining to be done. Always remember to allow for the angling-out of the raised letter walls.

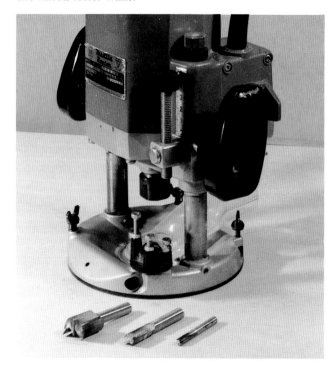

Fig 7.19 Standard router. The plastic insert takes a tube to an industrial vacuum cleaner. This greatly reduces the amount of dust and chips flung out by the machine and is to be strongly recommended.

118

The router is essential to making financial sense of many projects: relief work, lettering and general carving are all speeded up tremendously, with the added bonus that integral edges and frames are easily created as well.

The router can also be used in its own right to create letterforms. Such forms look 'router-generated', and are therefore very different from handcarved letters. The router is commonly used in a copying jig to produce house signs.

Raised lettering created with a router can be very attractive, but it is better to see this sort of work as being a different product altogether to carved letters. A router is used in the project on page 217, and if you have an interest in developing the use of this tool, there are two books I recommend: Spielman's *Router Basics* and *Making Wood Signs*, details of which can be found in the Further Reading section on page 228.

HAND ROUTING

The hand router and 'old woman's tooth' are tools which have largely been superseded by the electric router, but are still used by some woodworkers (see Fig 7.20).

Fig 7.20 Two types of hand router, designed for housing and other woodworking joints.

It is best *not* to try to finish off the surface with a hand router – the flat blades tend to tear the background. This is fine for joints (for which they are designed) but in the context of relief lettercarving the results are very disappointing and the tearing effect of the flat blade is difficult to control. The ground needs the far better finish produced by carving tools.

The best use for a hand router is where there are problems getting a sense of even depth and flatness to the background. After the initial stages of removing the wood with deep gouges, the hand router can be used to level over the ground before finishing with flat gouges. Never try to go the whole depth with the router.

However, with practice you should have no problem grounding out letters with carving tools only, and this tool is therefore largely unnecessary.

COMMON MISTAKES

Newcomers to raised lettering quickly come across two specific problems, both of which can be easily eliminated.

DEEPENING GROUND

You may find yourself in a situation where the background seems to get deeper and deeper. This often happens as the letters are being set in. Instead of the ground edge arriving at the right depth, the wood around the junction starts being excavated – that is, cuts are taken into the ground below the point at which they should stop. Cleaning up the ground edge then results in the ground being at a deeper level. When the next letter or part of a letter is set in, the excavating recurs, but from the new depth.

It is therefore very important to *control* the setting in. Start by keeping the shapes of the letters (the surface edge) accurate, and maintain cleanly cut walls with consistant angles. However, as the tendency is to concentrate on the surface shapes and walls, for some students setting in often means just pushing the cutting edge downwards and hoping the depth works out right, and if you set in too hard, the depth will be exceeded. Try and imagine the point – which is hidden to begin with – where the wall meets the ground, and *approach it carefully*, if necessary nibbling or paring to a neat halt. This takes practice, and the exercises in the following chapter should help you to develop the right technique.

If the ground becomes too deep and the appearance of the letters unacceptable, then cut your losses, plane off the surface, and start again. There is no need to level the board totally. Plane off enough so that the depth of ground returns to what you originally intended, and carefully redraw your letters from the original paper layout. If the sides of the letters slope outwards, there will be plenty of room and you can therefore see why *undercutting* raised letters can be potentially disastrous.

BREAKAGES

'Bits of the letters keep coming off.'

Raised letters are prone to breakage – corners and thin elements being particularly vulnerable. There are several reasons for this. It may be that the wood has too open a grain for the letterform, so that the fibres crumble rather than cut cleanly. Alternatively, perhaps there was a hidden shake or hairline crack which would automatically weaken the wood. To avoid such flaws and resulting breakage, identify any weak elements before carving starts, and remember to pare up to them carefully from a free edge, so that there is no pressure.

If the wood is sound and dense enough, the reason for breakages may be the pressure on the bevel of the carving tool, either as a result of leverage, or because the bevel's natural wedge-shape forces the grain fibres to one side, which can have adverse effects on weak parts. The solution to this is: first, don't use the carving tool like a small crowbar, and second, set in *lightly* around the weaker elements.

If you have chosen a letterform with thin elements, they can be strengthened by shaving off the top surface to bring it nearer to the ground before setting in. Be careful not to overdo this: changing the relative ground depth can leave the letterforms looking a bit disunited.

Neat breaks can often be glued back invisibly, and small C clamps made from bedsprings may help here.

FINISHING

The face of the raised letters can be cleaned up with a block and fine sandpaper (minimum 150 grit). Be *very* light with this, removing as little wood as possible. The danger is in what was the side wall becoming surface edge, with the letters enlarging or in other ways altering shape as a result.

Raised lettering can be painted, as can the background. Some examples of this will be seen in the projects. The edges of the lettering need to be painted particularly carefully to preserve the carved shape.

Village sign in Brazilian mahogany and oak by Steve Eggleton.

120

CHAPTER 8

RAISED LETTERING EXERCISES

AIMS

- To give a progressive scheme of work which builds into the creation of finished raised letters.

- To enable you to acquire a practical understanding of skills which are transferable to any style of raised lettering.

INTRODUCTION

Once again, modern roman is the practice alphabet, and once again you should use my drawings for your initial laying out. You will see how they are heavier than their equivalent incised forms for reasons of strength. You may find it helpful to refer back to Chapter 6 for extra information on the characteristics of specific letters.

EXERCISE PLAN

As with the incised exercises, this chapter starts with simple tool work, which is built up into the creation of complete, raised letters. To get the best out of this practical work, it is important that you have digested one exercise before moving on to the next.

There are two main areas to be dealt with: removing the ground (background), and outlining letterforms precisely.

The principles of carving raised letters are independent of style and by the time you have reached the end of the exercises you should be able to carve any suitable letterform you like.

You will find that the components or shapes which make up the letters are much simpler, and more easily produced than with incised letters. For this reason I have taken sample letters only, rather than covering every letter. The samples demonstrate the elements common to all letters and can be quickly and easily adapted.

Each exercise is divided in the same way as with the incised exercises. You will need a supply of prepared wood. I suggest boards of medium density wood, planed but not sanded. A list of the tools you will need is shown in Fig 8.1.

Tool List for the Raised Lettering Exercises
For lowering and levelling the ground, interspaces and counters
• no. 9 (deep) x 10mm (³/₈in) straight gouge
• no. 9 (deep) x 20mm (³/₄in) straight gouge
• no. 3 (flat) x 3mm (¹/₈in) straight gouge
• no. 3 (flat) x 6mm (¹/₄in) straight gouge
• no. 3 (flat) x 10mm (³/₈in) straight gouge
• no. 3 (flat) x 25mm (1in) straight gouge
For cleaning corners
• Skew chisel x 13mm (¹/₂in)
For clearing awkward areas within counters
• no. 3 (flat) x 10mm (³/₈in) shortbent gouge
• no. 3 (flat) x 25mm (1in) shortbent (spoon) gouge
• Left and right shortbent (spoon) skew chisels x 3mm (¹/₈in)
For setting in straight elements
• 40mm (1 ⁵/₈in) straight chisel
• 30mm (1 ¹/₄in) straight chisel
• 20mm (³/₄in) straight chisel
For setting in curved elements
• no. 4 x 15mm (⁵/₈in) straight gouge
• no. 5 x 16mm (⁵/₈in) straight gouge
• no. 6 x 6mm (¹/₄in) straight gouge
• no. 6 x 10mm (³/₈in) straight gouge
• no. 6 x 13mm (¹/₂in) straight gouge
• no. 6 x 15mm (⁵/₈in) straight gouge
• no. 6 x 20mm (³/₄in) straight gouge
• no. 7 x 6mm (1/4in) straight gouge

Fig 8.1

Be sure your tools are razor sharp with correctly flat bevels and their corners intact. The ground can be left straight from the gouge with no further finish providing the tools are sharp enough.

You will see how the low-angle grip (see page 17) predominates in the initial clearing of the ground around the letters, with the pen and dagger grip (see page 17) used for paring up the letters and finishing off.

Proceed slowly and practise each exercise until you are confident. Occasionally, I have broken points and techniques down within the method, so please read through the exercises first, and try to visualize what you will be doing, before you begin.

EXERCISES

Read through each exercise before beginning it. Have your selected wood prepared and firmly fixed to the bench with the grain horizonal. I prefer always to start with a planed (not sanded, as the grit can dull cutting edges) surface. Use a wider piece of wood than you would for incised lettering if possible. In addition to your carving tools you will also need the usual general tools for carving, such as a mallet and drawing equipment.

BASIC TECHNIQUES

R1 GROUNDING USING THE DEEP GOUGE

CONTEXT

In woodcarving, the term **grounding** or **grounding out** is used to mean reducing and cleaning up a background (or **ground**), down to a required level. I will keep the term in these exercises, using it to mean the whole process, which ends with a finished background.

In practice, unless the ground is only to be very shallowly reduced, grounding has two stages:

1 **Lowering the ground**

Here the main waste wood is removed down to a rough background surface which still needs flattening and smoothing. A deep gouge is used and allowance must be made for cleaning up waste which is left around the letters. Lowering by hand will be the subject of the next exercise. If you are using a router then this is the stage that the machine takes over.

2 **Levelling the ground**

The preliminary rough surface is levelled and cleaned up to a finish using flat gouges. This is the subject of Exercise R3.

In practice, different tools are used and the stages can seem quite separate. I have chosen to split the stages in the grounding process into two exercises to make particular points. The first stage literally lays the groundwork for the next: if the lowering is done well, levelling is very quick.

In order to be successful with the first stage, (lowering the ground), you must use the deep gouge properly. This quick exercise demonstrates how best to use the gouge, and its pitfalls.

CROSS REFERENCES

- Low-angle grip (page 17).

TOOLS

- No. 9 x 20mm (3/4in) deep gouge.

METHOD

1 Always work *across* the grain for the lowering stage. This way you don't have to worry whether you are going with or against the grain (see Fig 8.2). Hold the gouge in the low-level grip with the heel of the leading (or blade) hand resting on the wood, and its thumb extended along the handle. As always, it will be useful to be able to use both hands (see Fig 8.3). Remember to use your body weight as you work

Fig 8.2 Working with the grain. On the left you can see how the grain tears as the edge cuts against it; on the right you can see a shaving rising smoothly as a result of cutting with the grain. Working across the grain (centre), is the most straightforward option for roughing out or lowering the background.

Fig 8.3 Both hands in the low-level (or low-angle) grip must work together. The thumb extended along the handle extends the effective width of the front hand and increases its control. The heel of the front hand always rests on the wood.

and to control the forward push (from the back hand) with a braking action of the leading hand. You should be able to start and stop the gouge precisely at will.

2   Start the cut away from the near edge of the wood. Enter the wood with the centre part of the edge,

lower the handle, and push the gouge steadily forward. Keep the corners clear and move in as straight and even a line as possible. Lower the handle to bring the cutting edge out of the wood. The heel of the leading hand can slide over the surface of the wood for a long cut (see Fig 8.4).

1 Start cut

2 Lower handle as forward motion continues

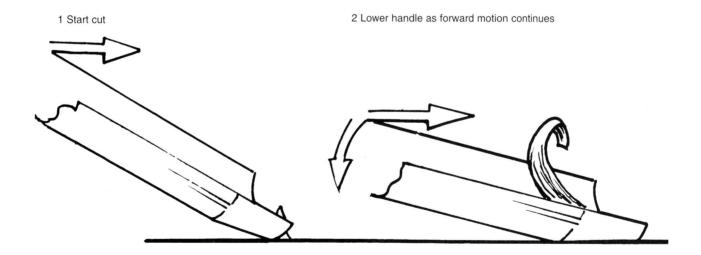

Fig 8.4 Keep the forward motion going after you enter the cutting edge (1), quickly lowering the handle (2) to a consistent depth of channel. Lower again to come out of the cut.

123

Fig 8.5   Taking the first neat shaving.

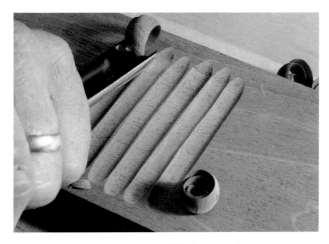

Fig 8.6   Making a series of parallel channels. This consistent way of working is the most efficient, and quickly gives a uniformly lowered ground.

Fig 8.7   The left sides of these channels run against the grain, and have torn it. Always place this side in the waste wood.

3   Make another cut next to the first. Try to maintain an even depth along the groove. This means maintaining the angle of the tool to the wood by fixing the position of the leading hand (see Figs 8.5 and 8.6). Control of the tool comes through achieving a *balance between the two hands*: the back or pushing hand, propelling the gouge forward, and the front hand exerting a braking action. Try to get a feel for this balancing effect, while remembering to relax and use your body weight.

4   Swap hands and repeat the cuts. Make a series of short and long straight cuts next to one another, trying to repeat the process evenly.

5   Make another series of cuts that curve to the left, then to the right, then in wave forms. Look at what happens to the grain on each side of the cuts. The grain will tend to split, or tear wherever the edge works against it (see Fig 8.7).

6   Make another, shorter groove with the deep gouge, but this time start near the left corner and rotate the tool clockwise as the tool passes forwards. This is sometimes called 'rocking' through the cut, and the gouge is rotated by the rear hand at the handle. This is a very important carving technique, and the result will be a slicing cut which you should find allows the tool to move through the wood more easily. The slicing cut is best used with a short tool stroke, as the corners of the tool must still remain above the surface of the wood (see Fig 8.8).

7   Make another cut, this time going deeper until one or both of the corners of the gouge is beneath the surface of the wood. The corner will tear the wood fibres instead of cutting them. The flatter the gouge, the easier it is to tear the wood fibres with the corner (see Fig 8.9).

8   Make another cut, and continue it to the far side of the piece of wood, allowing the cutting edge to exit on the far side. You will see that as the tool leaves the wood, the fibres burst away with it. These fibres have no support behind them, unlike the fibres that were cut with the tool directed *into* the body of the wood (see Fig 8.10).

Fig 8.8   Start the slicing cut towards one corner (above). Rocking the gouge along the cut will produce a smooth shaving that comes away more cleanly than when the gouge is simply pushed along without rotating (below).

Fig 8.9   If you allow the corner of the gouge to go below the surface of the wood, it will tear the fibres.

Fig 8.10   Unsupported wood is torn out as the gouge exits the far side. Always work into supported wood.

AIMS AND PROBLEMS

This exercise demonstrates some simple but basic rules, which apply to any gouge.

You must always *keep the corners of the cutting edge above the surface as you cut.* A corner beneath the surface ploughs up the grain uncontrollably and leaves a torn surface. This means that, unless you are willing to tear the wood – which in some cases is acceptable in the rough stages – then there is a limit to the depth a particular gouge will take you in one stroke, depending on how 'quick' the gouge is (see Fig 8.11). To go deeper, you must overcut the first passes with further passes of the gouge.

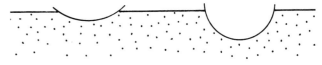

Fig 8.11   For the same width of gouge, a deeper cut will need a deeper (or 'quicker') gouge in order to avoid digging the corners in.

Gouges must work *into* a supporting mass of material, i.e. from the edge of your board, in. Fibres which are not supported will break away under pressure from the cutting edge. This may mean having to turn the wood round to work into the other side. This also has implications when it comes to shaping letters, as you will see.

125

You should also have seen the benefits in working *across* the grain at this stage, and these will become even more obvious with the next exercise, as will the advantages of a slicing cut.

An initial problem students often have is in starting and stopping the gouge precisely, at will. This is down to tool control – essential for all good carving – and comes only with practice. Continue to experiment with the gouge, especially with the balance between pushing and braking, which aids control. Lay down more and more grooves, both straight and parallel, as if you were ploughing a field.

VARIATIONS

Use different sweeps and sizes of gouge. If you haven't done so yet, *do* try to work with reversed hands. This will avoid awkward contortions as you work on, for example, a panel of carved lettering.

R2 LOWERING THE GROUND

CONTEXT

Although a lowered ground appears rough when compared with a finished one, in fact it needs to be precisely cut in a particular way so that the depth is uniform and matches your specification throughout.

The depth to which you take the deep gouge is very important. Its deepest point should lie just slightly above the final surface, so that when the ridges are removed (in the next exercise) the level is neatly arrived at. Keep your results to work on.

This exercise works to a line scored around the rim of the wood with a marking gauge. This line is precise, and gives a good edge to finish to. If you can, always use a gauge to mark the line on the side of the workpiece, rather than a pencil. In many cases you will need to estimate the depth. By eye is the best way, but a depth gauge can be helpful in the early stages until you have gained confidence to work by eye.

CROSS REFERENCES

- Depth gauge (page 112).
- Mallet (page 19).

TOOLS

- No. 9 x 20mm (³/₄in) deep gouge.
- Marking gauge.

METHOD

1   Begin with prepared wood and use the gauge to mark a line around the edge about 3mm (¹/₈in) below the surface (see Fig 8.12). This is also a good depth for the letter you will raise later, though in general terms the depth will relate to the size of the letters and the effect you want to achieve. Always work *across* the grain at this stage.

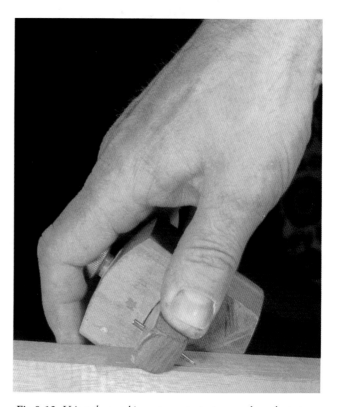

Fig 8.12 Using the marking gauge: start at an angle and rotate the pin down on to the wood surface as you push it away from you. Always keep the face of the gauge against the back of the wood.

2 Using the low-angle grip, position the cutting edge on the near side of the wood so that the corners are in the air while the lowest point of the sweep lies a fraction above the line. You want to come as near to the line as possible – even touch it – but *not* cut below it in any way.

3 Make the first stroke from the near edge with the gouge as before, starting slightly above the depth line. Carve across at an *even depth*, stopping short about a quarter of the way from the far side. You will eventually need to turn the wood around to complete the cuts from the other side (see Fig 8.13).

Fig 8.13 Magnified view of the line made by the marking gauge (which represents the final level of the ground) and the channels from the lowering stage. Note the consistency of depth. Levelling off will be quick, as you will need only to remove the small amount of waste down to the line.

4 Check your cut for evenness of depth – an even cut will have a uniform width. Make a second cut parallel to the first, but overlapping it by about a third. Remember to rest the heel of your front hand on the wood and control the tool and depth of cut as you go along, with the corners of the cutting edge always in the air.

5 Keep laying down overlapping grooves across the board, working from left to right, but stopping short of the far side. The result will look like a neatly ploughed field. Eye along the grooves to check for overall flatness. When you come to the left and right ends you can finish with a cut which passes along the gouged line, at a depth slightly above it.

6 Turn the board round and work from the other side, again starting from just above the line. It is not necessary to join groove to groove, just make sure that the grooves from both sides come together at the same depth (see Fig 8.14).

Fig 8.14 Starting from the edge, lay down a series of channels, stopping short of the far side. Then turn the wood around and finish off (there is no need to join the channels). The result looks a bit like a ploughed field.

7 Now take another piece of wood, and try and achieve the same effect using the mallet. Set the edge of the gouge in place and cut across the wood with a series of firm taps, checking for even depth. Then turn the wood round and finish from the other side.

AIMS AND PROBLEMS

The result should be an evenly-grooved surface that still appears level. There will be some crumbling of the crests between the grooves, but with sharp tools and tight-grained wood this should not be particularly noticeable, and will disappear when the surface is levelled.

Remember that a final ground must *appear* level across the lettering, although it need not be truly level in an engineering sense. It is the lowest point of the grooves, lying as they do slightly above the final levelled surface, that you need to pay most attention to.

Whether you need to use a mallet or not depends on the hardness of the wood as well as the strength of your wrists and the depth you wish to go. This sort of depth in medium-dense wood can normally be carved easily enough without a mallet, but feel free to use one at any time: mallets are there to help make any carving job easier.

If you want to go deeper, just repeat the ploughing process and drop another level. These levels are known as **lifts** (although it is the letters which are really 'lifted'). The depth of a lift is governed by the depth of the gouge (corners always being above wood). It may take two or three lifts to get to the necessary depth, and you only need to mark the final depth, estimating the transitional ones.

This methodical way of working has several benefits:

- It ensures an even depth across the work, retaining an overall flat appearance.

- This in turn supports the next levelling stage, which can then be completed very quickly.

- Working across the grain avoids trouble. Working in all directions can result in tearing below your depth by encountering adverse grain, especially when you have little depth to play with.

Some students don't find it easy to run an even level groove, but as always, skills such as this always improve with practice. The leading hand needs to lock the presenting angle of the gouge once the cut has started. An even depth of cut will also have parallel edges. Keep checking the appearance of the cut and making adjustments.

Repeat this exercise until you find you can 'plough an even field', and keep the results of this exercise for the next.

VARIATIONS

Explore different depths (or 'quicks') of gouge, and observe the effect on the depth of cut. Try working in all directions, and taking the ground down another lift.

R3 LEVELLING THE GROUND

CONTEXT

Once the ground has been lowered, it must be smoothed and flattened. Although giving contrast to the letters with texture is sometimes desirable, the heavy grooving that resulted from the last exercise would be very distracting. Texturing will be considered in Exercise R14.

The depth has been set by the previous stage, with the lowest point of the grooves lying slightly above, or even on, the level you are aiming for (refer to Fig 8.13). In fact, you will find the bulk of the levelling work has been accomplished if this lowering stage has been done properly: the job now is to remove, or level, the crests. Pay attention to the lowest point – the root – of the grooves, as this is the starting guide to the surface beneath.

TOOLS

- No. 3 x 25mm (1in) flat gouge. As a rule, the larger the surface to level, the wider the flat gouge you should use – this is the quickest way of working. So when clearing background around lettering, use the largest, flattest gouge you can, for as long as you can.

METHOD

1 Use the grooved wood from the previous exercise, or a new, prepared piece. Hold the flat gouge in the low-angle grip, swapping hands when required. Start anywhere you like on the board – the main thing is to work systematically. I tend to start on the right with my left hand resting on the wood so that I am always working away from the finished, levelled areas, ensuring they are kept clean.

2 Start working over the surface methodically, removing the crests down to the troughs of the grooves (see Fig 8.15). As you do this, the ground will quickly start levelling. Wherever you can, slightly rotate the handle of the tool so that the cutting edge slices across the wood. This slicing action will always give a cleaner cut (see Fig 8.16).

Fig 8.16 The slicing cut is similar to that shown in Fig 8.8, except that rocking is hardly possible with such a flat gouge. Start towards one corner, and drift the blade to the side while slightly rotating it, making a slicing cut to the opposite corner.

Fig 8.15 Levelling the lowered surface.

3 Work across the grain to begin with, and then with the grain where this is apparent. Whenever you find yourself going against the grain, react immediately and reverse the direction of cut.

4 Smooth the cuts together as you go along and either spread out from a given point or work in strips. Constantly look out for torn grain – it is very easy to snag the wood with the corner because the gouge is so flat (see Fig 8.17). If this happens immediately go over the torn grain and smooth it. Don't leave a trail of blemishes to be repaired later, because you'll find you'll never get round to it!

Fig 8.17 It is very easy to tear wood fibres with such a flat gouge. Clean up such tears as you go along.

5   Work over the whole surface, levelling and cleaning it. You should be able to run along the line at the edge, or in from it, and hopefully not need to turn the board round.

AIMS AND PROBLEMS

You should end up with a smooth flat-looking surface free from tears or prominent facets, and levelled neatly to the gauge line (see Fig 8.18). Eye the surface from the side to see how level and flat it looks. If your tools are properly sharp then the surface should have a polished look about it.

Fig 8.18 This is the sort of flat surface you should aim for, having a 'sense' of flatness, but with a light texture that shows it has been carved by hand.

If the initial 'ploughing' or lowering was uniformly done, paring over the crests will quickly give a uniform surface. Although some adjustment may be needed to the level, the main problem is in making sure the surface is free from grain tears.

It is a good idea to alter the light at this stage, and check over the surface. A change in light direction can be very revealing. Do not carve such a surface with the lighting directly above the work, as this will entirely eliminate any shadows caused by scratches and torn grain.

Don't get into the habit of shunting the blade forwards and backwards quickly under the blade hand. Precise, clean, flowing slices will remove the wood much quicker and give a fresher surface.

Some students ask why a flat chisel cannot be used to level the surface. Bearing in mind the point that we actually don't need a truly flat surface, it is impossible (without laborious effort) to avoid dropping the corners of a flat chisel into the grain of the wood and tearing it as a result. The flattest gouge, with the corners kept free, is therefore the best tool for the job.

If you want a really flat, smooth surface for the ground, proceed by using a sharp scraper to remove any light crests, and also any shavings, right into tight corners. Scraping is much quicker than sanding, and will get you to the end result quicker in the long run. Now sand in the usual way with progressively finer grits.

You have now completed what would be the finished background surface between letters. Next we look at the shaping of the letters themselves.

VARIATIONS

Prove the point about the flattest gouge being the best tool by using a flat chisel to try and level the surface. Then experiment with different sizes of flat gouge on smaller or flatter areas.

R4 USING THE V TOOL

CONTEXT

Using this tool has already appeared as an exercise in incised lettering, on page 92. Although I personally seldom have need of it in that context, it really comes into its own in raised lettering.

The tool has another name: the **parting tool**, and this gives away its more common use. In raised lettering it serves to separate letterforms from waste wood which is subsequently removed to form the background. The V tool is still incising, but instead of making grooves to be left as part of the lettering, the cuts are combined with those from other tools.

The V tool is used for a stage called **lining in** in relief carving. This is a rough setting of the outline prior to background removal and the setting in of the letterforms.

METHOD

Use a 60° x 16mm (³/₈in) V tool (no. 39 in the Sheffield list), and run through the incised exercise. Then try tilting the V tool to give a different angle of edge.

AIMS AND PROBLEMS

Once again, you will have noticed that the root of the V trench is rounded. The root, in the case of raised letters, will lie at the ground edge (where the ground meets the wall of the letter) when the background is removed. The shape is 'soft', and differs from the 'hard', sharper edges that result from using carving tools. This might or might not be a problem but you should be aware of it and be prepared to sharpen up the angle if the difference is noticeable.

As one side of the V tool cuts *with* the grain, the other cuts *against* it. In other words there may be a 'good' and a 'bad' side to the cut depending whether the grain is clean or torn. Both sides will be clean when the cut is across the grain. As the V tool will be used to outline some parts of the letters, it is very important that

the tool is always used so that the good side of the cut forms the edge of the letter, and the bad side goes on the waste side. There may not be a problem with a *very* sharp V tool and dense wood, but it is an excellent habit to get into and applies to relief carving as well.

This means that you must be clear on which direction to run the cut at any time, and many students find difficulty in telling the lie of the grain. This is explored in the next exercise.

As you now know, the V tool judders and snatches the grain as the curve of a cut gets tighter. The upshot of this is that V tools are really only suitable for *slow* curves. Tight bends in letterforms need the sweeps of carving tools to create them. However, the V tool *can* be used to outline simple raised letterforms. The 60° angle gives a 30° slope to the walls. This can then be set at the correct angle (normally about 10°) when the appropriate carving tools are used to set in the edge.

Exactly how much work can be done with the V tool, and how much by carving tools, depends on the style and profile of the letters. While the V tool cannot be used to outline tight curves, it can still come close enough to the letters to maximize waste removal before setting in. Its usefulness in this respect is clearly demonstrated in the sample letter exercises.

R5 GROUNDING TO AN EDGE

CONTEXT

The first three exercises looked at removing wood and finishing off a background – 'grounding' around the letterforms. This exercise looks at how waste wood is cleared away to an edge. This has to be done carefully to preserve the letter shapes and a uniform depth.

There are two edges to take care of: the **surface edge** (which gives the main sense of the letter shape), and the **ground edge** (which parallels the surface edge and creates a sense of contrasting depth). Whether the letters are outlined (set in) before or after the surrounding waste is removed, was discussed on page 115. I said that the general approach tends to be that most of the main wood is removed around the letters, and then inroads are made into the spaces and counters. Exactly to what ratio and to what degree these actions take place depends on the style of letter.

This exercise involves two simple shapes which can be outlined with the V tool (a square and circle) to demonstrate the method. Because the shapes are simple, the V tool can be used to give the *exact* profile. The ground around the shapes is reduced, and then cleaned up to the edge.

TOOLS

- No. 39 (60°) x 16mm (⁵/₈in) V tool.
- No. 9 x 20mm (³/₄in) deep gouge.
- No. 3 x 25mm (1in) flat gouge.

METHOD

1   Start with a fresh surface to your piece of wood, grain horizontal. Draw a square with sides about 50mm (2in) and a circle of the same diameter, leaving a similar gap between.

2   Start with the square, and begin your V cut in the waste wood *before* the square, running into the waste beyond. It doesn't matter how much you cut into the waste wood, as it will all be removed later. It is important however not to cut below what will be the finished ground.

3   Run the V tool up the right hand side, keeping the left edge of the groove against the line, to a depth of about 3mm (¹/₈in). If you have kept a consistent depth the cut will appear the same width along its length. Take more than one pass if necessary. Now run up the left side of the square in the same way (see Fig 8.19). Next, cut along the upper line, then the lower.

4   With the deep gouge, remove the waste around the square, working across the grain to a depth a fraction above that which was set with the V tool (as in Exercise **R**2). Come towards the edge of the square but don't use the deep gouge to clean up against the wall (see Fig 8.20).

Fig 8.19 Neat lining-in with the V tool, placing the surface edge of the groove along the drawn line.

Fig 8.20 Lowering the ground with the deep gouge.

132

5   Use the flat gouge to level the lowered surface, (as in Exercise **R**3). Start in the area around the square and come closer to it, cutting across and with the grain. Leave a little wood for cleaning immediately around the outlines (see Fig 8.21).

6   The ground should now be level around the square, but with a rough area immediately around its edge. The flat gouge can now be used to finish up to the edge, using the *walls created by the V tool as a fence* to guide the side of the blade. Start on the right side of the square with the blade parallel to the edge. Allow the blade to slide along the wall while paring away the ground. Do not angle the cutting edge into the square as you will cut the wall. You may need the V tool again if you have been uneven with the initial depth of cut.

7   You may find that the ground edge is a little ragged in parts, where the V tool depth was inconsistent. Leave this for now and finish off the other vertical side, then the top and bottom edges, cleaning up any V tool marks in the ground. Use the V tool to carefully define the square again, and return to the flat gouge to finish off (see Fig 8.22).

8   Now outline the circle with the V tool. Following what was said in Exercise **R**3 about V cuts having 'good' and 'bad' sides (i.e. with or against the grain), make your cuts so that the edge of the circle is always cut *with* the grain). To prevent awkward body contortions you need to reverse hands for the left and right cuts. Come to the edge as you did with the square, and marry the two cuts carefully. Use the waste wood as an approach run if you wish (see Fig 8.23).

9   As with the square, remove the waste with the deeper gouge, rocking slicing cuts as you approach the edge of the circle (see Fig 8.24). Level off with the flat gouge (see Fig 8.25). Again, you will find being able to swap hands a great benefit, and you may find you have to repeat the work with the V tool a little.

Fig 8.21 Levelling the ground. Allow the wall to act like a fence, guiding the blade along the neat junction.

Fig 8.22 The finished square.

Fig 8.23 Lining in the circle.

133

Fig 8.24 Lowering the background methodically.

Fig 8.25 Levelling up to the circle. In this case a second light cut with the V tool to firm up the line and the junction is now required.

Fig 8.26 Using the wall as a fence to guide the tool around.

10 Use the wall of the circle created by the V tool as a fence to guide the flat gouge around for final clearing up (see Fig 8.26). Work in the same directions as when running the V groove originally. Again, keep the edge back from the walls or you will cut into the circle.

11 Finally, you may have to touch up the ground edge with the V tool before finishing off with the gouge (see Fig 8.27).

AIMS AND PROBLEMS

The result of this exercise should be a clean-looking square and circle with the background neatly cleared away around them. The edges should be precise, and the depth uniform. Repeat this exercise until you get the hang of it.

This exercise brings out a number of important points.

TOOL CONTROL

Tool control is needed to prevent cutting the ground deeper in some places than others, or cutting into the walls of the letter itself, so altering its shape. Use the wall of the letter as a fence to maintain a crisp edge, the shape of which depends on the outlining.

Fig 8.27 The finished circle. Note the soft ground junction resulting from the rounded apex of the V tool.

EFFECT OF THE GRAIN ON TOOL DIRECTION

This is to be seen particularly in the direction of the V tool. For the square, the cross grain was cut first. If you had cut the side *along* the grain first, when you brought the other groove into it, the fibres in the corner would not have been supported, and the corner would probably have been knocked off. Try making a couple of cross cuts with the V tool to invoke this effect. As a rule, make the cross grain cuts first, and then those along the grain.

For the circle, the V tool must be presented so that the cut *with* the grain is *against* the letter, to prevent any damage to the letterform.

LEAVING IMMEDIATE WASTE

Waste is cleared away as near as possible to the letter, and then the letter finished off. Although I made two stages out of this to demonstrate the way the wall of the letter can be used as a guiding fence, there is nothing to prevent you finishing up to the edge of the letter straight away, as you are clearing the main background. Notice also how the V tool set the depth to which the ground was subsequently reduced, how the waste wood could be used to help the V tool line in a shape.

These principles will become even more evident when you begin to cut the straight and curved parts of actual letters.

VARIATIONS

Repeat the two shapes, tilting the V tool away so that the wall angle becomes steeper. Attempt some other large, simple shapes such as ovals, crescents or pentangles, but leave those with small internal angles until after the next exercise.

R6 SETTING IN

CONTEXT

The V tool, as you have seen, copes best with relatively simple shapes, but it is very quick and is normally the tool of choice to start carving with. It can be run around a whole word for preliminary clearing of the background, and where possible its groove brought close to the individual letter shapes, using the waste wood to make an approach if necessary.

The V tool, used normally, leaves a wall angle of about 30°. This is too sloping for most work, for which an angle of about 10° is better, as a slight tilt to catch the light is all that is needed. So, wherever the wall is to be left from the V tool, the blade must be tilted away, consistently, to make the walls steeper.

Depending on the style and size of letter, V tool work usually leaves the letter shape ill-defined, especially in the tighter curves and small details. These must be 'set in', or placed more precisely, and the ground tidied up to them. When the V tool is used before the setting-in of the carving tools, it is said to be **lining in**. One important function of lining in is to relieve the sideways pressure exerted by the edge and bevel of a carving tool as it is pushed, like a wedge, into the wood.

This exercise looks at simple setting in, following lining in, and illustrates the basic method. Further details and practice will arise when we tackle the sample letters. The tool grip, and the way the tools are manipulated, is very similar to that used for incising curves (see page 80). If you have been successful with these then you should have no problem with setting in. The trick is to control the depth so as not to cut into or disfigure the ground.

TOOLS

- No. 6 x 15mm (⁵/₈in) gouge.
- No. 5 x 16mm (⁵/₈in) gouge.
- Deep and flat gouges.
- V tool.

METHOD

1   Score only the surface of the wood by running the no. 6 gouge around in a circle (see Exercise ■15 on page 72).

2 Use the V tool, along with deep and flat gouges, to ground out the circle as in the last exercise. You needn't follow the curves exactly, as this will be the job of setting in. You will be left with a wall angle of about 30°.

3 Now present the gouge to the line at an angle of about 15° (estimated) to the vertical. Use the pen and dagger grip to push down from the shoulder and 'set in' the raised shape.

You will find that, because of the angled walls, the circle at the ground edge is *larger* than the one at the surface. As you create the angled walls with the gouge, the tool will dig its corners in. The lesson here is that you can only use the curve of gouge that matches the surface curve, if the walls are vertical (see Fig 8.28).

To cut walls at an angle you need to use a *flatter* gouge than the surface circle, and adopt the technique described in the incising exercises where the gouge is swept around the line with a raised leading corner (see page 73).

Fig 8.28 The gouge (with its sweep matching the circle at the surface edge), is pushed down at the angle of the walls. The circle at the ground is larger because the walls slope out and, unless the ground is very shallow, the corners dig into the walls.

4 Now make a second circle of the same size as the first, but choose a gouge that is a little flatter – I have suggested a no. 5 x 16mm (⁵⁄₈in).

5 Offer the gouge to the circle at the appropriate angle, but lift the leading corner. This corner always remains above the wood surface.

6 Lean the gouge towards the centre of the circle to maintain the correct angle of wall, and sweep around the walls of the circle, setting in up to the line (see Fig 8.29). The technique is described fully in Exercise ∎16 in the incising section (see page 74). Any gouge can be made to cut a quicker curve than its own sweep, but *not* a flatter one. When setting in letters, you can make one gouge do the work of many. The difference here is in maintaining a consistent angle to the wall of the circle. Remember it is the thumb of the blade hand which propels the blade while the fingers guide it; the gouge is rotated from the handle. Be careful to control the depth.

Fig 8.29 Using the corner of the gouge to slice around the circle. You need to pay attention to both the surface edge and the ground junction.

7 Now clear away the waste around this circle with a small flat gouge. Use the wall as a fence to guide the side of the tool (see Fig 8.30). Depending on the hardness of the wood, you may have to repeat the setting in to arrive at the depth you want. To get a precise junction between ground and wall, the merest stroke of the cutting edges may be all that is needed to finish off.

Fig 8.30 The finished circle: compare this with Fig 8.27, which shows the 'softer' result obtained by using a V tool.

8   Repeat this procedure with different sizes of circles, and then with a series of squares, setting in with chisels as you go. Although squares can be cut with a V tool, as before, use this as an opportunity to practice cutting them with the flat chisel.

9   Repeat with a fat L shape, using flat chisels. You must come *into* the angle of the L with the V tool (see Fig 8.31). Precede the chisels with stop cuts into the corner and, when setting in, give the chisel a slight slicing action down the angle of the internal junction (see Figs 8.32 to 8.34).

Fig 8.31 Lining in the fat L shape, running into *the angle.*

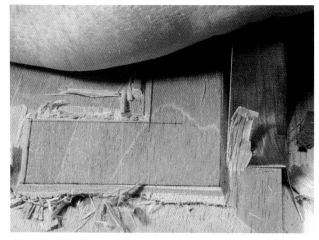

Fig 8.33 Use the wall as a fence to finish up to the junction.

Fig 8.32 After lowering and levelling, trim up to the line with as wide a straight chisel as possible.

Fig 8.34 The finished L-shape.

137

10 Next, draw two crescents about 50mm (2in) long and fairly fat. Place the first so its longer dimensions lie across the grain and the other at right angles – lying along the grain. Outline these crescents with the V tool, and lower and level the ground as before. The challenge here is that the points of both crescents have weak grain. There are two approaches: either bring the V tool towards the crescent so the fibres are supported, or leave a protecting amount of waste at the ends, and then set in, almost nibbling back, until the line is reached. Try both these methods, either at different ends of the crescents or in another set.

11 Now use the gouges in the same way as for the circles, reversed for the hollows to set in the crescents (see Fig 8.35).

Fig 8.35 Slicing around the crescent with the corner of the gouge. Note the supporting finger.

12 Finally, level off the waste with a flat gouge. You will find that you cannot use the inside walls as a fence to guide the tool, as you can with the outside walls, so be careful not to dig into them with the corner of your gouge.

AIMS AND PROBLEMS

The basic work here covers most of what is needed for setting in letters. Although most letters are more complicated and need more work, if you can successfully set in these shapes, you will be able to set in any others.

Several points arise from this exercise.

EDGES

Where you can use the sweep to set in an exact curve, do so, as this will give a perfect shape. However, it is more usual to use corners like the keel of a boat, to sweep around the shape.

CORNERS

The corners (and near edge) of the gouges are the principal means of setting in. If you use the tools correctly it is not necessary to match sweeps to curves. The method of using the corners to set in is the same as if you were setting in any relief carving, and for incising letters. It is one of *the* fundamental carving techniques. A very delicate touch is often called for, such as during the final setting of a junction.

ANGLE AND DEPTH

The trick is to control the tool so as to maintain the correct cutting angle and the correct depth, while at the same time following the line accurately. It is common for students to concentrate on one of these aspects and forget one or more of the others. The ability to achieve all three elements simultaneously will come – with practice!

MALLET

Hard wood, deeper ground or large letters may need the mallet for setting in.

V TOOL

The bottom of the V cut is rounded, and this may look incongruous when mixed with ground edges that are cut sharply with carving tools. This exercise will have demonstrated the differing appearance.

In these exercises we removed waste around the shapes and then set them in. You *can* set in first and then remove the ground afterwards. There are advantages and disadvantages to both approaches and these are discussed on page 115.

The method I have presented here (lining in; most waste removed; precise setting in) is the one I use most of the time. It avoids damage to short grain in letter elements through the wedge effect of the bevel, and allows me to locate the ground edge earlier. Sometimes, however, some preliminary setting in will occur first without the V tool – for example when grounding out a counter, such as the inside of the bowl of **B**. The next exercise concentrates on this.

VARIATIONS

Try a few amoeboid and geometrical shapes, as well as grounding to different depths and altering the wall angle to vertical.

ⓡ7 GROUNDING WITHIN A COUNTER

CONTEXT

There are two types of counters: open (leading into an interspace, e.g. **C**), or closed (enclosed within the letter, e.g. **B**). Their shape depends on the letter style.

In modern roman, the open counter is found in letters such as **C** or **H**, and may be bounded by curved or angular walls. Lowering and levelling wood into this shape is an extension of the surrounding work and the method is similar to that which we have been using on the surrounding area. Problems tend to arise with the smallness of curves or the weakness of certain elements, such as serifs or tails.

The closed counter occurs in **A**, **B**, **D**, **O**, **P**, **Q** and **R**, and needs a somewhat different approach. In **B**, the counters are small, and in **A** the counter is tightly angular. As a result, smaller tools, especially small flat gouges, may be needed to get into the available space, and a short bent skew chisel required to clean into corners. A router can be used to remove some of the waste, but getting into closed corners requires the skills we will develop here.

TOOLS

As well as the tools from the last exercise you will also need:
- No. 9 x 10mm (^{3}/$_8$in) small deep gouge.
- No. 3 x 6mm (^{1}/$_4$in) small flat gouge.
- Skew chisel.
- Front bent flat gouge and skew chisels (optional).
- Compass.

METHOD

1   Start with a circle. Draw one about 30mm (1^1/$_4$in) across on a fresh area of wood. This sort of shape is found fully in letter **O** and partially in **B** and **D**, for example. Alternatively, draw a circle which matches the sweep of the gouge.

2   Use the small deep gouge to remove wood from the centre to a depth of about 3mm (^{1}/$_8$in). Allow a little waste at the line to take account of the sloping walls (see Fig 8.36). Removing waste in this way gives a similar effect to lining in with the V tool. The wood fibres will crumble forwards towards the centre, when the sideways pressure of the setting in gouge is forced down into the wood. This pressure can cause the whole of a small counter to jump out, especially if a mallet is used, so be careful! You will find it takes less effort to push down the gouge, and that the required depth is reached earlier and with more ease.

Fig 8.36 Lowering the centre of the circle with small deep gouge.

139

3 Take the gouge in the pen and dagger grip and run it round in the usual way, setting in up to the line, down to the ground depth, and at the angle at which the walls should tilt (see Fig 8.37).

4 Use the flat gouge to level down the background up to the junction with the wall. It is practically impossible (as demonstrated with crescents in the last exercise) to use the convex walls of inside counters as a guide, so be careful not to run the corner of the gouge into them (see Fig 8.38). You may have to return to the setting in gouge and the levelling gouge, for the final delicate marrying of walls and ground.

5 Now try a square. Draw one about 30mm (1¼in) across. This sort of shape is found in the letters **E** and **H**, for example.

6 Use the V tool around the edge. Then remove the centre wood, as before, with the small deep gouge (see Fig 8.39).

7 Now use a chisel which is a little narrower than the side of the square, to set in the walls, tilting the tool at an angle. Nick a stop cut into the corners first (see Fig 8.40). It also helps if the heel corners have been ground back on the chisel. Leave the actual corners of the square until last. If you are working with hard wood you may need to use a mallet.

8 Level the counter with the flat (no. 3 x 20mm (¾in) gouge. You can use *straight* walls as a fence (see Fig 8.41).

Fig 8.37 Setting in with a slicing cut which winds around the circle at the appropriate angle. You will find that, having removed material in the centre, the remaining waste wood easily pushes over and crumbles.

Fig 8.38 Levelling with a small flat gouge. Take care not to run the corner into the wall.

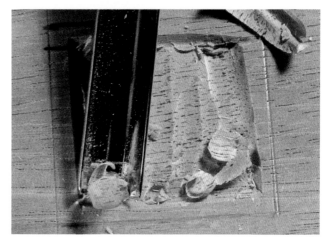

Fig 8.39 Lining in the square with the V tool, and lowering the ground with a deep gouge.

Fig 8.40 Setting in the walls with a chisel, which should be a little narrower than the sides of the square. Stop cuts will be needed in the corners.

Fig 8.41 Levelling the counter using as wide a flat gouge as is possible.

Fig 8.42 This is where a skew chisel comes into its own.

9 Slice down the walls at a slight angle away from the corners to finish them off, carefully merging the cuts.

10 Finally, draw an equilateral triangle with walls about 30mm (1¼in) long. This sort of shape is found in the letter **A**, for example.

11 Remove the centre waste with the deep gouge, and set in the wall with a chisel as before. Avoid the corners: as the angle of a corner moves from square to acute, the thickness of the chisel makes more of an impact and can damage the junction.

12 Level off the ground within the counter as far as possible, and then return to the corners. Use either a skew chisel or a chisel presented at a low angle to trim these to shape.

13 Finally, finish the ground up into the corners with the skew chisel. A bent skew chisel is even more suitable for this job (see Fig 8.42).

AIMS AND PROBLEMS

You should end up with a neat, sunken area within the shapes you drew, with clean walls and junctions, and to an even depth. In many ways, this exercise is a simple extension of lowering and levelling general background. The technique of removing wood first (either by lining in or by clearing away), to lessen effort or relieve sideways pressure, can be used with both open and closed counters as well as between letters.

A mallet can be used for setting in with hard wood. It will exert greater and more sudden sideways pressure, so use it with caution around weak parts.

There is a tendency to make the angle of the inside walls different to that of the outside, often less steep. Remember that in raised lettering the wall angle should be as consistent throughout as possible.

VARIATIONS

Try amoeboid and geometric shapes, different wall angles and different depths.

SAMPLE LETTERS

R8 I

CONTEXT

Use my drawing (Fig 8.43) as a guide to laying out. You may like to space out the letters in the exercises that follow out on the same piece of practice wood.

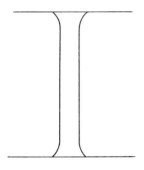

Fig 8.43 Layout for I. Letter height for exercise : 50mm.

TOOLS

- No. 39 x 16mm (⁵/₈in) V tool.
- No. 9 x 20mm (³/₄in) deep gouge.
- No. 3 x 25mm (1in) flat gouge.
- No. 1 x 35mm (1³/₈in) No. 1 x 20mm (³/₄in) chisels.

METHOD

1 The grain should lie horizontally. Lay out cap and base lines and draw the letter in between. Remember that relief letters are generally bolder than incised letters, and that the serifs are often a bit stubbier.

2 If you are grounding to the edge of the wood, you can mark the depth of 3mm (¹/₈in) on the edge using a marking gauge, unless you prefer to estimate the depth by eye throughout.

3 Refer to Figs 8.44 to 8.49. Run the V tool up the vertical sides first, beginning in the waste wood and tilting the V so that the walls of the letter are a little off vertical (about 10–15°). You can come up to the line and may be able to shape the serifs. If not,

come as close as you can and leave them for setting in. Similarly, line in horizontally the top and bottom of the letter.

4 Lower the ground around the letter evenly and methodically, working with the grain where you can.

5 Level the ground up to the root of the V trench. This and the previous stage I will refer to from now on as **grounding out**. You may have been able to actually finish the letter if your lining in was accurate to the shape, or you may need to use the V again to touch up the contours.

6 The root of the V groove is slightly rounded, and you may want to sharpen this to match other letters, or perhaps adjust the straightness of the upright, or the shape of the serifs. Use the 35mm (1³/₈in) chisel to set in the side walls, avoiding the serifs at each end. Use the 20mm (³/₄in) chisel for the top and bottom walls. Take care not to stab below ground level. Use the corner of an appropriate gouge to sweep around the serifs, merging them with the straights (at the same angle). Take care not to cut into the ground above or below the letter.

7 Finally, check all the ground junctions and clean off the pencil marks with a block and fine sandpaper, rubbing with the grain.

AIMS AND PROBLEMS

Congratulations! You have just finished your first raised letter! The resulting letter should have neat, true edges and slightly angled walls, on a clean levelled background. You may need to repeat the setting in to get to the depth, and problems sometimes occur at the serifs, such as corners breaking away because of the short grain. Try again, 'sneaking up' on the shape more by allowing extra waste at these points and paring back to set in.

VARIATIONS

Try the letter both thinner and thicker, to see what effect this has on its appearance. Then take some of these letters to a greater depth.

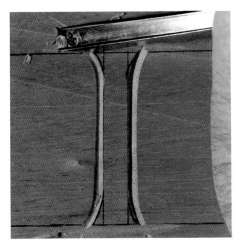

Fig 8.44 Raised letter *I* – lining in.

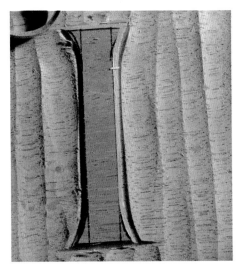

Fig 8.45 Lowering the ground.

Fig 8.46 Levelling the ground, using the wall as a fence.

Fig 8.47 Setting in to the cap and base lines with the 35mm chisel.

Fig 8.48 Slicing the walls of the serif.

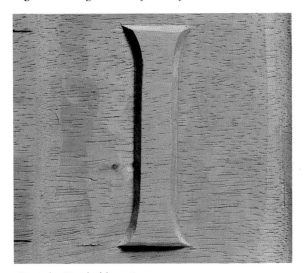

Fig 8.49 Finished letter *I*.

R9 H

CONTEXT

This letter introduces two open counters into the work.

TOOLS

As last exercise, plus 20mm (³/₄in) chisel.

METHOD

1 Draw out the cap and base lines, and the letter **H** (see Fig 8.50).

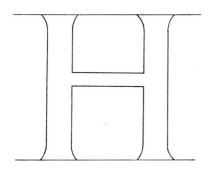

*Fig 8.50 Layout for **H**. Letter height for exercise : 50mm.*

2 Refer to Figs 8.51 to 8.55. Line in uprights outside and inside with the V tool. You will need to swing your body over to make the downward cuts into the top counter, or turn the wood around.

3 Line in the horizontal bar. Start in the middle and link up with the ends of the vertical V cuts.

4 Ground out around the letter using as large a gouge as the counter will allow.

5 Use the large straight chisel to set in the outside walls of the uprights.

6 Use the smaller chisel to set in the straight inside walls. Be careful to avoid the inside corner where the angled walls meet. You may also need stop cuts in the junctions of bar and stems to prevent the grain splitting out.

7 Use the gouge to shape the serifs.

8 Clean up the levelled ground to the walls.

9 Finish off the corners in the counters.

AIMS AND PROBLEMS

The resulting **H** should have neat, true edges and slightly angled walls, on a clean levelled background. You must be careful to control the cutting edges at all times so that you do not stab into the ground (in which case you might find yourself lowering it), or into the walls (in which case you may lose the shape or appearance of the letter).

There is a tendency to make the crossbar too thin because you are setting in *along* the grain, and fibres tend to come away. Use a slicing action as you cut down, as with horizontal incised trenches, which presented the same problem in Exercise **I**9 on page 55.

VARIATIONS

Try the letter at different sizes and thickness of stroke, and then take some of these letters to a greater depth.

Fig 8.51 Lining in the **H**. Where possible, use the waste to make the V tool approach, and carve the horizontal lines last.

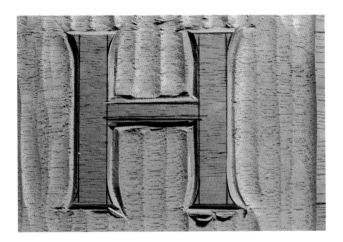

Fig 8.52 Lowered ground.

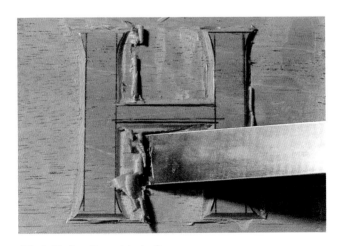

Fig 8.53 Levelling with the flat gouge.

Fig 8.54 Making stop cuts into the corners.

Fig 8.55 Finished letter **H**.

Ⓡ10 A

CONTEXT

This is the third letter made of straight elements, but **A** also has a closed counter.

TOOLS

- As in the previous exercise, plus small deep and flat gouges, a skew chisel and short bent gouges.

METHOD

1   Draw out the cap and base lines and the letter itself (see Fig 8.56).

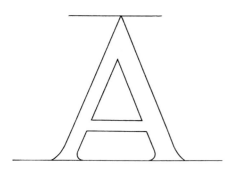

Fig 8.56 Layout for A. Letter height for exercise : 50mm.

2   Refer to Figs 8.57 to 8.62. Begin by lining out, to depth, with the V tool on the outside. Be careful at the apex: I suggest you come in from the waste *above* the letter. This way the apex is supported by fibres behind it and the 'good' side of the V groove is against the letter.

3   Line in the lower counter as for **H**, taking care of the corners. It is up to you whether you run a few lining strokes in the closed counter.

4   Ground out the background around the letter and into the lower counter. Make stop cuts into the corners. Lower the wood in the upper counter, but don't level it yet.

5   Set in the letter with straight chisels and gouge, as for **H**, including the closed counter. Be careful of the corner junctions. Serifs on either side of an oblique will need different gouges.

6   Finish the ground neatly up to the walls, including the closed counter, which will require smaller tools. This is where you may need the skew chisel to get into the apex of the counter.

AIMS AND PROBLEMS

The resulting **A** should have neat, true edges and slightly angled walls, on a clean levelled background. The ground of the closed counter should look as if it is continuous with that surrounding.

The apex is one point where you may come to grief, because its short grain makes it very weak. The same problem occurs with the other pointed letters: **M**, **N** and **V**, but not **Z**, where the grain runs *into* the points. When in doubt, leave plenty of waste wood around, and pare back when setting in.

Another place where problems arise is in the internal corners. Take care of these, again, 'sneaking up' on them if necessary.

VARIATIONS

Try different sizes of **A**, with different thicknesses of stroke, and take some of these letters to a greater depth. Try an **A** with a top serif as well (see page 106).

Fig 8.57 A lined in with the V tool.

Fig 8.58 Lowered ground.

Fig 8.59 Setting in, after levelling, with the wide chisel.

Fig 8.60 Here you can clearly see the stop cuts in the corners of the inner counter.

Fig 8.61 This corner of A's inner counter is very awkward to work, and the ideal tool is a shortbent skew chisel, as shown. Failing this, use a regular skew chisel.

Fig 8.62 Finished letter A.

℞11 D

CONTEXT

This letter brings in a simple curved element.

TOOLS

You will need all the usual tools for lining in and grounding out the surrounding area, along with:

- 30mm (1¼in) chisel.
- No. 4 x 15mm (⅝in) gouge.
- No. 6 x 7mm (¼in) gouge.

METHOD

1   Draw out the cap and base lines and the letter (see Fig 8.63).

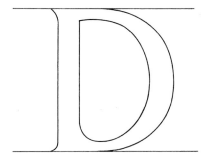

*Fig 8.63 Layout for **D**. Letter height for exercise : 50mm.*

2   Refer to Figs 8.64 to 8.69. Line in the outside, running the upright first, then the curve. To put the 'good' side of the V cut against the letter, you will need to work towards the mid-line on the outside, and you will find reversing hands will help for the upper stroke.

3   Line in the inside, taking care of the top corner. This time the V tool must run from the mid-line out.

4   Ground out around the letter and within the counter.

5   Set in the upright walls with the straight chisel, as well as the flat cap and base line portions of the letter.

6   Set in the serifs.

7   Set in both the outside and inside walls of the bowl using sweeping cuts with the gouge, held in the pen and dagger grip. Switch to the small gouge for the lower inner corner. Be careful to maintain the wall angle and not to run the corners below the ground depth.

8   Clean up to the walls. As always, you may need to repeat the setting in and levelling to get a neat junction to the required depth. A small flat gouge may be needed to cut around the tight inside curve of the lower junction.

AIMS AND PROBLEMS

The resulting letter **D** should have a flowing shape to the bowl, neat edges, and slightly angled walls, on a clean levelled background. The ground of the closed counter should look as if it is continuous with that surrounding the outside of the letter.

If you have practised Exercise ℞5 (Grounding to an edge) then you should have few problems. The challenge is in getting the shape of the bowl just right, with smooth lines. Most students find this a very satisfying letter to carve.

VARIATIONS

Try the letter at different sizes and thickness of stroke, and take some of these letters to a greater depth.

Fig 8.64 *Lining in.*

Fig 8.65 *Lowered ground.*

Fig 8.66 *Setting in the outer curve using the no. 4 x 15mm (⁵/sin) gouge, after levelling.*

Fig 8.67 *Setting the inner curve using the same gouge.*

Fig 8.68 *Using the smaller gouge to make the lower junction.*

Fig 8.69 *Finished letter D.*

Ⓡ12 B

CONTEXT

In many ways this is a similar letter to **D** but has smaller bowls. It is the only letter in the alphabet to have two closed counters, and these require a larger number of tools to carve. **B** provides excellent practice in closed-counter relief carving. It also requires gouge shapes not used elsewhere other than for **R** and **S**.

TOOLS

- All the tools for lining in and grounding out the surrounding area.
- 40mm (1⅝in) chisel.
- No. 3 x 3mm (⅛in) gouge.
- No. 3 x 6mm (¼in) gouge.
- No. 5 x 16mm (⅝in) gouge.
- No. 6 x 6mm (¼in) gouge.
- No. 6 x 13mm (½in) gouge.
- No. 7 x 6mm (¼in) gouge. You will find shortbent tools very helpful for the inner counters.

METHOD

1 Draw out the cap and base lines, and the letter. Note that this **B** has a hollowed base (see Fig 8.70).

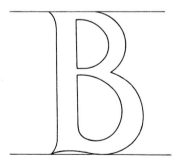

Fig 8.70 Layout for B. Letter height for exercise : 50mm.

2 Refer to Figs 8.71 to 8.75. Line in the vertical upright around the outside. Come close to the junction between the bowls but don't actually try to form it – it is best set in with carving tools.

Similarly, you can leave the hollow base for setting in. Line in as much of the inner counters as you can, but be careful not to cut into the walls.

3 Ground out around the letter and lower *only* the inner counters as much as possible.

4 Set in the uprights with straight chisels.

5 Set in the serifs.

6 Set in the outside of the bowls and the inner counters with appropriate gouges, making stop cuts into the sharp corners. Take great care when you come up to the junction of the bowls with the stem.

7 Finish off the ground up to the walls. Use smaller flat gouges to level the inner counters.

AIMS AND PROBLEMS

The resulting letter **B** should have flowing bowls, neat edges and slightly angled walls, on a clean levelled background. The ground of the inner counters should look as if it is continuous with that surrounding the letter.

The inner counters need smaller tools of course, and the deeper the ground the more these tools need to be shortbent. Because of the smallness of the inner counters, each lowering cut gives a big effect, and it is very easy to take the ground too deep here. Take it easy with the lowering, verging on the shallow to begin with.

You can see how the angled walls close down the counters and make the junction look thicker, compared with an incised letter. If the ground here were deeper, the walls would show up more and, depending on the size of the letter, may meet within the bowl. Make sure the walls are kept at an angle of only 10–15°.

VARIATIONS

It is worth exploring the effect of depth on the inside counters and the appearance of the letter. Take the background around the letter you have carved to a greater depth and see what happens. Try also the **B** at a different thickness of stroke.

Fig 8.71 Lining in.

Fig 8.72 The ground lowered around the letter and inner counter.

Fig 8.73 After levelling and setting in the outer curves, a stop cut is needed at the junction of the lobes, and you can see this clearly here.

Fig 8.74 Setting in the inner counters.

Fig 8.75 Finished letter B. The shape is one of the most complicated of the roman letters and requires gouge shapes not used elsewhere other than for R and S.

Ⓡ13 S

CONTEXT

S is made up of pure curves with open counters. It has tricky short grain at the serifs and is a good overall test of skill.

TOOLS

- Select from those in the previous exercise and use your judgement to decide which to use and when.

METHOD

1   Draw out the cap and base lines and the letter (see Fig 8.76). Remember that raised letters need to be a bit bolder than incised ones. Look at the serifs and the weak grain, and put a ring around these points with a different coloured pencil.

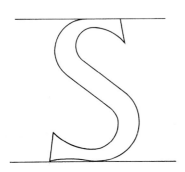

Fig 8.76 Layout for S. Letter height for exercise : 50mm.

2   Refer to Figs 8.77 to 8.81. Line in with the V tool to depth with the 'good' side of cut against the letter. Use the waste for your approach, and work out the best direction for the serifs. Come as close to the line, and as far into the counters, as possible.

3   Ground out around the letter and into the counters. It is easy to reduce the ground of the inner counters too much – rather like the **B** – so be careful here.

4   Set in, sweeping around the curves with the gouges, and if necessary sneaking up on the serifs. By all means use the whole edge of the gouge if it fits the profile of the curve. Try to get a continuous flowing line at a consistent angle.

5   Finish off the ground up to the walls. You may need to repeat the setting in, with delicate final touches of the cutting edge or corners.

AIMS AND PROBLEMS

S should have flowing curves, neat edges and slightly angled walls, on a clean levelled background. The ground of the inner counters should look as if it is continuous with that surrounding it.

S is a challenge both in gouge use and in tackling vulnerable corners. If you have problems then do repeat the attempt: it doesn't take too long, and when you have succeeded with this letter, there should be no letter which you cannot carve.

VARIATIONS

Try different shapes of **S**, and see again how lowering the depth makes the walls more prominent.

Fig 8.77 Lining in.

Fig 8.78 Lowering the ground into the open counters.

Fig 8.79 Levelling in progress.

Fig 8.80 A narrow gouge is needed for setting-in the tight curves.

Fig 8.81 Finished letter S.

153

ℝ14 TEXTURING GROUND

CONTEXT

The result of lowering the ground was a heavily textured surface which, after levelling, became a lightly textured surface. These are just two of the many options available when you raise letters (unlike incising, where a plain, untextured surface remains). In this exercise I want to explore alternative texturing options, including one where the background is not reduced at all.

Texturing can occur at the same time as lowering the ground, or may be a deliberate final stage, using tools not previously used. With a large area to be covered, the separate texturing of a ground can be a tedious process, so it is preferable to combine it with lowering and levelling.

When texturing the ground it is important to achieve a logical relationship with the letters. The texturing shouldn't just happen, washing up to the letterforms indiscriminately like flotsam on a beach. It must be laid down, and related to the letters deliberately, even if it is so understated as to be hardly apparent.

It is the *effect* of the background on the whole work that needs to be considered. The ground is a foil to the letters, setting them off by contrast or creating a complementary backdrop. Above all, its surface texture must never detract from the finished piece or confuse the viewer.

I have used the letter samples already carved for this last exercise, which combine to create a 'sampler' of different texturing effects, but you may choose to carve new ones.

CROSS REFERENCES

- Backgrounds (page 117).
- Froster (page 117).

TOOLS

- Various gouges from tool list.
- Froster.
- Hammer.

METHOD

1   Take a sample of fresh wood. Texturing this in separate units will give you a record for future reference.

2   Begin by texturing with gouges. Use a deep gouge to take short shallow cuts across the grain, slicing the edge as you rock the tool along its cut. Overlap the cuts and lay them down rhythmically, but not too uniformly (see Fig 8.82). The facets should be of a consistent depth in order to minimize torn grain and crumbling crests.

Fig 8.82 Texturing the ground using a deep gouge. The facets are best placed irregularly, or like scales, rather than in rigid lines. Depending on the wood, the crests between cuts can tend to crumble, so care is needed here.

3   In another area, try making the short cuts across the grain again, but deeper. If you work over the surface you can arrive at a considerable depth without a lowering stage.

4   Make similar cuts along and across the grain, then in an undulating pattern, and then randomly placed. Make the strokes longer and shorter, to the extent that the shortest ones create an almost pock-marked effect. Try to control the texturing strokes, using the same gouge, so that the left half of, say, a square is rough (heavier) texture, the right smooth (lighter) and the centre something in between.

5 Now try texturing around some of the letters you have cut previously, using different lengths and depths of stroke (see Fig 8.83). At the edge of a letter, you have to control the cut of the gouge so that it doesn't run into the actual letterform, which could be disastrous. This usually means ending in a short, tight, slicing action so that the edge ends up abutting the wall of the letter, and then cleaning down with the corner of a skew or fishtail chisel.

6 Next, try frosting. The frosting tool is struck vertically into the wood with a hammer or metal mallet (it will damage a wooden mallet). The best way is to suspend the froster a little above the wood, tensing the hand using a finger against the surface to set the height, so that when you strike the teeth punch the ground but the tool springs back up off the surface (see Fig 8.84). As you move your hand along the wood you can strike the froster rapidly so that it feels like a little piston, rapping on the surface. The alternative is to lift and place the froster more precisely each time. Use the froster to overlap lines of texture, as well as spreading out more loosely, while avoiding the actual appearance of lines. Then try using it on smooth, lightly faceted, and rough surfaces, and observe the different results.

AIMS AND PROBLEMS

You will see further texturing up to precise lines on pages 35 and 118. The trick is to make the texturing look as if it continues *behind* the letter and not as if it was affected by the letter being there. It is not quite the same as levelling with a flat gouge, as the deeper gouge must be used in the direction set by the texturing pattern.

If you are not lowering the ground, you will find it helpful to outline the letters with a small V tool or U-shaped gouge, running a narrow, light trough all round. This acts as a stop cut to the texturing and allows a little freedom for finishing up to the letter with the texturing gouge. The effect is different to when the groove isn't there.

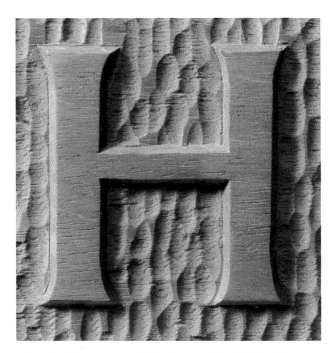

*Fig 8.83 Texturing around **H**. Compare this with Fig 8.55.*

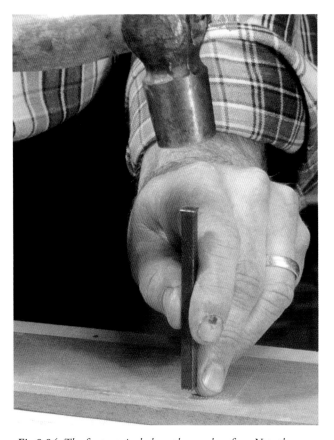

Fig 8.84 The froster poised above the wood surface. Note the supporting finger setting the height.

You will see how frosting or 'matting' as it is sometimes known, is quite a long process. You will achieve a more consistent textured surface, requiring less effort, when the wood has been smoothly finished. It is considered bad carving practice to use the froster to disguise a poorly cut surface, so you must regard texturing with this tool as an *additional* stage. The froster can also be used without lowering the surface, for a lightly contrasting background.

Several tools may be needed to get in the counters and between the letters. In fact, texturing as a whole adds to the time taken on the work, but can then save time by reducing the need to lower the background.

SUMMARY

If you have worked through the exercises, you will have come across practically all the problems you are likely to encounter with raised letterforms, and have the skills to deal with the ones you haven't. Other letterforms, for example, might need more delicate manipulation of the tools around edges or into corners.

Hopefully you have also tried some letters with vertical walls, of different thickness and to differing depths, and will now have a good idea of the impact these changes have on the appearance of the letters.

The next stage is to put the letters together and create meaningful words. You will see this being done in the project section, and there are endless possibilities: losing the spaces between letters, or staggering the letters without cap and base lines, for example.

The most important points to remember are:

- A delicate touch is needed with the cutting corners and edges, to achieve satisfactory finished junctions, (especially that between the ground and the edge).

- Tool control, especially with the gouges, is crucial to making a success of any carving, and this includes raised lettering.

- Increasing the ground depth has an effect on the letter appearance as the walls become more evident.

- Changing the wall angle also has a strong effect.

One last point: I discussed a general principle in carving on page 28: that as much work as possible should be done with the same tool before swapping it for another. This does not become evident until you cut a *series* of letters, but when you come to do this you will find it makes for more efficient working and usually adds flair to the carving.

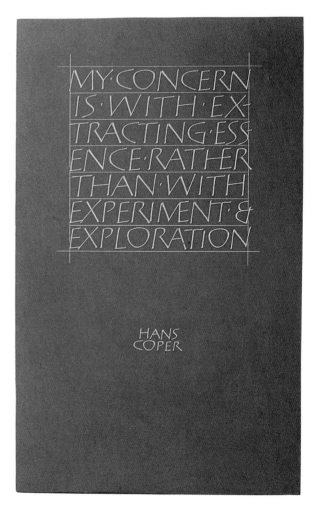

'My concern is with...' by Tom Perkins.

Opposite: 'Exuberance is Beauty' by Michael Rust.

PART FOUR

LETTERFORM

CHAPTER 9
LAYOUT

AIMS

- To define 'layout' and its purpose.

- To stress the importance of layout in relation to carving technique.

- To help with some of the problems students find with hand drawing, and to encourage practice in letter design and layout.

- To look at the important concepts of family resemblance, optical adjustments and colour in layout.

- To use the exercise style (modern roman) to demonstrate the principles of layout, as applicable to other letter styles.

- To give practical advice on setting about layout.

INTRODUCTION

This chapter applies to incised and raised lettering. (Though a few further points relating solely to the layout of raised lettering are discussed on page 113.)

Layout (also known as 'setting out' or 'drawing out') involves assembling and arranging letters *within given boundaries*. This means choosing the letterstyle and size, and perhaps designing or modifying the letterforms themselves. When the whole design for the lettering is completed, you have the 'layout', either on paper ready for transfer to the wood, or on the wood ready to begin carving.

Essentially, layout is the design stage of lettercarving, and as such is the most important. Once you are familiar with the techniques, the carving of the letters themselves becomes relatively straightforward.

What makes or breaks most examples of carved lettering is the layout: the design of both the individual letters and their arrangement. Good design can carry poor workmanship, but not the other way round (see Fig 9.1).

Fig 9.1   The layout of this eighteenth-century tombstone within the nave of a country church is typical of its time. The carver seems to have worked without much thought being given to the layout before he began. Note the astriction of TH and HE, the use of I in the month and the splitting of an all-important name.

Rarely do we find letters on their own. Letters are built into words, words into lines and lines into text. We normally take this for granted, but to *draw* and *carve* these same words requires an understanding of letter construction, spatial arrangements and which letterforms carve well.

Layout deals in a practical sense with the issues raised in Chapter 1: legibility, communication and aesthetic pleasure (see page 5), and what makes good lettering from a carver's viewpoint (see page 6). This chapter picks up these points and deals with them in detail.

To practise drawing and laying out you will need:

- Lots of paper, both plain and lined.

- A ruler and set square. An adjustable square is required for some letter styles.

- A selection of hard and soft pencils, and an eraser.

- A compass for some letter styles (modern roman being one).

MAKING A START

Students often ask how much they really need to know about layout. Why, for example, can't they just use dry transfer letters, such as Letraset (see Chapter 11, page 204); or even a computer. What, in other words, is the point of laying out letters by hand?

As is shown in Chapter 11, you can produce good lettered work by using common sense and getting someone, or some process, to lay out the text. 'Quick' methods, such as dry transfer alphabets do have their place, and can produce good work, but such methods remove a large part of the challenge, along with a great deal of the satisfaction and joy that can be had from lettercarving. Fine-carved lettering *starts* with design, and far from being a chore, this can be immensely enjoyable and satisfying in its own right. It also adds a sense of *control* over the whole work, and gives you the capacity to be infinitely and continually adaptable.

Although it has its subtleties, the underlying principles of layout soon become evident, and most are based on common sense coupled with some feeling for spacing and proportion. Many lettercarving students see themselves as not being able to draw – not being 'artistic' – but it is rare not to find a student with an eye for line, and this can be developed fairly quickly. The drawing skills necessary to outline letters are not the same as those needed for sketching, say, a tree or a face. Letter drawing requires good control of simple lines. Remember that your working drawings will disappear into the carving as it is completed, so they do not represent the final product.

The really important thing is to *engage* in lettercarving and design and keep exploring. The more you carve letters the better you will draw them, and vice versa. In both cases you are developing your eye and hand for a line. Practice makes all the difference to both confidence and competence. Skills of both carving and drawing can be built up slowly and surely if you follow two rules: start, and don't stop!

DRAWING PRACTICE

Practise laying out and drawing individual letters and text. Whatever letterform you want to carve, start with one letter – I and O are often good representatives of any style. Add another, and start adjusting the spaces in between according to the principles given later in this chapter. Build up elements of invented text as you begin to understand how the layout of the particular style works.

OBSERVATION

Besides such 'hands on' work, get into the habit of observing lettering. There are many sources of lettering available for the study of style and layout (see Fig 9.2).

Fig 9.2   *You can observe lettering everywhere. Develop your eye by looking at the layout critically: the spacing and the letterforms, whether you would want to change anything and why.*

159

Some are useful whatever level of drawing you are capable of, and it is a good idea to start a scrapbook or journal of designs. For example, lettering in churches and civic buildings and on gravestones. Letters carved in stone have many of the qualities of those carved in wood. Observe also the many other places where lettering appears: hoardings; shop fronts; vehicle sides and magazines, to name just a few. Books about lettering are also very useful. Some are included in the Further Reading section (see page 228), and these include studies of calligraphy. In all cases, do bear in mind the need for a style which *carves* (see page 6), as opposed to *printing* or *writing* styles.

RESEARCH

This is pro-active observation: searching out interesting letterstyles to study, rather than passively observing them. For example, trace over a letter style, using fairly large examples of the lettering, using a fine pen or pencil. Repeat this action many times, and you will eventually get a feel for the letterforms and be able to draw them straight on to paper.

PHOTOCOPYING

Because I have one available locally, using a photocopier is my sole method of enlarging or reducing my drawings. Having assembled, cut and pasted the letters to adjust the layout, I use the photocopier to change the size, and then recut and recopy, to help reach a final working drawing. In a similar fashion, photocopiers can give you good working drawings of lettering from many sources, without picking up a pencil!

LIGHTBOXES

A lightbox is an opaque screen through which a light shines. Any drawing resting on the screen will also illuminate through another sheet of paper placed on top, and a quick but exact copy taken. You can get the same effect using a window pane, and masking tape, or a sheet of Perspex (or toughened glass) rigged up over a lamp. Professional lightboxes have special cool bulbs. If you are using an ordinary bulb, do remember that they get very hot. Leave plenty of space between the lamp and the working surface.

FAMILY RESEMBLANCES

Three factors – family resemblances, 'colour' and optical adjustments – underpin the design of individual letters and their spacing arrangements. Layout comes to grief as a result of lack of attention to one or all of these three factors. Few people reading lettering, other than those who have an interest in calligraphy or letter design, consciously think about these points, but they are crucial to the effect of carved letters. There are no 'golden rules' to layout, or mathematics to be had, only guidelines, of which these three are the most important.

Different words are used to express the idea of family resemblance. **Style** is one, as in 'what style of letter?'. Other terms include **script**, **typeface** and **font** which come from different disciplines and are interchangeable. They all point to the same concept: a recognizable family of similar elements, hanging together and making a particular alphabet (see Fig 9.3). Indeed, with few resemblances between letters in an alphabet, there is no style at all.

Fig 9.3   Lettering on the back of a carved bedhead using a variation on modern roman. Every time you letter there is an opportunity to try some aspect differently.

Family resemblance is a 'rhythm', applied to lettering. The passage of the reader's eye, moving along your carved letters, will be smoothed by the repetition of forms. In the roman alphabet, for example, there is a strongly pleasing repetition in the regimental arrangement of thin and thick elements (see Fig 9.4).

Rhythm can be seen in many scripts throughout history, from Cyrillic to Turkish. When the meaning of the words is completely unintelligible to the reader, the rhythms, the repetition and symmetry of the letters, are still easy to see (see Fig 9.5). An attitude which says 'if you can read it, that's good enough' is very limited, wastes opportunities for creating attractive, readable letterforms, and will inevitably produce bad results. Lettering is more than just communicating a message, and insensitively formed or spaced lettering is awkward to read.

When you study a new letter style, look out for those shapes and proportions that give the sense of rhythm and family in an alphabet. Seek out similarities between the letters, and try to deduce what makes that particular alphabet hold together as a style, and differ from another. Given a few letters (including perhaps **I** and **O** – see Fig 9.6) you should be able to construct the whole alphabet in a particular style. If you have paid careful attention to family resemblances, you will also be able to ensure that they are consistently applied *throughout the whole composition.*

Be very careful about mixing completely different styles within any given arrangement of words. As a general rule it is safer to use the same style of letter, or close variations of them, throughout a particular composition. Emphasis and interest can be added changing the size, sloping the letters to make italic, or making the letters lighter or bolder, and so on. Mixing letter styles *within* words is something that should be avoided completely unless there is a real, conscious point to be made.

To sum up: it doesn't matter what style you choose to work in, consistency is important. You are free, as the carver, to interpret or change letterforms, but remember that whatever change you make to one letter, you must make the same change to *all* the appropriate letters you are carving in that style.

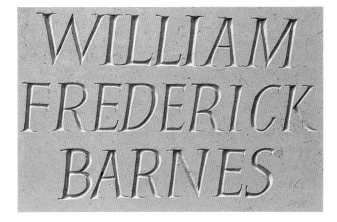

Fig 9.4 Roman lettering on a gravestone: always look for family resemblances and how the carver has dealt with spacing.

यकं विनिन्ये स जुगोप सप्त सप्तैव तत्याज ररक्ष पञ्च ।
प्राप चिवर्गं बुबुधे चिवर्गं जन्ने दिवर्गं प्रजहौ दिवर्गम् ॥ ४१ ॥
ऋतागसोऽपि प्रतिपाद्य वध्यान्न्याजीघनन्नापि रुषा ददर्श ।
बबन्ध सान्त्वेन फलेन चैतांस्त्यागोऽपि तेषां ह्यनयाय हृष्टः ॥ ४२ ॥
आर्षाख्यचारौत्यरमव्रतानि वैराग्यहासौचिरसंभ्रतानि ।
यशांसि चापव्रुणगन्धवन्ति रजांस्यहार्यौर्न्मलिनौकराणि ॥ ४३ ॥
न चाजिह्रीयौ र्दलिमप्रवृत्तं न चाचिकौर्गौत्यरवस्त्वभिधाम् ।

Fig 9.5 This is Sanskrit. Not only do I not know what it says, but I have no idea how to pronounce it, or from which end one reads it! Nevertheless rhythm, pattern and flow are readily and pleasingly apparent in the structure.

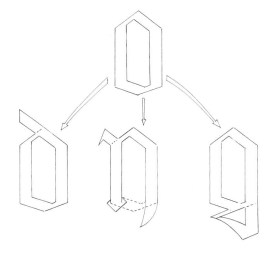

*Fig 9.6 These forms of the Gothic letter style (see Chapter 10) were all developed for carving from the letter **O**. If you understand the structure of **O** and the structure of **I** in any alphabet you should be able to construct the rest of the letters.*

161

COLOUR

The word 'colour' is used by many letterers to describe the optical spacing or arrangement of letters as they form words and text. It does not mean colour in the normal sense of pigment.

Lettering consists of letters *and* spaces. Colour in the context of lettercarving refers to the spacing of letters, but simply saying 'letter spacing' does not give the flavour of what the letterer wishes to achieve. Different combinations of letters appear to have different amounts of space between them (interspace) because of their shapes and the presence of counters. The aim of the letterer is to make the spaces look and feel as if they are of equal amounts – of equal weight. It is very important to understand that the *space* between letters is not the same as the *distance* between them: actual distances will vary between letters in order to equalize the sense of space. The space must be judged optically and the distance set accordingly (see Fig 9.7).

Many samples of lettercarving fail because of inadequacies in spacing rather than in the letterforms or the carving itself. However, it is common for a beginner to lettercarving not to see any difficulty at all: they gather a particular alphabet of letters from somewhere, place them together into the required message, and carve whatever appears.

In the vast majority of printing – and this book is no exception – letters occupy spatial boxes which are assembled in a similar way, without taking into account the shapes of the letters or their counters. We are so used to this 'mechanical' spacing that we experience no problem at all in reading it. However, legibility is only one criterion with which to judge a sample of lettering, and does not take account of aesthetics. The result of setting letters down beside each other without any thought for spacing is almost always an unevenness of colour – a lack of overall harmony in the spacing which manifests itself as a broken rhythm (see Fig 9.8).

If the spacing between two letters is too wide, the word can appear split, or part of it may be taken as belonging to the next word (see Fig 9.9). If, on the other hand, the letters are too close together, then the reader's

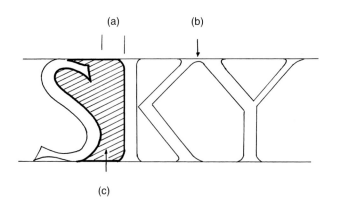

Fig 9.7   The distance *(a) and (b) will vary as the letterer attempts to create a uniformity of* space *(c) between letters.*

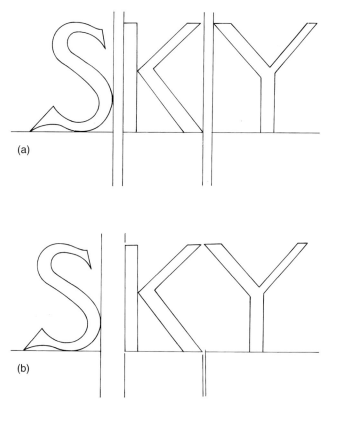

Fig 9.8 (a) 'mechanical' spacing: letters are treated as blocks and allowed the same distance between each. (b) optical spacing: here, the distance between letters is adjusted to allow for their shapes, resulting in a uniformity of colour through balanced interspaces.

162

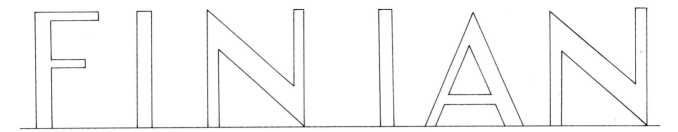

Fig 9.9 If the spacing is too wide, or irregular, the letters will not be scanned smoothly by the eye.

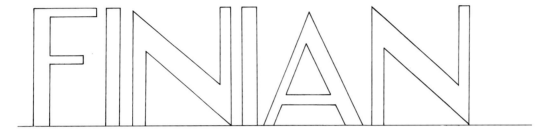

Fig 9.10 Too close a spacing makes letters harder to read as the eye tries to separate them.

eye will have trouble disengaging them (see Fig 9.10). Uneven spacing causes the eye moments of confused jumping, and the smooth flow of meaning to the brain is ruffled. Such effects may be apparent in only one place, but even this can be enough to spoil the impression of the whole.

Even colour will arise when the correct optical spacing has been satisfactorily achieved, and must take into account family resemblances and optical adjustments (see page 169). This is one of the great challenges and joys of lettercarving.

You can develop your sense for letter arrangement quite quickly, but be prepared to practise and not be discouraged by initially unsuccessful results. Give thought to achieving an evenness of colour in all letterstyles, right from your initial rough layout sketches. Carefully consider the spacing of letters, of words, and of lines of words, and seek to achieve an evenness of appearance in the whole work.

ASSESSING COLOUR

I don't know any better method to get an even sense of space when assembling letters than to half close your eyes and squint at them. This causes conceptual appreciation of the letterform to be screened out in favour of simple perception of form and space. You can see the lighter, overlarge spaces, and the dark 'tightness' of text more easily. It can help further to shade in the letters on the paper to make the contrast a bit stronger. Other, similar tricks include turning the paper upside down, or looking at the lettering through the back of the paper, reversed against the light. Anything to see the pattern of letters as an abstract rhythm.

It can help to cover up all the letters except the two previous to the one you are drawing. This means only three letters are visible at any one time, of which the last one is being drawn. Refer to the optical space between the two previous ones to position the third letter. A whole row of letters and interspaces can look complicated and overtax your judgement. When you have drawn in a few letters, by all means uncover the previous ones to assess the whole, but work specifically a letter at a time.

When you look at a particular word with a view to spacing the letters, *start with the most difficult spacing combination.* Establish a pleasing optical space between these letters, and use this spatial colour as your standard. Work outwards from this first spacing and arrange the other letters in the word one at a time to get a similar sense of space.

Look carefully for *repeating patterns*. Straight components next to each other, or curves, or any particular combination of elements will need the same amount of space each time it recurs. You can check for this with dividers.

There is a particular problem with regard to colour in incised lettering: the trough is half illuminated like the surface, and half in shadow. This causes the space between the letters to appear *wider* than if the letters were uniformly shaded, and errors of over-wide spacing tend to be exacerbated. If anything, err on too close a space rather than too wide. If you are uncertain about whether incising might affect your layout, shade in the letterforms, on paper, as if light was coming from one side and striking one wall, leaving the other in shadow (see Fig 9.11). However, do *not* black them in as this will not appear the same as when the letters are incised.

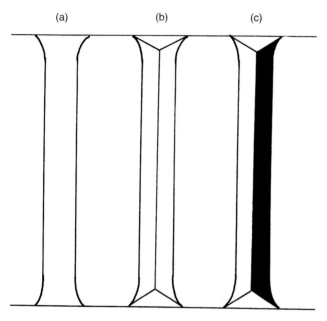

(a)   (b)   (c)

Fig 9.11 The normal drawing of letters is open (a), but drawing in the junctions (b) or shading in one wall (c) can sometimes give a better idea of their eventual three-dimensional appearance.

COLOUR OR SPACING BETWEEN LETTERS

When arranging letters, consider the shape of the letters themselves (the letterform), the space *within* the letters (the counter or counter space), and the space *between* the letters (the interspace). There are balances to be struck between the spaces within and around the letterforms, and the letterforms themselves.

The best way to start getting a hang of spacing and the concept of even colour is to move a few letters around. If you are coming to a new style this exercise will give you a quick feel for the spacing. The following exercise uses modern roman.

1   Draw, or photocopy, between cap and base lines, a large number (several dozen) of assorted letters. Make them quite big – about 50mm (2in) – and include straight (e.g. **I, L, H**), diagonal (**A, V**) and curved letterforms (**O, G**).

2   Cut out a dozen or so individual letters, keeping fairly tight to the sides while maintaining the cap and base lines.

3   On another piece of paper, draw another set of cap and base lines.

4   Take any two letters, place them between the cap and base lines, and adjust the distances between. See what effect moving the letters nearer and further apart has on the sense of space between them.

5   Now try arranging three letters, and see if you can get a feel for when there is *equal weight* – i.e. a balance of interspace – between the letters on either side and the middle one (see Fig 9.12).

6   If you can find variations on three letter words such as BAT, HAT, SAT etc. you will see how changing the initial letter means adjusting the distance with the second letter to have an even colour across the word. Alternatively, you can find words in which you can change the last or middle letters (see Fig 9.13).

7   Add more letters one at a time and continue balancing space.

Fig 9.12 Try varying the distance between the letters of a three-letter word to see the effect it has on the interspacing. This will also enable you to see how lengthening or shortening an element can help the optical balance. Note how A looks shorter (see page 169).

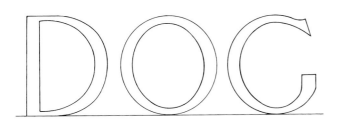

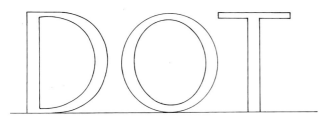

Fig 9.13 Experiment with words made up from three letters, altering one letter at a time.

You will find that when straight vertical stems (such as **I** and **H**) are next to each other, *less* distance is needed between the letters compared with two curved shapes (such as **C** and **O**) to get a balance of space. This is because, as two uprights are brought closer together, the interspace tends to tighten and the uprights read as one. The space must be loosened up (the distance increased) to counter this effect (see Fig 9.14). Conversely, circular letters have a lot of space in the open counters around them already, so they need to be pulled together to tighten up the space (see Fig 9.15).

Fig 9.14 Straight vertical stems appear to close down the space between. To counter this they need wider spacing.

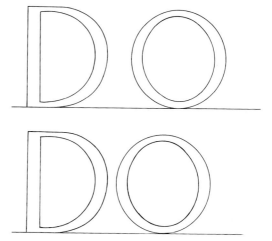

Fig 9.15 Curved letters appearing together have more space above and below them than straight-element letters, and need to be brought closer together.

Other letter combinations create their own colour problems. For example, if you put two Ts together, a large space is created which can appear as a hole in the line of letters. The way to bring them closer together is by shortening the inner cross arms of the Ts a little and carefully opening up the neighbouring letters to get an evenness of colour. Depending on the text and style, it may even be possible to overlap the letters (see Fig 9.16).

Two **As** in a word is a rare event, as is two **Vs**, but **LA**, **CA**, **RA** and **TY** are quite common combinations. Other letter styles may have combinations of letters with a similar problem of two fixed counter spaces coming together. There is scope here for shortening the arms of **T**, or the leg of **L**, as well as carefully tightening the outer hook of the serif on **A**.

The opposite can happen when combining letters with opposite shapes of counter spaces, such as **AV**, **LV** and **AY**. To get an even colour, letters such as **A** and **V** can be brought closer, so that the serifs lie on the same vertical line, or even overlapping a little. The leg of the **L** can be lengthened to take up space (see Fig 9.17).

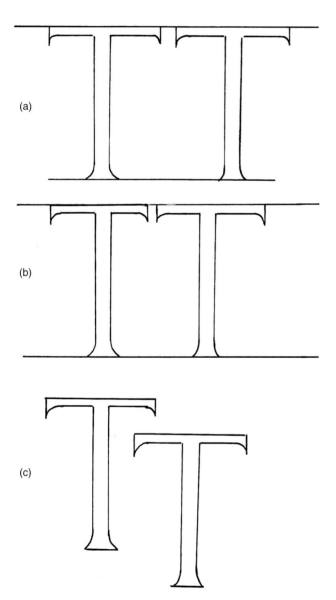

(a)

(b)

(c)

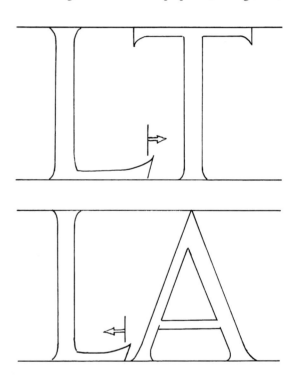

*Fig 9.17 Lengthening and shortening the leg of **L** to cope with the impact of the next letter.*

The exercise and this discussion will, I hope, have made you familiar with some of the basic principles of colour in lettercarving. To sum up:

- Evenness of colour (space) within a word will mean letters having different distances between them.

Fig 9.16 (a) two Ts together create a large open space beneath the neighbouring arms. Shortening these arms (b) can help reduce the space, and it may sometimes be possible to stagger the letters (c).

- Two adjacent, upright, straight stems will require more space between them than rounded letterforms. The distance between two such uprights is the greatest distance between any two letters.

- Two adjacent curves must be brought closer together. This combination is the least distance between any two letters.

- Some elements of the letters may be shortened (or lengthened) to increase (or decrease) the interspace.

Remember that there must be an even colour throughout the spacing of the *whole word* and the rest of the text, so some extra balancing elsewhere may be necessary.

You can see how important it is to work out the spacing on paper first, and I *always* advise this, no matter how simple the job. Quite sensitive adjustments are often necessary to letterform or interspace to get an even colour.

Widening space is easier than saving it, and (as has been seen) there are many ways in which small adjustments will even the optical spacing. If the available room for the layout is tight, more drastic assaults on the interspace may be called for. The following are a few well recognized expedients in roman lettering, and most letter styles are open to this sort of tightening. Use them carefully; if overdone, reading becomes more difficult.

- Use the ampersand as a space-saving device.

- Apply overlapping to suitable letters such as **OO** or **TT**, either on the same line, or staggered beyond the cap and base lines.

- Merge serifs. Where an upright and an oblique (e.g. **HA** or **EV**) come together, the sides of the serifs in the interspace can be run smoothly into each other (see Fig 9.18).

- Merge letters. **HE** in 'the' is especially useful for this.

- Capitalize on opposing counters. Letters such as **AV**, **AT** or **AC** can easily be brought in quite close to one another.

- Reduce the width of letters. For example, making circular letters such as **O** more oval will lose space and darken colour.

- Reduce space where verticals such as **M** or **N** appear next to another vertical stem. Leave out the serif on that side, ending the angle squarely. Conversely, the serif can be subtly lengthened to colour in too wide a gap, say when next to **A**.

- When trying to fill in space by increasing letter width, make the weight proportionally somewhat heavier, otherwise letters begin to feel lightweight.

Fig 9.18 Running serifs together when space is tight can improve the appearance of a word.

COLOUR OR SPACING BETWEEN WORDS

Once each word has been evenly coloured, the words themselves must be given a sufficient gap to show the conceptual break, but not so much that the flow falters. The original Trajan inscription had no spaces between words, but such presentation is alien to us.

The amount of space between words varies in the same way as that between letters, because of the different amount of space in the counters. Whatever optical space value is given, it must be consistent between words to maintain a uniform balance of colour in the text (see Fig 9.19). In modern roman the amount of space required will be somewhere between one half and the full height of a letter (i.e. the distance between the cap and base lines). After a full stop (period) about half the established word space again is needed to give a sufficient sense of pause.

Fig 9.19 *This panel of lettering, carved in mahogany with text taken from a Yuma curing song, is a very good example of the way the space between words needs to vary to create a balanced effect.*

One trick that is sometimes used to help space words is to imagine inserting an invisible letter – normally an **I** – between words, still taking into account any counters in the spacing.

COLOUR OR SPACING BETWEEN LINES

Space is left between lines so that when the eye returns from the end of one line it is clear where the next one starts. Exactly where breaks occur depends on the text, the style of alphabet being used, and what sense the lines make. The breaks in lines should be natural, in the sense of adding to, or at least not interfering with, the meaning. The main contribution that the breaking of the lines can make is one of adding emphasis.

Fitting words into lines can be quite a problem, and this is where ways of expanding or compressing interspaces comes in useful. As a guide, the distance between lines will normally be found somewhere between a minimum of one half the letter height and a maximum of the full letter height.

Long lines are tiring to read. A line length somewhere between 50 and 70 characters, including punctuation and word spaces, is usually enough.

Additional space is needed when a style of alphabet has ascenders and descenders (e.g. roman lower case), in order to keep these elements apart. Similarly, avoid putting ascenders and descenders too close together.

Look out for 'snail tracks' (also known as rivers), and holes in the lettering, and adjust words to remove or diminish them. Once again, squinting through half closed eyes will help show them up.

Centring the text is often a simple and effective solution to line arrangement, and easier to arrange than a block of justified lettering. The effect of the two approaches is very different and should not be seen as having the same impact or power. The outline of centred lettering can look ragged if many differing lengths of line are presented. It also takes up more lines than justified lettering. On the other hand, a square-looking block of words can be monotonous.

OPTICAL ADJUSTMENT

As you worked with the modern roman letterforms in the exercises, you will have noticed that a certain amount of adjustment from what would seem to be the 'natural' letter shapes was advised, and often necessary. There are several reasons for this.

Changing the letter shape may be needed to adjust the optical space between a letter and the one following or preceding it (such adjustments are dealt with in the preceding section on colour). For reading purposes, letters are normally set between straight and parallel cap and base lines. These tram lines, while not actually present, have a virtual reality: our eyes imply the presence of the cap and base lines by linking all the tops and bottoms of the letters (see Fig 9.20). It is this implied alignment which causes many problems, and a bit of optical trickery is necessary to keep a uniformity of appearance and equality of height – so important for the rhythm of the text. This problem disappears if the letters are placed irregularly, and not between formal lines.

These points are best demonstrated by taking examples from roman letters where optical adjustments are well established. The visual sense of what is happening varies between letter combinations, but you will be able to see these principles at work in many other letter styles too.

The apexes of pointed letters (**A**, **N**, **V**, **W**) appear to float short of the virtual cap or base line when placed next to a strong horizontal stroke or neighbouring serif lying on the line. To counter this apparent shortness the points should be extended slightly beyond the appropriate cap or base line. Circular letters (**C**, **G**, **O**, **Q**) have a similar problem, and are also extended a little beyond the cap and base lines.

If the centre bar of **H** or centre arm of **E** is placed on the mid-line to give a 'natural symmetry', the eye makes the top counter larger, causing the letter to appear unstable. Raising the bar or arm a little, and thereby increasing the size of the bottom counter, lowers the centre of gravity and stabilizes the letter (see Fig 9.21). For similar reasons the lower bowl of **B** should also be enlarged, so stablizing the shape.

Fig 9.20 Although the cap and base lines are absent, the mind creates them. Pointed letters, especially when next to strong horizontals, appear to float in a large amount of space and not quite reach the line, as would be the case with the A here.

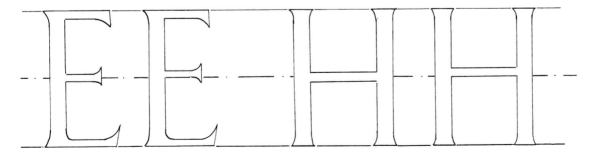

Fig 9.21 The top counter of a symmetrical letter is seen to be larger than the bottom counter. Raising the crossbar a little above the centre line compensates for this giving the letter more visual stability.

Curved parts of letters change from thin to thick. If the thick parts are given the same thickness as the vertical stems, they actually appear thinner by comparison. Thickening the curved parts a little more by their maximum widths results in all the components appearing to have optically equal weight.

If serifs are carved with a circular look – i.e. quite geometrically, and bracket-like – then a truly flat end to a serif will appear to bulge. The circular effect of the brackets appear to pinch the stem just beyond the brackets, and the eye compensates for this. To counter this effect, the serif should be merged into the stem, avoiding a geometric appearance. Some lettercarvers slightly dip or hollow the end-line of the serif as well.

To sum up, whatever style you may choose to work with, be aware of these sorts of effects and trust your eye to reveal both uniformity and imbalances as you play with the shapes or positions of your letters. The shaping of individual letters as well as their spacing needs a certain 'visual literacy': a sense of what is actually happening as you observe what is in front of you. In lettercarving, it might mean sensing whether a letter is leaning forwards or backwards, or whether it is *desirable* that it should; or if a letterform is top heavy, or has a sense of line or shape which is ill-matched to other letters.

It is this development of your visual sense that makes lettering so challenging and interesting. There are very few people who don't have an ability to judge what they see in this way, even if they are not aware of it, and the sense can certainly be strengthened and developed with experience.

WORKING PARAMETERS

How layout fits in the whole lettercarving process, with practical ideas and guidance on how to go about the layout, is discussed in the preliminary drawing stages (see Chapter 3). As part of the initial rough stages of laying out, you will need to make decisions about certain limiting factors. There are three:

- The physical boundaries you are working to.

- The size of the letters you will be carving.

- The style or form of those letters.

Such details relate to the purpose of the lettering in the first place, and must be worked out right at the beginning, in the rough sketches, otherwise there is a real danger of wasting a lot of time later on.

BOUNDARIES

The dimensions of the wood or the text within the wood may be given to you, or you may be left to suggest an overall size to the piece of work. Whichever, you will need to consider not just the size of letters but how close you want them to come to the edge of the available surface (see Fig 9.22). Lettering normally needs some space around it, and sometimes space *within* it, in which to 'breathe'. If you don't take this into account, you may think you have more space available for the letters than you really have. It is usual, given the eye's predilection for a sense of gravity and stability, to allow more space below the lettering than above. If the work is to be framed, you must take this into consideration also.

Normally, cap and base lines are the first guides to be drawn in. More often than not, they are straight and parallel, serving to make reading easier. However, there are no rules to say that parallel cap and base lines are obligatory – it is possible to taper them, perhaps to invoke perspective. There are many 'loose' styles, including a more 'rustic' roman, where letters can be staggered and arranged to different patterns. It all depends on the work and the degree of freedom you are allowed.

Not all surfaces will be flat. They might curve in all directions, such as on the side of a vase. Some surfaces may be flat in one plane but curve in another, say around the edge of a plate or the base of a lectern. Such differing planes will affect the layout and the way the letters must be cut. Some of the projects later in the book are examples of these circumstances.

LETTER SIZE

The size of letter is perhaps the most important factor in layout. This is not just because of the relationship of letter size to the available surface dimensions, but also

Fig 9.22 *Letter A by Tom Perkins, carved in Welsh slate, 30cm (12in). Note how the dynamic shape of the letter relates so perfectly to its boundaries.*

because of the practical purposes to which the lettering will be put – for example, the distance from which the words will be read. A *minimum* height for the letters on a house sign is about 50mm (2in), more if the sign is further away.

As letters increase in size (say above 50mm (2in)) they should be placed wider apart. Larger interspaces are also required between words and lines making the whole easier to read. Another point to bear in mind is that heavier letters appear larger than lighter ones, perhaps because more effort is needed to read them.

Several problems arise as the letters get smaller. As a rule, letters under 15mm (¹/₂in) – although some carvers would say 25mm (1in) – don't work well, for three reasons. First, the effect of the grain gets greater, especially with coarser grained woods. Second, executing the letters needs far greater precision: a small stroke with the chisel may not be much to a large letter, but with smaller letters the effect is proportionally greater. Third, the leeway for lining up the letters is less. A slightly untrue cut to the edge of a small letter may throw it out of vertical, whereas in a large letter the effect may not even be noticeable.

LETTER STYLE

A competent carver can probably carve *any* letter style, even the most outrageous! The question is whether a carver would *want* to work in a particular style. Just because a style *can* be carved, it doesn't mean it *has* to be, or that it is desirable to carve it. (I discussed 'carvability' in Chapter 3, and the styles suggested in this book have been chosen because they are suitable for use on a wide range of subjects.)

When you select a style, consider its fitness for the purpose. Is it appropriate to the message and the setting? Fairground-style letters would not be appropriate in a

Gothic church, nor would a set of instructions or a directional sign look right or sucessfully convey its message if carved in a gently flowing script. Each style has an emotional impact which is appropriate for some scenarios but not for others.

Style also includes the 'weight' of the letterforms (see page 104). Think of bold letters as a sort of shouting, or at least speaking more loudly. So a bolder, heavier, letter would be suitable for a house sign. A lighter letter would be suitable for more refined purposes such as the initials on the back of a hairbrush or mirror.

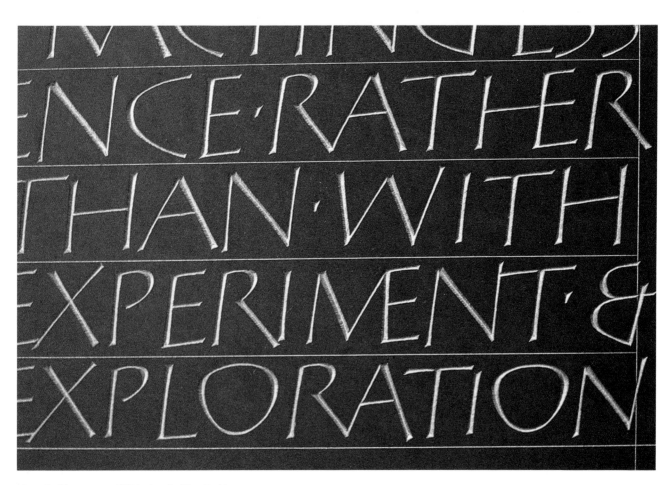

Detail of lettering in Welsh slate by Tom Perkins.

CHAPTER 10

LETTER STYLES

This chapter introduces some new letter styles to show how the techniques you have learned working with modern roman can be applied elsewhere.

There are a huge number of letter forms in regular use – one only has to look at computer fonts and manuals of dry transfer lettering. Whether they carve well is another matter, and it pays to be selective. Most letterers find they need only a small number of styles which they understand deeply and are able to apply in a wide variety of contexts.

There is only space to introduce a few alphabets. You will find many more, as well as different approaches to lettercarving, in the books listed in the Further Reading section (see page 228). The ones shown here are those I know carve well – that is, quickly and efficiently, allowing for a flow in the work, and this is partially because I have adapted them to carving in wood. You are free – and encouraged – to disagree with my adaptations and refer to other sources to make your own decisions.

The styles that follow are: traditional roman, lower case roman, versal, uncial, and Gothic. In each case, I have taken a representative letter to show the basic procedure for carving, and assumed familiarity with the information and exercise work which has gone before.

TRAJAN ROMAN

Trajan roman differs from modern roman in a number of ways. You will notice that:

- Its stress is rotated at about 10° anticlockwise.

- The thick strokes are one-tenth of the letter height.

- The strokes on **E** and **F** are closer to being the same length.

- There is a variable amount of waisting.

- There are subtle bends in the obliques.

- There is a sense of roundness in such letters as **C** and **D**, even though they are not necessarily compass-struck.

Trajan roman in its original form is subject to some variation. Individual carvers had their own way of doing things, even though they followed some common rules. As a result, the uprights will be found to have differing amounts of waisting, for example. Woodcarvers have always tended to cut parallel trenches when copying traditional roman. This is more in keeping with woodcarving techniques, and has its own elegance.

Details on waisting letters are to be found in the versal letterstyle. Otherwise, there is little to be said about carving the traditional roman style that is not covered in the incising exercises. If you familiarized yourself with modern roman, then the small but crucial differences in the basic structural form and layout should prove to be no problem (see Figs 10.1 and 10.2).

Fig 10.1 G in traditional roman style.

Fig 10.2 *The Trajan roman alphabet. Waisting and curving of elements are not included for ease of carving in wood.*

LOWER CASE ROMAN

Small letters (known as minuscules or lower case) are a later development from handwriting and printing, and as such are more intimate and less monumental. The change and evolution of small letters can be studied by looking at old manuscripts and printed material. Those we are familiar with today have been established for about 400 years and come from what are now illegible precursors.

Fig 10.3 The lower case roman alphabet.

The lower case roman alphabet is shown in Fig 10.3. Many letters are similar to capitals, but others differ, having more curved parts – such as **d**, **g** and **q**, and their reversed forms **p** and **b**. Some letters have an almost inverted form (e.g. **f** and **t**, **p** and **d**, and of course ascenders and descenders make their appearance. Other features you will not have encountered with upper case roman are: the addition of dots to **i** and **j**, and cross bars at the height of the cap line. You will also notice that **a** and **g** have several variations. However, lower case roman letters have approximately the same ratios of width as the upper case letters.

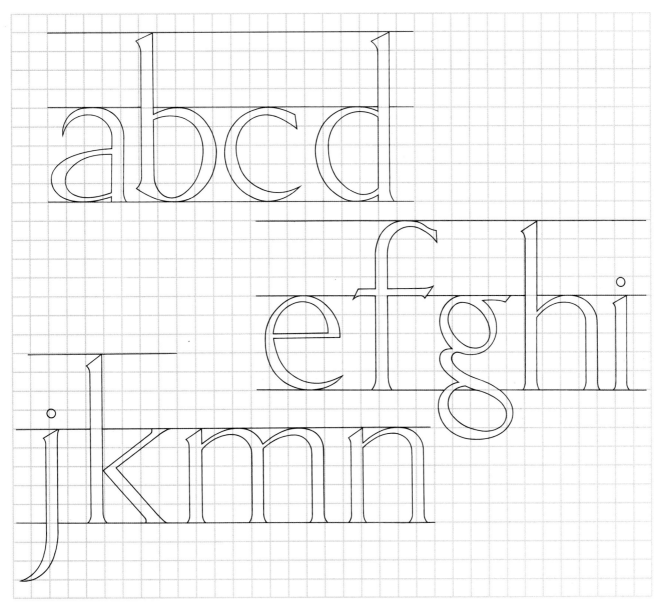

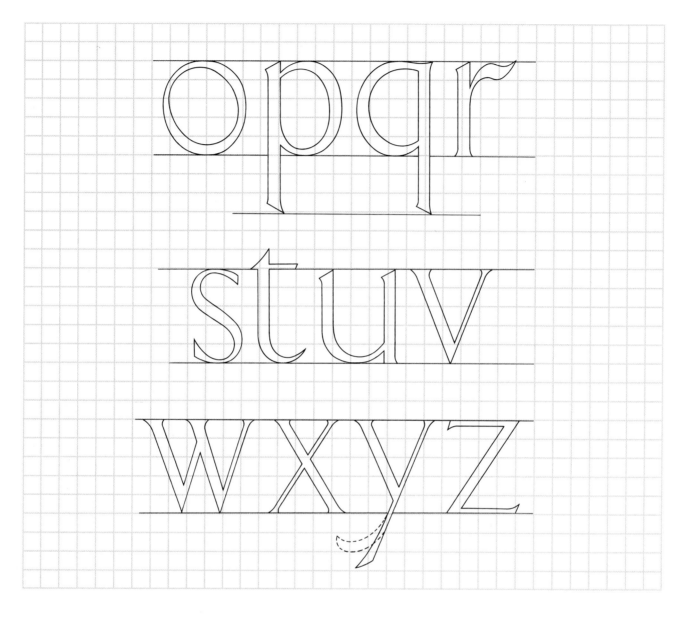

SAMPLE LETTER: b

The letter **b** includes uprights as well as curves, and the method for carving it incorporates many of the techniques you will have encountered in the exercises.

METHOD

1   Refer to Figs 10.4 to 10.9. After drawing out the letter, cut the vertical trench first.

2   Cut the serif.

3   Stab the centre line of the bowl.

4   Remove the outside wall with a slicing cut.

5   Run the inside wall round and into the upright.

6   Finish off the lower part of the bowl and serif.

Simply *slanting* roman lower case letters does not produce an italic form. Although italic letters *are* sloped (by about 10°), the square forms are more condensed, and the circular forms more oval. Nor are italic letters joined together. For further information from which to construct a carveable italic alphabet, refer to *The Art of Hand Lettering*, by H. Watzkov, details of which can be found in the Further Reading section on page 228.

Fig 10.4 Letter **b** in lower case roman. The angled cuts to the vertical trench are made first.

Fig 10.7 Removing the outside wall with a slicing cut.

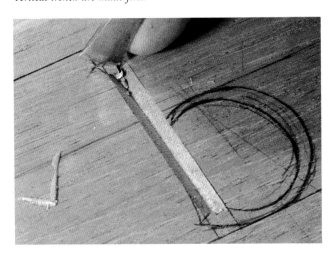

Fig 10.5 Finishing the cap serif.

Fig 10.8 Running the inside wall into the upright.

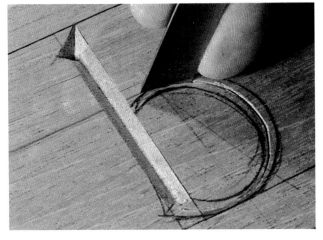

Fig 10.6 Making a stab cut to the bowl.

Fig 10.9 Finished letter **b**.

VERSAL

This is a very elegant letterform in which the straight strokes are waisted, producing an open look. Shown in Fig 10.10, it exists only as a capital form and was originally drawn with two strokes of the pen, with the spaces filled in.

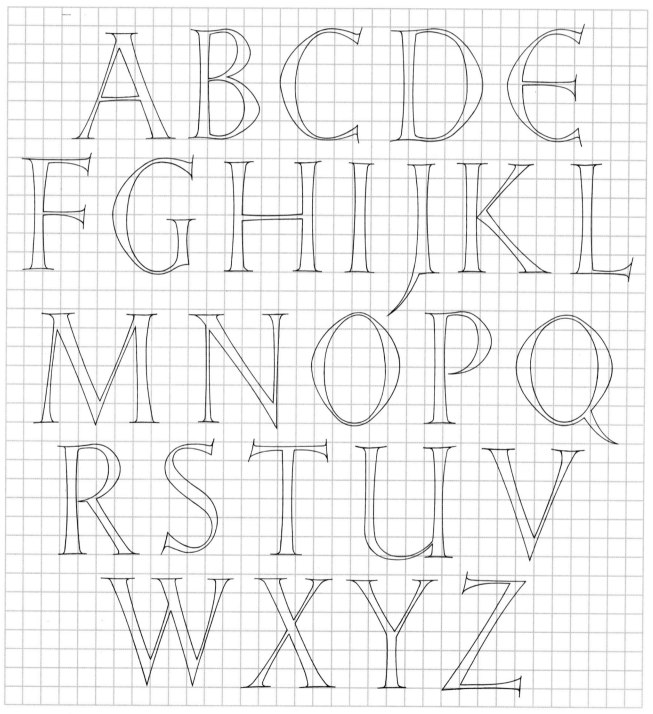

Fig 10.10 The versal alphabet.

Some characteristic features of the basic versal letterform besides the waisted uprights are the vertical stress, the thin cross serifs and horizontal elements, and the curves of the letters **B**, **D** and **P**.

SAMPLE LETTER: A

Because the ratio of thick to thin strokes is quite extreme with smaller letters, the thin strokes tend to disappear. You may need to stab the roots of the thin elements to produce enough shadow.

Incising curved parts and grading thick to thin is not difficult, as the gouges are manipulated in the usual way.

The main difference in terms of carving this letterstyle is in the waisting of the straight parts (see Fig 10.11). For this you will need a skewed fishtail chisel for pushing along the sides and shaping them. A skew to the edge of about 20° is sufficient.

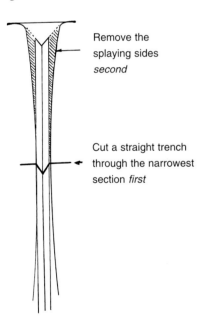

Remove the splaying sides *second*

Cut a straight trench through the narrowest section *first*

Fig 10.11 Versal letters require a particular approach when carving the uprights, due to their characteristic waisting. The technique for cutting straights involves incising a shallow trough the width of the narrowest section first. This 'primary trough' is then deepened and widened towards the serifs to produce the waisted shape. It is not so much that a versal letter is made narrower during carving but rather that it is widened from its narrowest point.

METHOD

1   Refer to Figs 10.12 to 10.18. Draw out the letter accurately, and then cut the primary troughs to both obliques with a wide chisel.

2   Make stop cuts for the serifs with the skewed fishtail chisel.

3   Start with the thick oblique, and use the skewed fishtail chisel in the pen and dagger grip to run up the sides at the right-angle, starting at the thinnest point of the trough – in the middle. Place the long point on the root of the trench and push forward with your thumb.

4   Control the edge at the surface and the point in the root as you slice smoothly up towards the end wall of the serif. Follow the line at the surface. As the trench gets wider, it must get deeper.

Fig 10.12 Making a straight cut up to the waist lines.

Fig 10.13 Using the skewed fishtail chisel to make stop cuts for the serifs.

5   Repeat this on the other side. You will have to swing your body to the side to produce the lower half of the obliques. Alternatively, you can reverse the chisel and pull it towards you with your fingers. Here, the chisel is used rather like a knife.

6   Finish the serifs on this oblique.

7   Repeat the waisting on the thin oblique, running it into the serif end at the top.

8   The crossbar can be formed with wide flat gouges, offered back to back, or waisted with the fishtail chisel as before.

9   As a final touch, create the hair lines to the serifs by stabbing with the corner of the fishtail chisel.

Fig 10.16 Finishing off the serif. Treat the thin stroke and the crossbar in the same way.

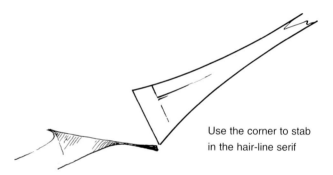

Use the corner to stab in the hair-line serif

Fig 10.17 Use the corner of the fishtail chisel to create the hairline serif.

Fig 10.14 Running up the side at the right angle using the pen and dagger grip. For this slicing cut the thumb is the major mover and pivot.

Fig 10.15 Slicing round with the fishtail chisel on the inside wall into the serif.

Fig 10.18 Finished letter A.

SAMPLE LETTER: D

METHOD

1 Refer to Figs 10.19 to 10.22. Incise and waist the upright as for the letter **A**, and cut the one-sided serifs at both ends.

2 Stab in the centre stop cut in the usual way.

3 Cut the outside angled wall first in a clean curve running into the top wall of the serif.

4 Cut the inner wall, running the trench also into the serif.

5 Thicken the centre of the bowl with a deeper gouge and merge in.

6 Create the hair lines to the serifs by stabbing with the corner of the fishtail chisel.

Fig 10.19 Stabbing the centre of the lobe after the upright is finished.

Fig 10.21 Running the inside angle cut into the serif, making a trench of the thinner part of the lobe.

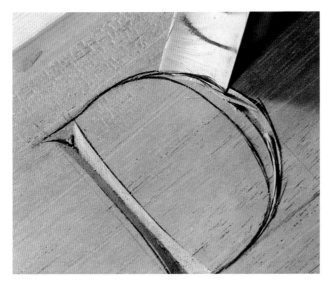

Fig 10.20 Making the outside angle cut. A change of sweep may be needed where the lobe bulges at the centre.

*Fig 10.22 The finished letter **D**.*

UNCIAL AND HALF UNCIAL

This letterstyle, shown in Fig 10.23, is sometimes called Celtic, and is quite an ancient one, having affinities with Greek. It was the first real alternative to Rustica (a looser form of roman) and was developed by scribes somewhere around the fourth century, who used it to copy Christian manuscripts.

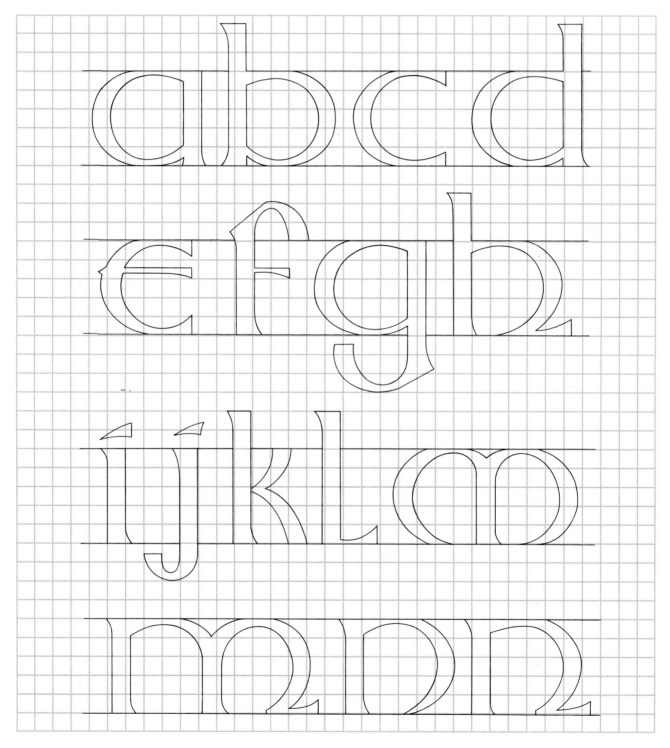

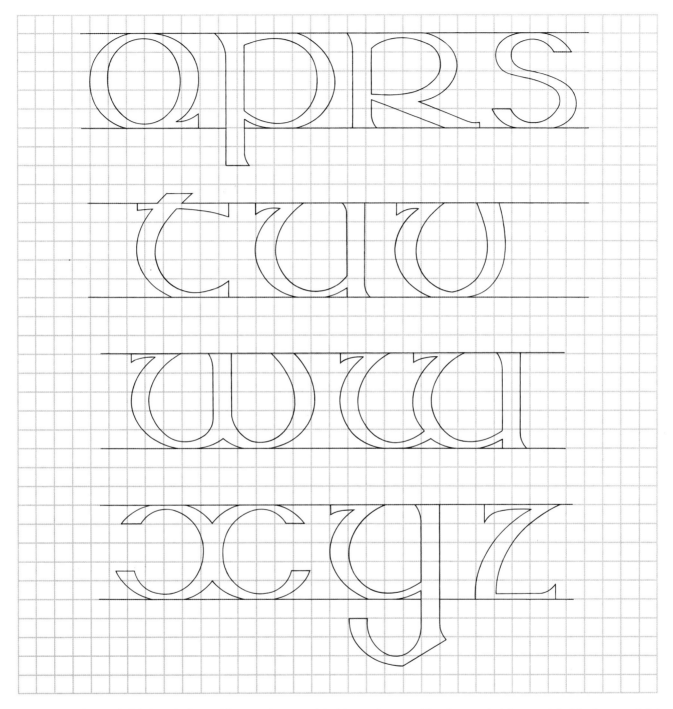

Fig 10.23 *The uncial alphabet. The flattened horizontal sections of the lobes on the cap and base lines can be left out, and the lobes kept rounded.*

Uncial derives from capital letters and is itself a capital form, taking its name from the Latin *uncial* – an inch – which was the height. Both uncial and half uncial were in use up to the end of the eighth century, when they were replaced by more fashionable Carolingian pen styles. They bear a close resemblance to one another, many of the letters having the same features and only varying in their size. In half uncial, the embryonic ascenders and descenders of uncial become more prominent, and appear to be the precursor of many lower case letterforms.

Uncial and half uncial often appear dark and condensed. Originally penned with a broad nib held horizontally, the letters have wide curving forms with a strong vertical stress and round counters. The serifs are more 'clubbed' than bracketed.

Although originally a pen letter, the style adapts well for carving. There was a wide variation in the way scribes penned this broad letter style. The letter style I have developed here is part extract, part synthesis of these, taking the most legible forms and working them into a coherent family that is straightforward to read. For capitals I use larger versions of the letters.

The letters can be drawn with a compass, giving a regular pattern, and this is especially useful when they are quite large (see Fig 10.24). They can also be drawn out freehand somewhat more informally and loosely. A point to note is the flat, thin horizontal section to the lobes at the cap lines.

If you research this style you will find many interesting alternatives to some letterforms; I have included a few common variations with the alphabet.

SAMPLE LETTER: **h**

The carving is quite straightforward. I have chosen this letter because it has both straight and curved parts.

METHOD

1   Refer to Figs 10.25 to 10.31. Draw out the letter **h**, and cut the vertical trough with a centre cut and angled side cuts.

2   Finish the one-sided serifs at both ends.

3   Stab the centre of the bowl into the horizontal top part.

4   Cut the outside wall.

5   Run the inside wall into the heel of the foot.

6   Use a fishtail chisel or flat fishtail gouge to incise the triangular-shaped foot, finishing the end with a skew chisel.

7   Finish the horizontal section either with the skewed fishtail chisel, pushing it as in the versal letter style on page 178, or with a flat chisel. Merge carefully with the curve.

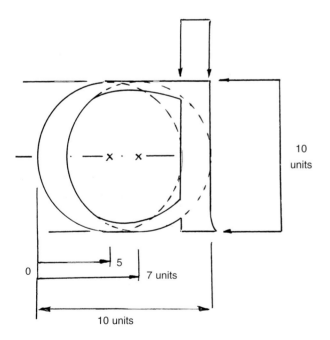

Fig 10.24 Layout of a typical uncial letter. In larger sizes the lobes can be struck with a compass, as here.

Fig 10.25 Incising the upright trench.

Fig 10.26 Finishing the end wall.

Fig 10.29 The end wall of the foot may need the sharper angle of a regular skew chisel to finish off, as here.

Fig 10.27 Making the centre stop cut to the lobe.

Fig 10.30 After the flat horizontal section has been removed in the normal way, merge in the lobes with the fishtail skew, or a flat gouge.

Fig 10.28 Removing the foot of the fishtail skew chisel.

Fig 10.31 Finished letter **h**.

GOTHIC

Gothic, sometimes referred to as Old English, is a heavy, formalized script deriving from around the eleventh and twelfth centuries (see Fig 10.32).

Fig 10.32 An example of Gothic lettering.

There was a wide variety of schools and styles of Gothic lettering. Indeed, so formal and dense did it eventually look that it was sometimes called 'blackletter', which, to modern eyes, is hardly more than an unintelligible pattern. The name Gothic was a term of abuse given to the style by renaissance scholars, who thought it barbaric.

Gothic letters carve well, because of the style's regularity, and can include a large number of straight elements. Pen flourishes can be included or ignored, as you wish.

I have taken extracts from different letterforms to produce a synthesis of Gothic. Gothic capitals are very ornate, and there is no standard type. They tend to be rounder than the small letters, which makes them stand out as initial letters. Capital and lower case alphabets are shown in Fig 10.33. *Never* write a word in capitals-only using Gothic, as it will be difficult to read. Use capitals to start a word only, and think about missing them out altogether. I have not shown them carved here: they can be cut with the normal techniques I have discussed in the incising exercises.

Fig 10.33 The Gothic alphabet in upper and lower case forms. Note that the upper case letters are ordered by letter structure. I have not included a grid or cap and base lines for the upper case letters because the letterform is so variable.

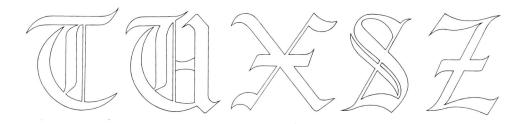

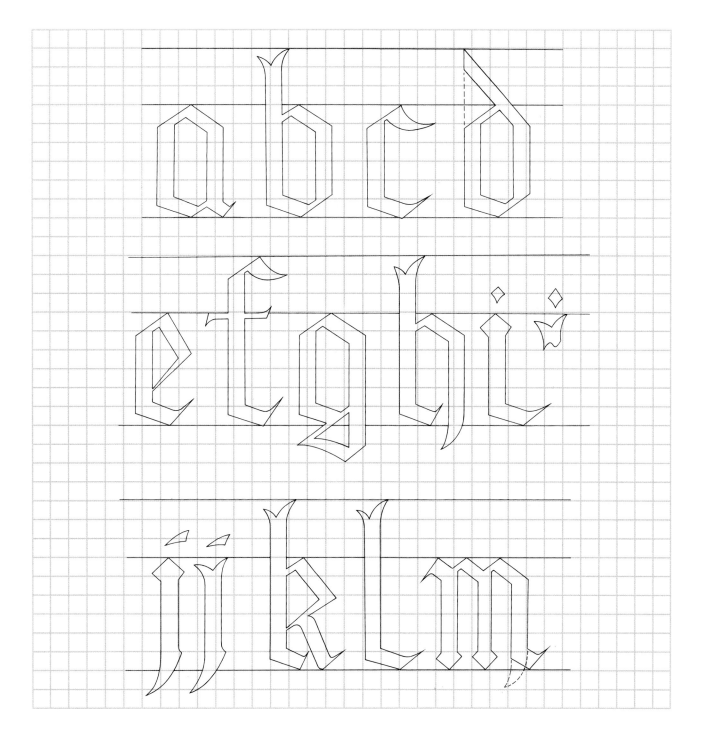

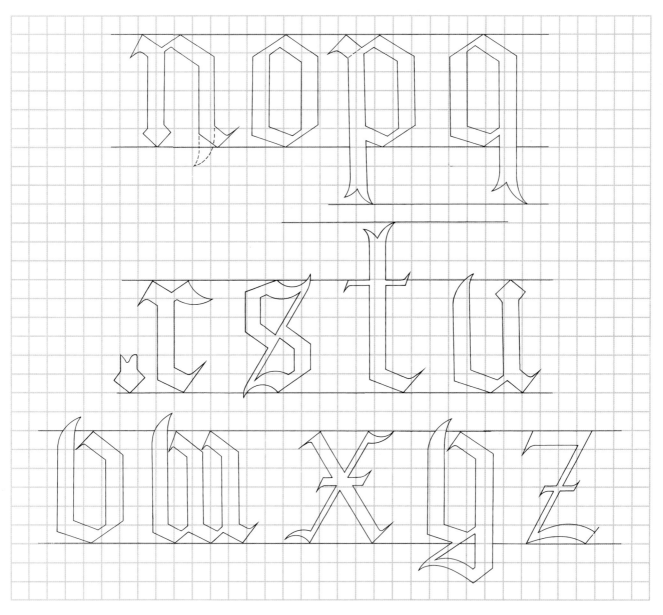

There are several useful points to note about the style. You will see that there is a contrast between thick and thin strokes, to which applies the same rules as roman, and a stress of about 40°, making a difference in the appearance of the upper and lower angles (see Fig 10.34). The ascenders and descenders are normally quite short. In the style I have chosen to show here, I have lengthened them a bit, and added forked ends. Spacing is normally quite tight, one of the reasons why Gothic can be so dense and illegible, but I prefer to make the spacing a little looser.

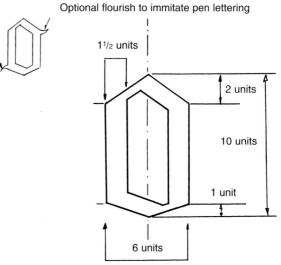

Optional flourish to immitate pen lettering

1½ units

2 units

10 units

1 unit

6 units

*Fig 10.34 Layout of the letter **O** showing the proportions of the letter in the Gothic style.*

SAMPLE LETTER: **a**

This letter shows the basic features of all the other letters.

METHOD: BASIC LETTER

1   Refer to Figs 10.35 to 10.40. Draw out the letter, and incise the uprights first.

2   Make stop cuts into the junctions (see incised Exercise ■13).

3   Stab the centre of the obliques.

4   Use a fishtail chisel to cut the oblique walls and junctions.

5   Use a smaller fishtail chisel to cut the tail, reverting to the wider one for the end.

Fig 10.37 Making the inner angled cuts to the thin elements.

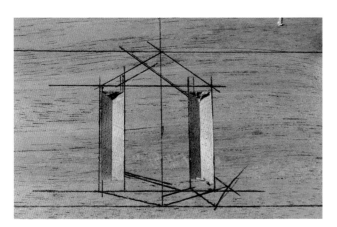

Fig 10.35 The upright trenches have been removed. Remember to select a chisel that will avoid biting into the angled walls in the junctions.

Fig 10.38 Making the outer angled cuts.

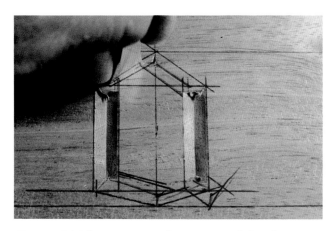

Fig 10.36 Making stop cuts to the junctions and thin elements.

Fig 10.39 A small fishtail chisel is the best tool for the tail.

189

Fig 10.40 The finished letter a.

METHOD: LENGTHENING THE ENDS OF THE ASCENDERS AND DESCENDERS

1 Refer to Figs 10.41 to 10.43. Cut the trench of the ascender with a wide chisel, stopping short of the fork.

2 The fork is made of two crescent cuts. Stab in centre of the right hand curve – which is a continuation of the thick upright – with a medium gouge, from the root of the trench to feather out on the surface at the end.

3 Incise the angled walls and finish this side of the fork completely.

4 Stab and incise the left fork, which is somewhat smaller and more bending to the left than its partner, merging in the left wall with the upright.

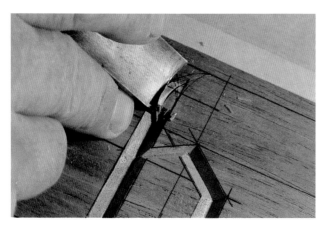

Fig 10.41 The larger section of the fork should be cut first, as if it were an extension of the upright.

Fig 10.42 Bringing in the smaller part of the fork.

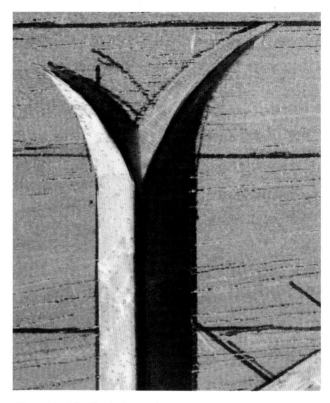

Fig 10.43 The finished ascender.

Opposite: 'Type Face' by Bridget Powell.

190

PART FIVE

PROJECTS

CHAPTER 11

INCISED LETTERING PROJECTS

INTRODUCTION

Examples of the fine work of many carvers are scattered throughout this book. These are principally in wood, but occasionally in stone. I hope close inspection of these pieces will both guide and inspire you in your lettering.

The incised lettering in this chapter, and the raised ones in the following chapter, show a further variety of approaches to lettering with a range of applications. You can follow them exactly or use them as springboards for your own ideas.

References are provided to the details of the actual lettercarving to be found in the main text of the book, but I have commented, where appropriate, on any unusual points, in particular on the background to the designs I chose.

Obviously, carved lettering needs a vehicle – it must be carved *into* something. Sometimes the available wood will suggest a layout for the letters. At other times, the workpiece will need to be specially made.

The choice of text may be out of your hands carving a specific job for a client: a sign or an inscription, for example. If you can choose your own text, then you need to think very carefully about what you want to say.

Poems, aphorisms and injunctions (in the sense of commands such as 'do not walk on the grass') are all popular and common choices, along with quotations. The choice is vast, and you may find it helpful to bear the following in mind when you are trying to decide what to carve.

- In carving, what you say is bound up with how you say it – the *aesthetics* of the result. Try to be sure that your text imparts as much viewing pleasure as reading pleasure.

- Leave some 'mystery' – some room for the viewer's imagination. You might choose to use only the first line of a poem, as I have done in the first project.

- Remember that what may be profoundly meaningful to one person may well appear sententious, even vacuous, to another. Don't just try to please other people – please yourself first – but try also to see your text as if you were a complete stranger just happening upon it. Be wary of homilies, clichés and slogans.

INSCRIPTED POST

This carving is a large post which now stands in the garden, gently reminding visitors – and myself – to look around and enjoy being there (see Fig 11.1). I like the idea of lettering slabs of wood and leaving them in out-of-the-way places to be discovered.

The post is several hundred years old, and was in poor condition, but I felt it had the potential to be rejuvenated, which led on to the idea of adding some appropriate decoration in the form of an inscription.

DESIGN

The text comes from Kathleen Raine's beautiful poem: 'The Moment', the first lines of which run:

> Never, never again
> This moment . . .

These lines have three 'units' of sense. I have taken the liberty of altering the arrangement, making four units, one for each side of the post:

This moment
Never
Again
Never

I feel this works well, and keeps the sense of the original lines. The post is orientated so that one comes across 'this moment', followed by 'never' whichever way round the post, then 'again'. If you decide on a similar experiment, make sure you have obtained permission to use the material you choose, assuming it is still in copyright.

Fig 11.1 The finished oak post, with words from 'The Moment' by Kathleen Raine, in a quiet corner of the garden. I was kindly given permission to use the text of this poem by Golgonooza Press, Ipswich.

WOOD

The old oak post had splits, nails and woodworm and needed cleaning up carefully to protect the cutting edges of my carving tools. I first removed or punched down the nails, and then wire brushed and planed up the surfaces roughly, before removing any wormy wood (see Fig 11.2).

I now knew what surfaces I actually had to work with, and could decide which parts of the wood to use for which parts of the text.

Fig 11.2 Cleaning up the wood to protect the carving tools and find out what surfaces are available to work with.

LETTER STYLE AND LAYOUT

I chose versal (see page 178) for this carving. It is lightweight, has loose capital letters, and makes the post look a little as if someone had graffitied the wood while waiting by it for a friend.

I kept the letters in line with the edges of the wood (i.e. vertical), all about the same size and all starting from roughly the same height up the post.

I have so far advised laying out the letters on paper first. However, here I drew letters directly on to the wood with a white and very sharp watercolour pencil (see Fig 11.3). I allowed the letters to flow individually and the layout to be guided by the splits and defects in the post, spacing each letter in relation to the next, in the hope of achieving a spontaneous effect. You need to be confident in the letter style and its carving to do this successfully; if in doubt rough it out on paper first.

CARVING

Incising took place exactly as described on page 179. The *vertical* grain meant that I needed to make stop cuts to the upright ends of the letters before cutting the initial trenches, but not to the horizontal ends. This is the opposite of normal procedure, when the grain runs *across* the text (see Fig 11.4).

I decided to work as if the surface was smooth and sound. If the letter ran across a small crack, of if bits of old wood broke off, I mainly ignored it, knowing that weathering would do further damage in any case as time went by. You can see the results of this approach in Fig 11.5.

FINISHING

The level to which you are prepared to allow such a piece to weather, along with its location (exposed or sheltered), will dictate the amount of finishing you undertake. This of course applies to all projects destined to be sited outdoors.

After carving, the white crayon was wire brushed and wiped off, the top end of the post bevelled, and woodworm fluid was brushed over its whole.

The letters were then painted in acrylic (red ochre) and varnished (letters only). I wanted them not to be too clear at a distance, but rather invite the viewer to closer inspection (see Fig 11.6).

The ground end was soaked in preservative and then the post was cemented in position in the garden, after which the whole was brushed with several coats of Danish oil.

Fig 11.3 Drawing out the letters with white watercolour pencil. The lines may be a little broad, but the chisel will cut precisely, so you need to be confident in carving the letter style.

Fig 11.4 Shaping the versal waisting with a skewed fishtail chisel. Remember that when carving into vertical *grain, stop cuts are required in the upright ends instead of the horizontal ends.*

Fig 11.5 The lettering to the four faces of the post, working around, and sometimes over, the blemishes and cracks in the wood.

Fig 11.6 The incised lettering after painting but before oiling.

HOUSE SIGN

Simple house signs are good projects for students of lettercarving to start with. The work is straightforward, can be finished in a reasonably short space of time, and always makes a welcome present (see Fig 11.7).

Fig 11.7 The finished sign for 'The Yard', carved in yew.

DESIGN

A sign of this type, giving specific information or directions, needs to be seen from a distance. The letter height should be a minimum of 50mm (2in), and in this case I made the height 80mm (3¹/₄in). As I expected the wood to darken, the letters were picked out in white paint, to give the greatest visibility in poor light.

WOOD

I selected a piece of well-seasoned yew for the sign, and chose to keep its wavy edge on the upper side. Yew will take quite fine carving and, if treated, weathers well outside.

LETTER STYLE AND LAYOUT

I decided on modern roman, for its simplicity and clarity. I transferred the letters to the wood using the method described in Chapter 3 (see page 26) from a working drawing (see Figs 11.8 and 11.9).

If you look at the drawing, you will see that I have altered the heights of **H** and **A** to create an even colour and an interesting layout. When the sign is glanced at in passing, this height difference is not obvious. The leg of **E** and the arm of **T** are also altered to take account of interspace.

I extended and joined the lower serifs together to parallel the even, bottom edge of the wood, while the irregular tops to the letters echo the wany edge above. The position of the shorter word allows a knot in the wood to fill in the empty space above it, while the larger, more important word has more clear grain around it.

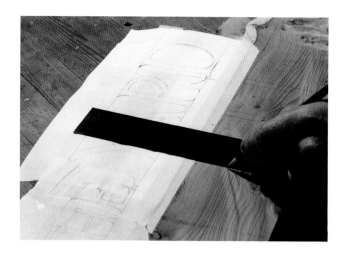

Fig 11.8 The working drawing used for the sign.

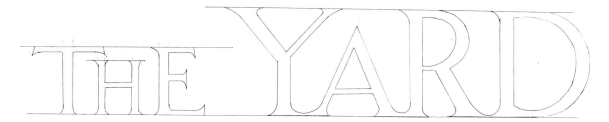

Fig 11.9 Transferring the paper layout to the wood using the method described in Chapter 3. You can see that cutting and pasting has taken place in order to achieve even spacing.

CARVING

The letters were carved exactly as in the incised exercises, with the sequence of cutting as described in Chapter 3 (see Figs 11.10 and 11.11).

The grain in yew wood tends to be somewhat wild in places, and needs a responsive approach. Sometimes the grain rises from below the surface, and a cut which at first seems to be with the grain (for example, down one side of a trench) turns out to be cutting against it. This problem also besets the carving of tangential slices of trees, which some carvers prefer for house signs.

FINISHING

When the carving was complete, inspected and passed, the letters were primed and painted for outside siting (see Figs 11.12 and 11.13). I used a very fine belt sander to clean up the board and letters, and because of the sapwood in the wavy edge, I treated the wood with woodworm fluid and, when dry, rubbed in several coats of Danish oil. I always recommend a fresh coat of oil before and after winter. I have seen signs carved 20 years ago still looking good due to this kind of regular care.

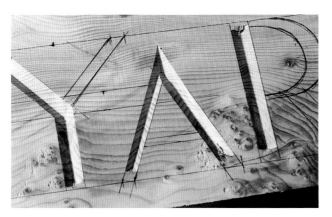

Fig 11.10 I used the techniques described in Chapter 5 to carve the letters. The straight elements were cut first, using the same chisel for as long as possible. Because of the size of the letters, I needed to cut the uprights in carefully merged sections.

Fig 11.12 The finished carving.

*Fig 11.11 After the straights, I tackled the curves. Note how the **D** serif is joined to that of the **R**. The end walls of both serifs are continuous with the outer wall of the letter **D**, and the serifs and lower part of the **D** are best finished off at the same time.*

Fig 11.13 The painted letters, just prior to sanding and finishing.

BOWL

Bowls and platters make good vehicles for lettercarving, and are often commissioned to commemorate weddings or anniversaries because they are functional as well as decorative. Placed by a window, the horizontal edge of a bowl will usually pick up good cross light, showing up carved lettering to excellent effect (see Fig 11.14).

Fig 11.14 The finished bowl in olive ash, 35cm (14in) in diameter.

DESIGN

The bowl in this project is quite thick and robust looking. I wanted the strong mass of the wood to be evident, countering and enclosing the light space within.

The outside diameter of 350mm (13¹/₂in) and the diameter across the hollow of 230mm (9in) gave me enough rim to make a real feature of the lettering. Remember, the smaller the rim, the smaller the lettering. This can introduce problems (see page 170), as can a rim that is anything but flat!

When lettering the rim of the bowl or platter there are two options: the words can be read either by *including* the bowl or by *excluding* it. The effect is quite different. Including the bowl means the lettering will cause the viewer to look *across* the bowl to the other side.

Excluding the bowl means that the lettering will cause the viewer's eyes to travel around the edge. As a rule, the first option – as in this project – is always preferable.

The text itself is a favourite aphorism of mine, taken from the Buddhist tradition:

> Clear Heart
> Light Mind

By running the text around the rim, the meaning can be 'stretched': you can start the text from any point, read around the bowl and it will still make sense. Reading 'heart light, mind clear' is equally thought-provoking.

WOOD

Being simple shapes, bowls and platters are generally made from interesting wood, with lots of figure. However, as discussed in Chapter 2 (see page 21), strong figuring can create problems for the lettercarver. A balance needs to be struck in this sort of case between the need for interesting wood, and confusion of legibility on account of the figure.

The wood for this project was a mild, air-dried olive ash which has a certain amount of figuring but which I hoped struck the right balance. Legibility was further assisted by using bold letters.

LETTER STYLE AND LAYOUT

I used uncial (see page 182) as the letter style. I felt its strong, rounded appearance was sympathetic to the roundness of the bowl.

For quick rough sketches, I measured the circumference of the rim at the centre line of the letters, to get the length in which my text had to fit, and drew my initial idea in a straight line, deciding on the size of letter and what space above and below I would allow on the rim.

When my rough sketches were ready, I drew out the circular rim on to paper with a compass, and made the final drawing, allowing for uprights orientating to the centre of the bowl (see Fig 11.15).

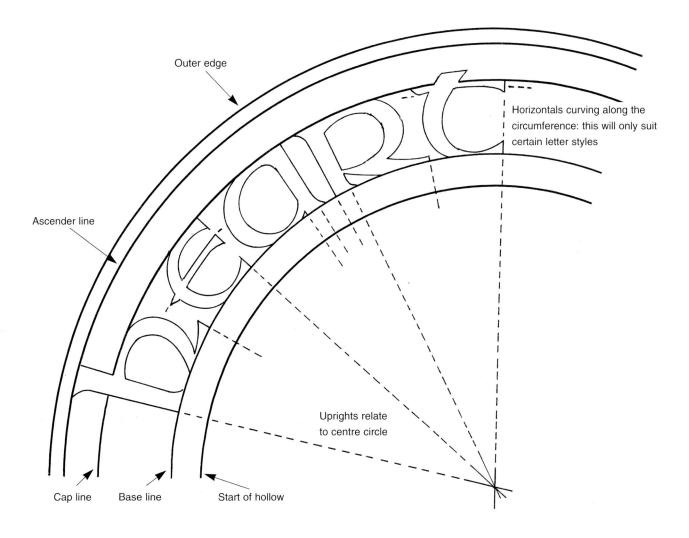

Outer edge

Horizontals curving along the
circumference: this will only suit
certain letter styles

Ascender line

Uprights relate
to centre circle

Cap line   Base line   Start of hollow

Fig 11.15 The final working drawing, showing how the letters orientate to the centre of the bowl.

Two devices were useful for transferring the text to the bowl: a pencil guide for constructing cap, base and ascender lines (see Fig 11.16) and a centre finder for the uprights (see Fig 11.17). The construction of the pencil guide is shown in Fig 11.18.

CARVING

Holding the bowl securely is vital. I held the bowl in the chuck which turned it, gripped in shaped blocks in a vice. Alternatively, use three dowels in a board, and soft wedges or a batten across the rim with clamps.

Carving this letter style is described in Chapter 10, and begins with the uprights, as shown in Fig 11.19.

Fig 11.16 Holes in the pencil guide are used to mark important lines such as the cap and base lines.

Fig 11.17 *Using the centre-finder to mark accurate uprights.*

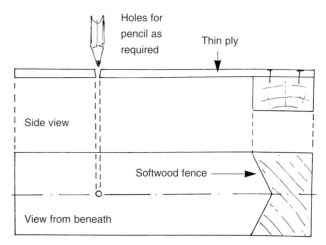

Fig 11.18 *Construction of the pencil guide I use for marking out platter and bowl rims.*

Fig 11.19 *Incising the uprights. Care has to be taken here because some cuts are with the grain and will therefore need stop cuts at the ends.*

FINISHING

After cleaning the rim with a block and fine sandpaper, I finished the bowl with Danish oil. If a bowl or platter is to be used for food, treat it with an edible oil, such as walnut.

SMALL TABLE

This small table is an example of how you can combine a painted and gilded image with some complementary lettering.

A Goldlaufkäfer (*carabus auratus*) is a beautiful beetle, which was chosen as the subject because it makes an interesting design, and its name, in German, presented attractive lettering possibilities (see Fig 11.20).

The beetle was painted by artist Karin Vogel in acrylics and metal leaf, using biology books as reference material. The lettering on the table was designed to act as a foil to this centrepiece. With pieces such as this, always carve the letters *first*, as this allows you to lay out and remove drawing lines without fear of damaging the painted image.

DESIGN

I can't think of an easier way to make a table than to let four legs into a thick block of wood. In this case the legs were turned with a spigot to fit a matching hole. Alternatively, you could shape the legs and mortice them in. Of course, you could choose to carve into a ready-made table.

The table has a glass insert, 6mm ($1/4$in) thick. The glass protects both painting and lettering from the ravages of tea cups, as well as giving a flat surface and keeping dust out of the trenches. Toughened glass is preferable to ordinary glass, especially with larger tables. However, this is not available in such small sizes, so in this case I had to make do with ordinary glass.

I began by rebating the table top by 7mm ($1/4$in), using a router (see Fig 11.21). This allowed protection for the glass edge, which was polished for safety after it was cut.

This table is 300mm (12in) square, with the top 40mm ($1^5/8$in) thick. It stands 270mm (11in) from the floor, and the legs have strong spigots 25mm (1in) in diameter which go at least half way into the top. The design I chose is shown in profiled cross-section in Fig 11.22.

Fig 11.20 The small table made from olive ash, 30cm (12in) square. I removed the glass for the photograph.

Fig 11.21 Routing the recess for the glass. After removing the waste wood the surface was carefully flattened with a scraper.

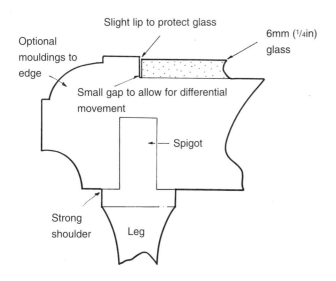

Fig 11.22 *Cross-section through table showing construction.*

The cross-section labels:
- Slight lip to protect glass
- Optional mouldings to edge
- Small gap to allow for differential movement
- 6mm (¹⁄₄in) glass
- Spigot
- Strong shoulder
- Leg

WOOD

I used olive ash – in fact, the other end of the plank from which I made the previous project. If you are following my method, make sure the wood is seasoned and stable. Ideally, you should keep it in the room you intend the table to live for about two months before you carve it. Otherwise, you risk warping, which will cause the legs to be thrown out of true.

Before laying out and carving, the wood must be prepared square, the recess for the glass routed and scraped flat, the edges moulded (if that is what you desire), and holes for the leg spigots bored.

LETTER STYLE AND LAYOUT

I used Trajan roman as described in Chapter 10 for the name of the beetle. I felt that its classical feel suited the fact that the beetle could be regarded as a labelled specimen. In this respect, this letter style would be suitable for any Latin names.

Although 'Goldlaufkäfer' is one word, I split it to allow some framing of the beetle, which was to be placed on a diagonal. I also placed larger letters in the corners, to emphasize the frame.

The letters were laid out on paper and then transferred to the wood, using a ruler and set square (see

Chapter 3, pages 26–7). The working drawing for the lower part of the lettering is shown in Fig 11.23, and the laying out process in Fig 11.24.

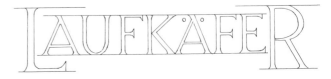

Fig 11.23 *The layout for the lower part of the lettering. The letters at each end echo the corners of the table.*

Fig 11.24 *Setting out on to the wood.*

CARVING

The letters were carved as in the modern roman lettering exercises, adapted to the traditional roman style discussed in Chapter 10 (see Figs 11.25 to 11.27). The two small dots of the umlaut were incised with a small quick gouge. Note that I placed the umlaut dots to either side of the **A**, rather than above it, as it suited the aesthetics of the layout and maintained balance in the design. The completed letters are shown in Fig 11.28.

FINISHING

After carving, the letters were painted with acrylic gold paint, as was the inside edge of the recess. The surface was then cleaned with fine sandpaper on a block to

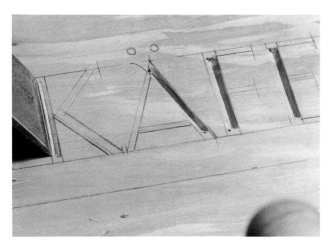

Fig 11.25 Incising the uprights. You can see that at this stage I had the umlaut above *the A.*

Fig 11.26 Finishing off the serif to the apex of the A.

Fig 11.27 Incising the curves. This pattern of carving is that described in Chapter 3.

Fig 11.28 The finished letters before painting.

bring up the crisp edges of the letters and preparing a smooth ground for the beetle painting (see Fig 11.29). The surface beneath the glass was varnished, and the rest of the table treated with Danish oil.

Fig 11.29 The letters were painted with gold acrylic paint ('renaissance gold').

DRY TRANSFER LETTERING

While the process of lettercarving, as you will by now know, embraces not only the satisfying discipline of carving, but also those of layout, planning and the understanding of letterforms, it is also possible to carve letters using dry transfers in whichever font, or style, you desire. This is, of course, a shortcut, but it does have its uses, especially if time is short, or if the carving element of lettering is that which you enjoy the most. Dry transfer alphabets are commonly available, and there are hundreds of letter styles to choose from, produced by such firms as Mecanorama and Letraset.

Even though these lettering sheets come with suggested systems for spacing letters, you will find that, with experience, the best layout will always be achieved by using your trained eye along with the principles of spacing and colour (see Chapter 9). Remember that, while still requiring the techniques covered in the exercises, different letterforms will probably require the use of different tools to carve them successfully.

This project shows how I used dry transfer letters to carve another house sign, this time for my own house, The Poplars (see Fig 11.30). The project uses a letter style not previously encountered, a new method of transferring the lettering to the wood, and a new carving technique, using the V tool.

Fig 11.30 *The finished sign, carved in iroko. The letters are approximately 75mm (3in) high, and were painted white to make them stand out.*

LAYOUT ON PAPER

Once you have selected your letter style, draw the cap and base lines and carefully lay out the lettering on to the paper. Follow the guidelines for 'colour' discussed on pages 162–4 rather than any mechanical rule of thumb which might be incorporated into the transfer sheets. If you are intending to enlarge the forms, remember that slight errors will scale up accordingly.

Now work out the final size. The quickest, and perhaps the only way of doing this if you are not familiar with the letter style, is to enlarge a drawing to the size you want using a photocopier. I needed to enlarge my example in two halves to fit the copier, and then join them together.

Look carefully at the final layout. Any magnified discrepancies in the arrangement of letters will be evident on the final large size. Be sure to cut and paste to get the arrangement just right. If necessary, re-copy for a clear unambiguous working drawing.

TRANSFER TO THE WOOD

After the wood has been prepared to size, the lettering can be transferred using the method described on page 26, before carving.

However, I chose another option which gave me perfect lines to work from. I simply stuck the paper on to the board, and carved through the paper and glue into the wood – an excellent example of a Good Idea that worked!

I diluted white PVA wood glue with two-thirds water. Then I wet the wood with it, and clamped the paper flat with a board overnight (see Fig 11.31). By diluting it, I tried to get the glue strong enough to hold the paper in position, but weak enough to allow it to be peeled off easily when the sign was finished. Wallpaper paste is another obvious choice of adhesive, though I have yet to try it.

I suggest you experiment first, as the type of wood will affect the glue bind. If you get the glue mix wrong, wet the paper, and it should rub away, although the work will still need cleaning up afterwards, whatever

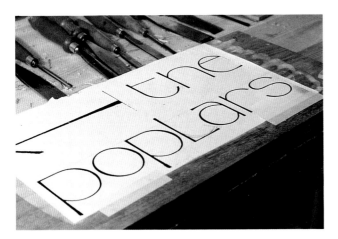

Fig 11.31 The paper layout of the transfer letters, glued to the wood with thinned PVA wood glue.

Fig 11.32 Carving straight through the paper with a V tool.

happens. An oily 'outdoor' wood, such as the iroko I used in this example, will also release the paper more easily than less oily woods.

CARVING

I ignored the paper surface and concentrated on the edge lines of the letter silhouettes. In this case, I had chosen a Letraset style with quite thin, curving strokes, known as 'Camellia', so most of the work could be done with a medium (60° no. 39) V tool. The letters were chased accurately to their edges, as smoothly and cleanly as possible, varying the depth as appropriate to the width and size of letter (see Fig 11.32).

For the larger elements, I drove the V tool with a mallet, taking care not to bury the corners of the tool, and finished off by hand. I switched to a narrower angle of V tool (45° no. 41) for the thinnest elements of the letters to get a deeper cut for the width. The bottom of the grooves must be kept clean with the cutting edges of the V tool working *with* the grain where possible. I used a fishtail chisel to finish off all the ends neatly – crisp and square. A skew chisel would have done this job just as well.

When carving was completed, I peeled away the paper to reveal the incised wood underneath (see Fig 11.33). I had a good look at my efforts and found a few places where the now-carved lines could be touched up (see Fig 11.34).

Fig 11.33 Peeling back the paper.

Fig 11.34 Touching up the edges by eye.

FINISHING

I then brushed primer, and exterior paint into the grooves of the letters, painting right to the edges (see Fig 11.35). I didn't worry if the paint went over the edges, as I cleaned the whole surface afterwards with a fine belt sander. The neatly cut letters came up very well (see Fig 11.36).

Take care if you decide to use a belt sander, as it is easy to take too much wood away, and alter the shapes of the letters, especially with the thinner parts. If you don't have a sander, use a block and sandpaper instead.

After the application of an outdoor preservative the sign was finished and ready for hanging.

Fig 11.35 Painting the letters for extra clarity in an outdoor setting.

Fig 11.36 After painting, a very fine grit on the belt sander cleaned off the excess paint down to the bare wood. The sign was then finished with Danish oil.

CHAPTER 12

RAISED LETTERING PROJECTS

INTRODUCTION

Raised lettering lends itself well to inclusion with relief carving of one sort or another. The reason for this is the obvious similarity in technique between raised lettering and raised carving: to some extent it doesn't matter whether the ground is being lowered around a letter or a flower, a similar procedure is involved.

Like incised letters, raised letters can also be painted. This allows the carving to become a vehicle for what is virtually a three-dimensional painting, with its own particular charm and feel.

As with the last chapter, I have tried to include a variety of ideas and approaches in projects that follow, referring to other relevant sections of the book and raising points particular to each project as I go along.

LARGE, SIMPLE SIGN

This project differs a little from the work covered in the raised lettering exercises (see Chapter 8), in that it is large, bold and vigorously carved, leaving a textured background.

I carved this sign for my son's treehouse, and chose the German word meaning, literally, 'air palace' – our 'castle in the air': *Luftschloss* (see Fig 12.1).

DESIGN

The tree house is made from rough, hefty-looking timbers taken from the stable block that was restored into my workshops. I thought the sign should similarly look a bit rough-hewn, perhaps a little boisterous, with the background coarsely textured. As there was plenty of space, I went for something big and bold!

Fig 12.1 'Luftschloss': the castle in the air.

WOOD

I used a plank of elm about 25mm (1in) thick and 200mm (8in) wide, and overlength. The plank was straight from the saw and well-seasoned.

LETTER STYLE AND LAYOUT

I took my letter style from the book *Buchstaben* by Kurt Koch (details are given in the Further Reading section on page 228). The letters were to be 160mm (6¼in) high. I drew on a base and cap lines, but only intended using them for some of the letters.

I drew the first letter freehand, directly on to the rough wood with a light pencil, firming it up with a heavier one when I was happy with the shape (see Fig 12.2). I then placed the letter next to it in the same way,

207

Fig 12.2 Drawing out the letters freehand.

but *above* the base line. I worked my way along the board a letter at a time, arranging them spontaneously: some on the line, some in the air, as their shapes seemed to suggest. Finally, I fixed the lines with a marker pen.

Most lettering starts with work on paper, and this is by far the best way in most instances. But with large letters in a free style and loose arrangement a more direct method can produce results that are more satisfying to carve.

CARVING

I did 95% of the carving using two tools: a 13mm (^{1}/2in) V tool and a 25mm (1in) no. 9 gouge, using a mallet. Starting with the V tool I ran a deep trench around the letters, bearing in mind the various points about the use of the V tool on page 131. I went deeper than I intended the ground to be and got into the tightest curves of the letters as closely as possible (see Figs 12.3 and 12.4).

Fig 12.3 Outlining the letters with a large V tool.

Fig 12.4 Close-up of the V-tool work. The tool is tilted away to give the correct wall angle, and always passes with the clean cutting side to the letter.

I lowered the background about 6mm (^{1}/4in) with the deep no. 9 gouge, leaving a cleanly cut, textured surface right up to the letters (see Fig 12.5). I then used a slightly shallower gouge to set in the tight curves which the V tool couldn't really deal with, and also went quickly over the ground, breaking patterns that were too regular in the texturing (see Fig 12.6).

Finally, I went around the letters again with the V tool, creating an outlining groove. This groove, plus the texturing, threw the letters into greater relief (see Fig 12.7).

FINISHING

I used a fine belt sander to clean up the faces of the letters, enhancing them against the rough background. If I had sanded the board first, I would have been

Fig 12.5 Lowering the ground using a large deep gouge.

sanding a very large part of the surface that would be cleared away in any case. By sanding at this late stage, I also prevented my carving tools coming into contact with sanding grit, which always has the effect of dulling keen edges.

Since no other part of the tree house is 'finished', in the sense of being treated in any way, the sign too has been left completely 'in the white', but if extensive weathering becomes apparent, I will seal it with Danish oil or an exterior varnish (see Fig 12.8).

Fig 12.6 Setting in the more tightly-curved walls (those which caused the V tool to snatch) with a slightly shallower gouge than that used to lower the ground.

Fig 12.7 Some of the letters, and the tools used to carve them. A groove around the perimeters of the letters made with the V tool helped them to stand out even more against the tooled background.

Fig 12.8 The finished sign took about 2¹/₂ hours to carve, including drawing and sanding. This short working time can be attributed to the use of the mallet for most of the work, leaving the background textured and not levelled smooth.

BREADBOARD

This is a 'classic' bit of 'treen', the name given to domestic woodware used by poorer and more rural communities in the past (see Fig 12.9).

Fig 12.9 The finished breadboard in mahogany, 26.5cm (10½in) in diameter, with words for bread in various languages around the edge.

Treen always looks simple and rather rustic, but should still be well made. I have seen breadboards similar to the one in this project in many kitchen shops, imported at a cheap price and badly carved, with the carving almost obliterated by sanding. This project gave me, and will give you, a chance to make a piece of good-quality treen using the correct methods.

DESIGN

I think raised lettering looks very good on items such as breadboards. It seems to impart a generous, welcoming feel, whereas boards with incised letters seem rather formal. The lettering can even be a little uneven (rather like bread), which is fortunate as small raised letters are difficult to carve to a uniform size (see page 170).

The lettering should always be placed in a way that will avoid its being damaged by the bread knife. In the drawing of the profile, the top of a letter lies *below* the cutting surface. *Never* letter on to the cutting surface itself.

As text, I chose words for 'bread' from various countries: *brød* (Norwegian), *pain* (French), *bara* (Welsh), *pão* (Portugese), *Brot* (German), *pan* (Spanish), *leipä* (Finnish) and *chleb* (Polish).

Between words I incised simple ears of wheat with a V tool. You could choose to carve raised wheat-ears, or a more elaborate design altogether, but in general, simplicity is usually the key to success when working on items such as this.

WOOD

I used an offcut of mahogany, salvaged from a joiner's shop, for this project. Beech and sycamore were the most common woods for this work, as for most other treen, because they would have been the most readily available.

I turned the board to the profile you can see in Fig 12.10. Whatever method you use to produce the board, think of where you will place the letters first. Lower the surface to the ground above and below where the letters will be (this is very easy when turning on a lathe). Then shape the rest of the board edge. Establishing the ground depth in this way saves time, by removing a lot of waste and giving you a reference depth to work from.

LETTER STYLE AND LAYOUT

I designed my own block-like letter style, in which most letters were the same width; it reminded me of batches of bread loaves. This style is extremely easy to carve, with no interspaces, consisting of straight lines, some rounded corners, and minimal differentiation between letters (see Fig 12.11).

The height of the letters was 20mm (¾in), and I had created the cap and base lines when I turned the board. I laid out the words on paper, worked out the spacing between them and drew them directly on to the wood using a home-made centre finder based on the pencil guide I used in the bowl project in Chapter 11 (see page 198).

Fig 12.10 *Turning the board allowed me to set the depth of the ground above and below the letters.*

Fig 12.12 *The jig I used to make the upright lines along the radii. You can see that the letters were designed to taper a little towards the cap line.*

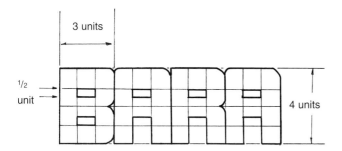

Fig 12.11 *The letter style I used was one I designed myself, though I have seen similar styles elsewhere.*

Fig 12.13 *The method I devised to hold the board. The nibs can be quickly loosened with a screwdriver to re-position the workpiece.*

CARVING

It is easier to carve the board if you can find some way of raising the rim above the bench, fixing it at an angle. The method I devised to do this is shown in Fig 12.13.

I started with a chisel the width of the letter height, and separated the letters with V trenches (see Fig 12.14). Next, I levelled the ground between the words, using a flat gouge and leaving a light texturing to contrast with the smooth surface of the rest of the board (see Fig 12.15).

A V cut with a small chisel was all that was needed for the counters, and I used a small flat gouge to remove the wood between letter legs (see Figs 12.16 and 12.17). I then rounded selected corners with a small gouge and skew chisel and the letters were done. The wheat-ears were then carved by means of simple toolwork using a V tool (see Fig 12.18).

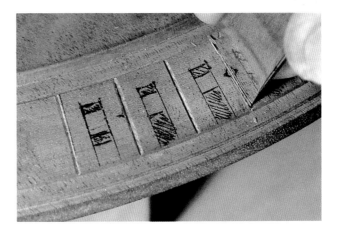

Fig 12.14 *Separating the letters with a chisel by carving a V trench between each.*

211

FINISHING

You need to finish items intended for use with food with an edible oil, and in this case I chose walnut oil, which has a pleasant, nutty smell. Re-oiling will be necessary with the walnut oil or whatever salad or cooking oil is to hand, especially if the board gets washed or gets very wet.

An aerial view of the finished board showing all the lettering is shown in Fig 12.19.

Fig 12.17 Removing wood to define the letter legs.

Fig 12.15 Levelling the ground between the words with a flat gouge.

Fig 12.18 Carving the wheat-ear pattern between the words using a V tool.

Fig 12.16 Using a small chisel to cut the closed counters. More emphasis can be given here if you punch the V cut down further.

Fig 12.19 The finished board after oiling.

NAME STAMP

This is a new use for raised lettering, and one I had never tried before. I made the stamp for my son Finian, to whom this book is dedicated. The finished stamp is shown in Fig 12.20.

Fig 12.20 The finished name stamp – spot the not-so-deliberate mistake!

DESIGN

First of all, I realized that the letters would have to be carved in the wood backwards so that they would print the right way round. The stamp would also need to be gripped comfortably, and so required some kind of handle. The obvious answer here was to turn a handle, but in the end I came up with a different solution, shown in Fig 12.21.

Finally, I needed to use a tight-grained wood, so that the letters would not absorb the ink, but carry it successfully onto the paper.

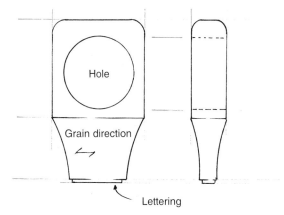

Fig 12.21 Construction of the stamp with a simple handle which required no turning to make.

213

WOOD

I chose maple, a tight-grained hardwood. Boxwood would have been even better, especially for fine detail.

I started with a piece 60mm (2³/₈in) square, 20mm (³/₄in) thick, with the grain running across the letters. These were only 10mm (³/₈in) high, as the rest of the wood was destined to be shaped into the handle.

LETTER STYLE

I used a simple block script, drawing the letters backwards, straight on to the wood between scored cap and base lines (see Fig 12.22).

Observant readers will already have spotted my error during the laying out. Although I *thought* I was drawing all the letters backwards, I actually drew the letter **a** the right way round, meaning it would *print* backwards!

What amazes me is that I didn't notice until the trial printing, despite all my advice in this book to check and double check spelling and layout. After slapping my forehead with the flat of my hand I decided that, rather than repeat the procedure and 'get it right' for the book, I would leave it as a salutary (if humbling) lesson.

CARVING

In this form of raised lettering it is only necessary to lower the ground enough to clear the paper for printing. However, it is good discipline to make the ground neat (see Fig 12.23).

I cleared wood above and below the word using a deep gouge, up to the cap and base line; and then around each end, thus isolating the word. Next, I separated the individual letters by making grooves with an appropriate chisel (see Fig 12.24). A smaller chisel then took away wood from square parts of the counters (see Fig 12.25). I then used small gouges to set in the curved parts of the counters (see Fig 12.26). The carving was quite quick and simple. My main aim was to get crisp surface edges from which to give a tidy print.

Fig 12.22 Drawing out the letters directly on to the wood.

Fig 12.23 Lowering the ground around the word as a whole.

Fig 12.24 Separating the letters with a chisel. A V tool could be used for this job, but a chisel guarantees a straight line.

It was at this point that I tested the printing using an inking pad (available from stationers) and realized my mistake! Despite this, the actual printing was quite successful. I touched up one or two edges and checked the print again (see Fig 12.27).

FINISHING

I bored a large grip hole in the handle, and shaped the wood on the bandsaw, finishing with sandpaper for a comfortable grip. Then I gave the letters several coats of acrylic varnish to seal the pores and this improved the printing.

There is obviously scope here for further exploration. You could, for example, draw the design on to paper, use light to get the design reversed on to the back, and then glue the paper to the wood. You could then carve directly through the paper, as demonstrated in the dry transfer lettering project in Chapter 11 (see page 204).

Fig 12.25 Removing the square counters. A stop cut on the insides of the legs prevents the grain breaking out.

Fig 12.26 Finishing off the rounded counters using a small gouge.

Fig 12.27 The inked-up stamp ready to go.

CARVED AND LETTERED SIGN

This sign requires more exact raised lettering than that carved for the large sign in the first project, or the breadboard with its small rustic letters. It also shows the way in which raised lettering combines well with carving and the use of colour (see Fig 12.28).

*Fig 12.28 The finished sign in sycamore, 60 x 25cm (23^1/$_2$ x 10in). The height of the letter **a** is 70mm (2^3/$_4$in).*

The sign was made for a local court house with gardens open to the public. I chose to colour it with stains, rather than paint it, and this affected my choice of wood. I preferred the softer effect of stains, expecting the colours to wash out with time. I reasoned that the sign could be painted later, but not painted first and stained later if I didn't like the effect. Luckily I did.

DESIGN

I felt a soft Art Nouveau effect would suit the particular garden where the sign would go. The first task was to lay out the letters satisfactorily (see Fig 12.29). I then overlaid the word with tracing paper and sketched several flower arrangements within the width of board I had available. When satisfied, I made a working drawing which combined the flowers and the words.

Finally, to add interest, but without needing to change the working drawing, I shaped the outline of the board, allowing the flowers to broach the top edge and the leaves to act as borders in parts. During this shaping process, I also allowed three areas for the fixing holes. Fixing is always worth considering early on, for all signs.

WOOD

I used sycamore, which, while not being a wood I normally like to carve, does have the quality of being almost white. The problem with using wood stains is that any colour in the wood (normally shades of brown) will mingle with that of the stain, turning clear colours muddy. You can of course opt to bleach your chosen wood, but using a 'white' wood, such as sycamore, some maples, and holly avoids the problem altogether.

216

Fig 12.29 The Art Nouveau style used for the text is called 'Arnold Bocklin'.

Garden

LETTER STYLE AND LAYOUT

I chose an Art Nouveau-like style called 'Arnold Bocklin'. This is a soft rounded letterform, but strong and solid, which satisfied the criteria I mentioned for raised lettering on page 10. I used dry transfer letters and a photocopier to space and lay out the word to the size I wanted, in order to create my working drawing.

Only when I was happy with the lettering did I start to work out a pleasing arrangement of flowers, creating flowing curves to contrast with the straight line of the text. I then realized that there was scope for making the outline of the sign more interesting, so that it seemed as if I worked from the inner letters outwards. I used very old carbon paper to transfer my final drawing to the wood, firming up the lines afterwards.

CARVING

Before carving, the board was bandsawn and the edge cleaned up with a spokeshave and a fine rasp (see Fig 12.30). I used the bandsawn waste pieces to form a fence and support for the following routing stage.

I chose to rout the ground to depth first. If you don't have a router, the techniques of lowering and levelling the ground described in the exercises can be used (see pages 128–30). In either case, mark the depth around the edge with a marking gauge. When routing, it is extremely important to allow for the angled walls of the letters if this is what you have decided on, and not go up to your drawn lines (see Fig 12.31). You may find it helpful to mark a second line in a different colour to work to.

Fig 12.30 Bandsawing the profile of the board.

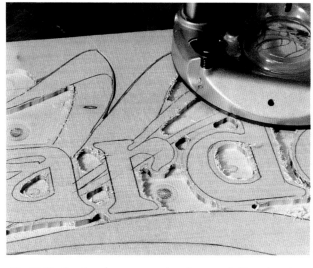

Fig 12.31 Routing the waste wood to the ground. Note that the offcuts from bandsawing have been replaced to act as a clamping fence and a support for the router. Remember to leave space around the letters for the out-sloping walls.

Levelling the ground and setting in around the letters and in the counters took place as described in the raised lettering exercises (see Fig 12.32). Without the flowers this will produce your finished sample or raised lettering. Remember to use the same tool as long as possible and allow the shapes of the tools to do the work, cutting clean profiles, even if this is not exactly to the pencil line (see Fig 12.33).

The stalks and leaves were lowered to half the depth around the letters and set in, in the same way as the letters themselves (see Fig 12.34). They were then carved to shape, working into the flowers and main leaves at full depth. There should be no need to use sandpaper (see Fig 12.35).

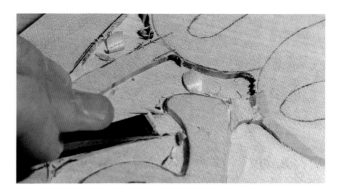

Fig 12.34 Taking down the stalks to the required depth before shaping.

Fig 12.35 Starting to shape the lower leaves.

FINISHING

The completed carved sign (see Fig 12.36) was then stained using water-based stains, rubbing back a little with finest wire wool to reveal the wood underneath at the high points and edges, giving a slightly 'worn' feel. Several coats of Danish oil sealed it from the weather. I prefer using Danish oil to exterior varnishes, as it gives more of a sheen than a gloss, and so far it has proved very satisfactory.

Fig 12.32 Levelling the ground as in the exercises (see page 128).

Fig 12.33 Levelling the closed counters. Cutting clean profiles is very important, even if you are not cutting exactly to the pencil line.

Fig 12.36 The sign carved and ready for colouring. The letters themselves were left uncoloured.

Opposite: 'Love' by Tom Perkins.

PART SIX

RESOURCES

NUMBER				PROFILE OF

Straight Tools	Long Bent Tools	Short Bent Tools	Back Bent Tools	2 1/16	3 1/8	5 3/16	6 1/4	8 5/16	10 3/8	11 7/16	13 1/2	14 9/16	16 5/8	20 3/4	22 7/8
1	–	21	–												
2	–	22	–												
3	12	24	33												
4	13	25	34												
5	14	26	35												
6	15	27	36												
7	16	28	37												
8	17	29	38												
9	18	30	–												
10	19	31	–												
11	20	32	–												
39	40	43	–												
41	42	44	–												
45	46	–	–												

CARVING TOOL SHAPES & PROFILES

CUTTING EDGE

26	30	32	36	38	MM
1	1⅛	1¼	1⅜	1½	Ins

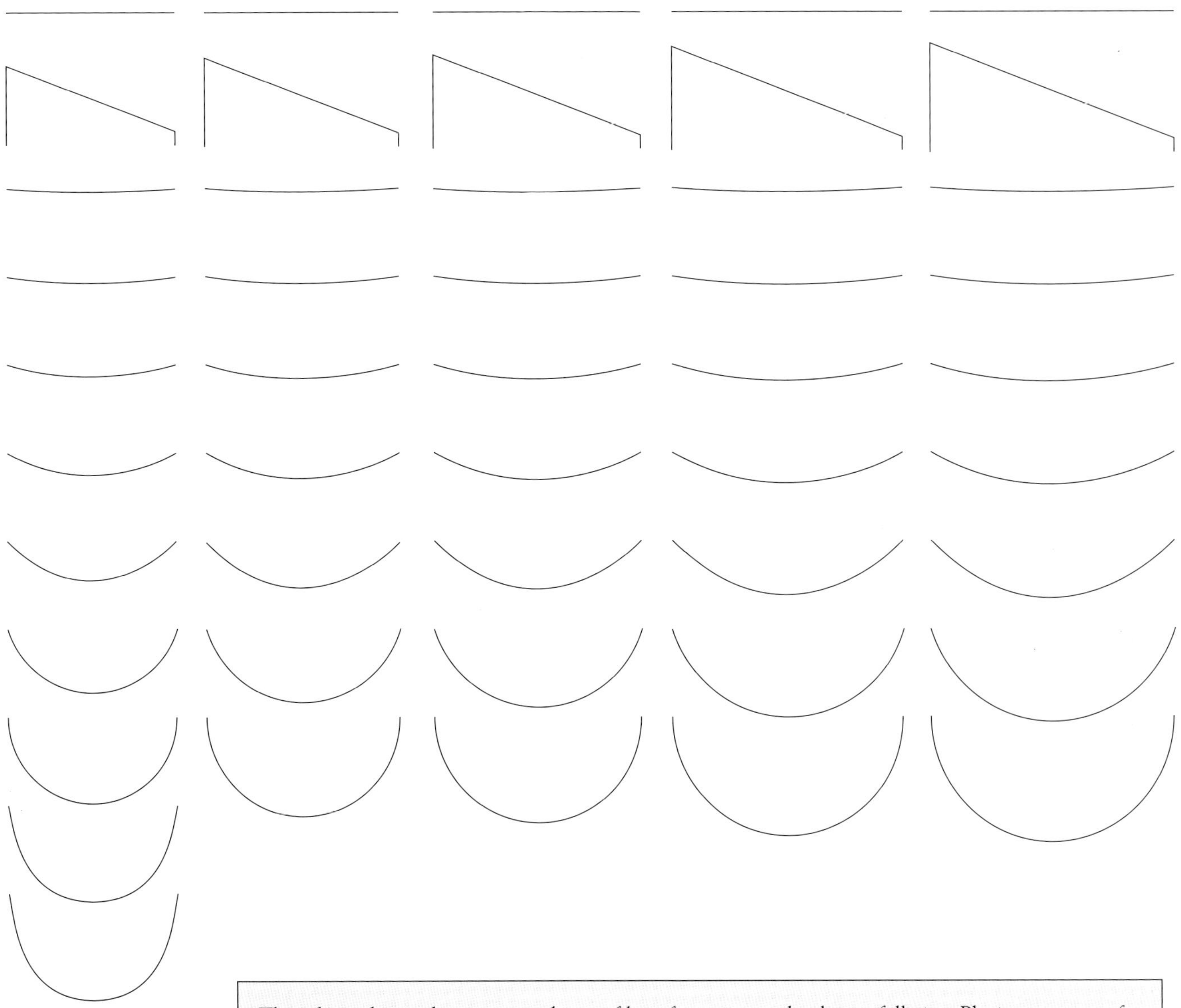

This chart shows the cutting edge profiles of carving tools, drawn full size. Placing a gouge, for example, lightly over the appropriate curve will give you both its size and number. Tools up to 2in (50mm) are also available. This system has been used in Britain for well over 100 years; a continental system stacks the tool profiles, but I have found the layout presented here the most useful to work with.

GLOSSARY

alignment the way a given text relates to the margins or boundaries in which it appears. 'Aligned left' means the lines start neatly one above the other from the left margin but will end irregularly on the right depending on the words. 'Aligned right' means the opposite, with the right ends of the lines forming a neat edge. 'Justified' means the lines of text line up at each end forming a regular block of text. It is far more difficult to space the letters and words of a justified text well than of a text aligned to one side. 'Centred' means the text is aligned symmetrically around a vertical mid-line.

alphabet every language creates its words from a finite number of symbols which are normally arranged in an agreed order as an alphabet. See **letterform**.

ampersand a **character** used since the nineteenth century to symbolize 'and'.

angle in incised lettering, the **internal angle** is that at which the two walls of an incised trench meet at the **root**. It normally has an angle of about 60°. In raised lettering, the **wall angle** is the angle of the walls from a vertical off the ground, and is normally about 5–10°. The **cutting angle** (in lettering) is the angle at which the carving tool is placed relative to the surface of the wood. In incised lettering this is normally about 60°. See also **apex** and **stress**.

apex the pointed upper tips of letters such as **A**, **M** and **N**. The lower tips have no special name and are often referred to as simply the 'lower angles'.

arm a straight letter component which goes from the main **upright**, either horizontally or upwards, and has a free end, e.g. the horizontals in a roman **F**, or the ascending oblique of the letter **K**.

ascender a part of a letter which extends above the cap line and the main mass. Seen particularly in 'small' letters, such as **b** or **d**.

background see **ground**

bar see **crossbar**.

base line the line on which a row of letters sits. Sometimes called the 'footer' or 'footer line'.

beaked serif this occurs as the long side of an oblique-stroke serif is drawn out, and when a letter such as **A** ends in a serif to the cap line, rather than a point.

blackletter see **Gothic**.

block letters a simple square-looking letter style, of uniform thickness, without serifs. Recognized as modern although actually ancient.

bold see **weight**.

border the space or margin around a whole of a body of text, however large or small it may be.

bowl the shape formed by the curved stroke in letters such as the roman **B** or **R**. Also commonly called the 'lobe' or 'loop'.

bracket term sometimes given to the outward splaying curve of one half of a **serif**.

cap (capital) line the line up to which a row of letters reaches. Sometimes called the header or header line.

case, upper and lower these terms originate in the printing trade, and describe in which box (top or bottom) a printer would find the printing blocks for different letters. Upper case (capital) letters are also known as **majuscules**, and lower case (small) letters as **minuscules**.

centre angle see **root**.

centre line see **mid-line**.

centred lettering see **alignment**.

character a particular letter, sign or symbol, distinctive of a language. See **alphabet**.

chasing a way of incising with the tool held low and cutting along the surface. A technique associated with, and arguably more appropriate to, engraving or stonecarving. Occasionally used for lettercarving in wood, but not recommended.

chip carving incising a surface so that the chips of wood are removed to form a design. Chip carvers tend to use special knives rather than carving tools.

colour the uniformity (or not) of letter spacing, affecting its legibility and aesthetic appearance. 'Even colour' occurs when there is a balance between all components of the **letterforms** in a text, including the spaces within and between them.

component any part, or element, of a letter.

condensed text in which the **interspaces** are tighter than normal. The appearance is heavier and the text more difficult to read, but sometimes condensing is necessary if the overall amount of space is limited.

counter the space brought about by components of a letter. An inner, or closed, counter is a space fully enclosed by the letter (e.g. in roman **A** or **B**). An open counter is a space within the overall form of the letter which is connected with the area surrounding it (e.g. roman **C**).

crossbar also called a bar or cross-stroke. A horizontal component crossing from one side of a letter to another, such as in the roman **A**.

cursive a script that is flowing or running, with the letters joined together and very much a product of sweeping brush or pen strokes.

cutting angle see **angle**.

descender the part of a letter that extends below the base line and the main mass. Sometimes called a **tail** and seen particularly in 'small' letters, such as **p** or **y**.

diagonal see **oblique**.

edge there are two important edges to carved letters: the surface edge where the original surface of the wood will become the corner of a wall of a **raised** letter, or descends into a **trench**, and the ground edge, being the junction between the **ground** (background) and the wall of a **raised** letter.

face see **wall**.

family resemblance the shared features of a particular letter style. The family resemblance which makes and defines the **style**.

figure the patterning on the surface of wood caused by the colour and configuration of the **grain**.

flourish a common ornament to be found in **cursive**, penned scripts. Such fancy curves are easy to create with a pen but can be taxing to convert into carving.

font the **style** of a letter.

footer (footer line) see **base line**.

frosting also called 'matting' involves stippling a ground with a special many-pointed punch. Such texturing creates a dull, shadowy contrast to the smooth surface of raised letters.

Gothic various similar styles with Germanic origins but ultimately derived from roman lettering. Also called Old English and **blackletter** when it is particularly dense.

grain used sometimes confusingly by woodworkers to mean either (1) the wood fibres themselves or (2) the way they lie in relation to the surface with implications for how they need to be cut.

ground in raised lettering this is a short way of saying 'background' – the reduced surface surrounding the letters.

ground edge see **edge**.

half-uncial see **uncial**.

hardwood timber from deciduous trees (such as oak), as opposed to coniferous trees (such as pine). Not to be confused with 'hard wood'.

height the vertical distance between the **cap** and **base** lines.

horizontal the part (**component**) of a letter running parallel with the **cap** or **base lines**.

incised lettering any style of letter cut into a surface.

inner counter see **counter**.

interspace see **spacing**.

italic a slanted letterform named from a style used by Italian scribes during the renaissance. The small letters have developed into the **minuscules** we know today and are not joined together as they are in **cursive** writing.

justified see **alignment**.

layout the setting down or 'setting out' of lettering – anything from one letter to a whole text – in preparation for carving.

leg a straight letter component which goes from the main **upright**, either horizontally along or downwards, to connect with the **base line**, and has a free end e.g. the descending oblique of **K**.

letterform the shape or configuration of a symbol (letter) contributing to an alphabet. See **style**.

ligature where two letters are joined, or where two serifs are joined at the base of the **uprights**.

light see **weight**.

lining in a stage in relief carving where the approximate shape of the subject is outlined with a V tool.

lobe (or **loop**) see **bowl**.

lower angle see **apex**.

lower case see **case**.

mid-line a line drawn halfway between the **cap** and **base** lines. In some styles, drawing the mid-line helps to construct the letters. Also called the centre line.

modern roman a style closely related to classical (Trajan) roman but distinguished in details such as the angle of **stress** and the weight of letter.

monogram a single **character** made by combining several letters. Interweaving is needed for a proper monogram, not just the placing of letters next to each other.

oblique a diagonal straight element in a letter. Sometimes referred to as rising (or right, or ascending) as in the roman **Z**, or falling (or left or descending), as in the roman letter **N**.

proportion the relationship, or ratio, between the **width** of the character to its **height**, or the width of a part, such as an upright stroke, to the letter height. The appearance of letters is altered considerably by quite small changes in proportion.

raised lettering also known as relief lettering. The surrounding wood is removed to allow the letters to stand proud (stand out) from the **ground**.

roman a letter style developed during the Roman empire and considered by many to be depicted at its best in Trajan's column in Rome, which was carved about 114CE. For this reason it is also called 'Trajanic'. The incised style comes from a pen style known as 'quadrata'.

root the line created at the angle where the two descending walls of an incised letter meet. Sometimes called 'centre angle', but this can be a little confusing as one can talk about the root (incising it cleanly for example) without being interested in the angle.

router an electrically-powered machine for removing waste wood or cutting mouldings. Hand routers are also available but less commonly used.

rustica a looser pen style than the **roman** quadrata, and still in use during the fifth century, this style evolved into **uncial** and other more cursive hands.

sans serif literally 'without serif'.

serif the splaying ends of some letter styles. Each curving side of the serif is sometimes called a bracket. Serifs can be of a variety of shapes, from hairline cross-strokes to blocks, and are an important feature in the appearance of the letterforms. The head or cap serif lies on the **cap line** and the foot or base serif on the **base line**.

setting in the technique where the precise lines of an edge are formed using selected gouges, usually occurring after initial **lining in**.

shading where the widest part of a curve thins down to the narrowest. The widest part (having the heaviest **weight**) of the shading will be at right angles to the line of stress.

slope some letter styles, such as italic, slope or slant to the right of vertical. Other styles can be slanted (around 10–15° is enough) when there is a need for emphasis, creating sloping **uprights**.

softwood timber from coniferous trees (such as pine), as opposed to broadleaf or deciduous trees (such as oak). Not to be confused with 'soft wood'.

spacing the arranging of letters in the **layout** for legibility and harmony.

stab (stab cut) usually a vertical cut into the wood with a gouge or chisel. The edge leaves and enters the wood and does not travel along it removing a chip or shaving.

stem the principle, straight vertical component of a letter from which other parts such as **arms** or curves originate. It most often passes from cap to base line and is also known as the **vertical** or **upright**.

stop (stop cut) a cut with a blade corner into the wood to control the grain and prevent the fibres splitting out with subsequent cuts. Commonly in the form of a **stab** cut.

stress applies to any curved parts of letters where there is a **shading** from thick to thin (heavy to light). The line of stress passes between the thinnest points, which occur near the cap or base line, and is measured as so many degrees off the vertical. The degree of stress affects the appearance of the letter style.

stroke a term arising from pen or brush lettering but which to carvers, in default of anything better, is useful to refer to any single component of a letterform.

style a particular and recognizable pattern of letter shapes making up an alphabet. See **family resemblance**.

surface edge see **edge**.

tail see **descender**.

trench a long narrow V-sectioned channel out of which incised lettering is formed. Other common terms are V groove and V cut, but trench can also be applied to square and round-sectioned channels. 'Trough' and 'groove' are also common terms.

typeface a printing term meaning a **style** of letter.

uncial also known as 'Celtic' lettering. A style arising between the third and fifth centuries CE, characterized by curved and compressed letterforms. Half uncial is very similar to uncial, but was written at half the size and has many more features of small letters, such as ascenders and descenders, that we recognize today.

undercutting cutting beneath or under some part of a carving to increase the shadow and make it stand out more. It is never a good idea to undercut **raised** letters as this weakens them considerably; on the contrary, the **walls** of raised letters are often left angled out a little, like buttresses.

upper case see **case**.

upright a straight **stroke** rising vertically. This may be the main **stem** rising from the base line, as in roman **T**, or a shorter element, as in a roman **Y**, or a hanging element, as in **G**. Also referred to as the vertical or the stem.

versal an elegant capital letter style, characterized by **waisting**, vertical stress, and hairline **serifs**.

vertical see **upright**.

waist (waisted) a straight element of a letter which thins towards the middle, giving a lighter, more elegant and sensitive form. Waisting is sometimes incorrectly called 'entasis', which is an architectural term for the slight thickening, or convex curvature, of a column, the opposite of waisting.

wall in incised lettering, side walls are those which run along the main body of a trench, and join together at its base to form the **root**. Side walls may either be straight or curved. Curved walls may be inside (nearest the centre of radius) or outside (furthest away). In raised lettering, the walls are the side faces of letters, between the surface and the **ground**. These may be angled or vertical to the ground.

waste wood that is to be removed during carving.

weight how 'heavy' a letter appears, and thus the appearance of the whole text, depends on the thickness of its parts in relation to its height. Thicker, heavier-looking letters are termed **bold** and the thinner, **light**.

width usually given as a proportion of letter height.

LIST OF SUPPLIERS

The following firms produce useful and often very instructive catalogues. I suggest you phone first, as some catalogues are quite substantial, and you may be asked to pay for them.

UK SOURCES OF CARVING TOOLS AND EQUIPMENT

ASHLEY (EDGE TOOLS) ILES
East Kirkby
Spilsby
Lincs PE23 4DD
(01790) 763372
- Supply their own make of carving tools, some carving equipment, and sharpening products.

AVERY KNIGHT AND BOWLERS
James Street West
Bath
Avon BA1 2BT
(01225) 425894
- French Auriou woodcarving tools.

BRISTOL DESIGN (TOOLS) LTD
14 Perry Road
Bristol BS1 5BG
(01179) 291740
- Supply their own make of carving tools, second hand carving tools and other woodworking equipment, and sharpening products.

CRAFT SUPPLIES LTD
The Mill
Millers Dale
Buxton
Derbys SK17 8SN
(01298) 871636
- Pfeil carving tools, as well as other carving, sharpening and finishing products.

HENRY TAYLOR (TOOLS) LTD
The Forge
Peacock Estate
Livesey Street
Sheffield S6 2BL
(01142) 340282
- Supply their own make of carving tools, sharpening products, punches, rifflers, knives and adzes.

JOHN BODDY'S FINE WOOD AND TOOL STORE
Riverside Sawmills
Boroughbridge
N. Yorkshire YO5 9LJ
(01423) 322370
- Supply Henry Taylor and Ashley Iles woodcarving tools, carving and sharpening equipment, and finishing products.

TILGEAR
Bridge House
69 Station Road
Cuffley
Herts EN6 4BR
(01707) 873545
- Supply Pfeil woodcarving tools, a full range of sharpening products, clamps, bench vices and holdfasts, and finishing products.

ALEC TIRANTI LTD
70 High Street
Theale
Berks RG7 5AR
(01734) 302775
- Supply Henry Taylor woodcarving tools, a full range of sharpening products, carving equipment, frosters, and decorative punches.

US SOURCES OF CARVING TOOLS AND EQUIPMENT

WOOD CARVERS SUPPLY, INC.
P.O. Box 7500
Englewood
FL 34295-7500
Phone Voice & Fax: 941-698-0123 (24hrs daily)
Toll Free phone voice 800-284-6229 (US callers only, 24 hours daily.)

- Carry a wide range of Lamp and Henry Taylor woodcarving tools, and other carving and sharpening equipment. 70-page catalogue free on request.

WOODCRAFT
210 Wood County Industrial Park
P.O. Box 1686
Parkersburg
WV 26102–1686
Phone: 800-225-1153
Fax: 304-428-8271

- Supply Pfeil carving tools and a variety of woodcarving and sharpening equipment.

'Captain's Table' by Douglas Williams.

FURTHER READING

Barton, W. (1990) *Chip Carving Patterns*. New York: Sterling.

Bostock, J. (1959) *Roman Lettering for Students*. London: The Studio Ltd.

Denning, A. (1994) *The Craft of Woodcarving*. London: Cassell.

Evans, G. and Cash, G. (1988) *Applied Lettering*. London: Studio Vista.

Grasby, R. (1989) *Lettercutting in Stone*. Oswestry: Anthony Nelson Ltd.

Hart, T. (1965) *The Young Letterer*. London: Nicholas Kaye.

Koch, K. (1990) *Buchstaben*. Eulenbis: Eulenkopf-Verlag.

Koch, K. *Technik und Kunst für Shriften in Holtz*. Eulenbis: Eulenkopf-Verlag.

Norbury, I. (1987) *Relief Woodcarving and Lettering*. London: Stobart & Sons.

Pye, C. (1994) *Woodcarving Tools, Materials and Equipment*. Lewes: GMC Publications.

Spielman, P. (1981) *Making Wood Signs*. New York: Sterling.

Spielman, P. (1986) *Router Handbook*. New York: Sterling.

Wheeler, W. and Howard, C. (1963) *Practical Woodcarving and Gilding*. London: Evans.

Wotzkov, H. (1967) *The Art of Hand Lettering*. New York: Dover.

ABOUT THE AUTHOR

Chris Pye
The Poplars
Ewyas Harold
Hereford HR2 0HU

Photo: Ruhi Farmer

Chris Pye has been carving professionally for over 20 years. He originally studied with the late master woodcarver Gino Masero who strongly influenced the way he works, and from whom he first learned the rudiments of lettercarving.

As a general carver, Chris Pye's work is almost all commissioned, and covers a broad spectrum: from lettering to heraldry; figurework to abstract sculpture; fine butterflies to large bedheads. Shortly after he started carving he worked for a house-sign company, being paid per letter. He found, hundreds of signs later, that he had not only developed an efficient and precise way of lettering, but that he made a bit of money at it too! Since then he has made a deeper study of lettercarving and teaches it regularly to students.

Chris Pye has a City & Guilds Certificate for Further Education and runs adult classes in woodcarving for all abilities. He writes regularly for *Woodcarving* magazine: articles, tool and book reviews, and has written two previous books: *Woodcarving Tools, Materials and Equipment* (1994) and *Carving on Turning* (1995).

He was born in Co. Durham in 1952, but has lived a large part of his life in the south west of England. Now he lives in the Golden Valley, Herefordshire, where he runs local and residential woodcarving courses.

Chris has been a Buddhist since he was a teenager, and this deeply affects his outlook and attitudes to life and work. He was ordained into the Western Buddhist Order in 1990. He is married to Karin Vogel, psychotherapist and painter; his elder son is in art college, his younger at primary school. Other interests include his family, sculpture in general, painting, writing and – at the moment – tree houses.

INDEX

A 95,106–7,166,179–80,189–90
  incised 64–7
  raised 146–7
Abel, John 111
alignment 222
ampersand (&) 104,167,222
angle *see* cutting angle; internal angle;
  wall angle
angled cutting 44–6,75–82
apex 12,106–7,146,169,222
Arabic numerals 107,108
arm 12,222
'Arnold Bocklin' style 217
ascenders 13,190,222

B 91–2,96,150–1,176–7
'backcrank' grip 18
background *see* ground
Barton, Wayne 9,16
base line 13,169,170,222
beaked serif 106,222
blackletter style 186,223
block letters 211,222
boundaries 170,171
bowl (lobe or loop) 12,222
bowl project 198–200
breadboard 210–12
breakages 120

C 85–6,96
'Camellia' style 205
cap line 13,169,170,222
  squaring to the cap line 106
carbon paper 27
carved and lettered sign 216–18
carving 28
  incised projects 194,197,199–200,
    202,205
  raised lettering 115–16,208,211,
    214–15,217–18
carving tools 15–18
Celtic letter style 182–5,198,225
centre finder 199,200
chasing 222–3
chip carving 223
chisels 15,16
  fishtail 16,51,52,54,179
  removing from work 41
  for serifs 50–1
  shortbent 16,114
circles
  incised 72–3,81–2
  raised 132–5
clarity 5
cleaning work 19,28–9
closed counters 12,139,223
colour 162–8,223
  assessing 163–4
  spacing between letters 164–7
  spacing between lines 168
  spacing between words 168
communication 5
condensed text 223
congruence 6

consistency 45,161
corners 138
  removing heel corners 51,114,115
costing 29–30
counters 12,169,223
  grounding within 139–41
crescents 76–81
crossbar 12,223
cross-sections 13,34–5
cursive script 223
curved letters 37–8,70–87,165,170
  C 85–6
  circles 81–2
  crescents 76–81
  O 83–5
  S 87
  vertical stabbing 71–6
curved/straight combinations 88–94
cutting angle 3,32–3,36,44–5,138,222

D 89,96,148–9,181
Danish oil 197,218
density, wood 21,114
depth of cut 32–3
depth of ground 111–12,128,138,210
  deepening ground 119–20
descenders 13,190,223
design 1,23–7,29–30,158
  incised projects 192–3,196,198,
    201–2
  raised projects 207,210,213,216
  see also drawing/drawings; layout
drawing/drawings 19,23–6,39
  firming up 25–6
  practice 159
  rough sketches 23–5
  transferring 26–7
  working drawings 26
  see also layout

E 61,97
edges 116,138,223
  grounding to an edge 131–5
edible oil 200,212
Eggleton, Steve 120
elm 21,114
external shaping 116–17

F 60,97
family resemblance 104,105,160–1,
  223
fence and wedge fixing method 22
figuring 21,223
finishing 28–9
  incised projects 194,197,200,202–3,
    206
  raised lettering 120,208–9,212,215,
    218
flat-bottomed section 34
flourishes 106–7,223
frosting 35,117–18,155,156,223

G 90,97
gluing paper to wood 204–5
'gluing up' wood panels 20–1
Goldlaufkäfer (*carabus auratus*) 201
Gonzalez, Ray 7
Gothic style 186–90,223
gouges 16,71–6
  fishtail 16,52,54–5
  grounding with deep gouge 122–6
  levelling ground 129–30
  selection for incised curves 75–6
  shortbent 16,114,115
  sweep and curves 71–2
  texturing with 154–5
grain 197,223
  incised lettering 54,55–7,58,64,76,
    94
  raised lettering 10–11
    grounding and 126,128,129–30
    V tool and 94,131,135
grips 16–18
ground 117–18,223
  depth of *see* depth of ground
  texturing 117–18,128,154–6
ground edge 116,131,223
grounding (grounding out) 114,
  122–30
  within a counter 139–41
  using deep gouge 122–6
  to an edge 131–5
  levelling the ground 122,128–30
  lowering the ground 122,126–8

H 59,98,144–5,184–5
half uncial 182–5,225
hand routing 119
hardwood 223
height, letter 9–10,11,13,104,223
holding work 22,114
hollowed serif 14,54–5
horizontal 223
horizontal trenches 55–7
  junctions with vertical trenches
    59–62
  serifs 57–8
house signs 196–7,204–6
Hurst, Deborah 3,111

I 98,142–3
incised lettering 9–10,11,28, 31–94,
  223
  alternatives to incising 35
  alternatives to the V section 34–5
  colour and 164
  depth and angle of cut 32–3
  exercises 37–95
    curved letters *see* curved letters
    drawing out letterforms 39
    straight/curved combinations
      88–94
    straight letters *see* straight letters
  internal symmetry 33
  large lettering 36
  projects 192–206

bowl 198–200
dry transfer lettering 204–6
house sign 196–7
inscripted post 192–5
small table 201–3
stab and stop cuts 32
stabbing the root line 34
inscripted post 192–5
internal angle 12,13,222
internal shaping 116
internal symmetry 33
italic 176,224

J 88,98

K 69,99
knives 16
Koch, Kurt 207

L 61,99,166
large lettering 36
layout 113,158–72,224
  colour 162–8
  family resemblances 160–1
  incised projects 193–4,196,198–9,
    202,204
  observation and research 159–60
  optical adjustment 169–70
  raised projects 207–8,211,214,217
  working parameters 170–2
  see also design; drawing/drawings
leg 224
letter height 9–10,11,13,104,223
letter to letter transfer method 27
letter shaping 116–17
letter size 170–1
letter styles 160–1,161,172,173–90,
  225
  Gothic 186–90,223
  incised projects 193–4,196,198–9,
    202,204
  lower case roman 175–7
  modern roman *see* modern roman
  raised projects 207–8,211,214,217
  Trajan roman 4,14,173–4,202,224
  uncial and half uncial 182–5,198,
    225
  versal 178–81,193,225
letter width 13,104–6,167,225
lettercarving process 23–30
  carving 28
  common mistakes 30
  costing 29–30
  drawings 23–6
  finishing 28–9
  transferring the drawings 26–7
lettering
  'good' 5–7
    carver's standpoint 6–7
    viewer's standpoint 5–6
  history of 4–5
letters
  naming of parts 12–13

spacing between 164–7
levelling the ground 122,128–30
ligature 224
light and shadow 8–9
lightboxes 160
lighting 22,130
line: stabbing to a 42–4
line (pin) serif 14
lines: spacing between 168
lining in 115,131–5,135,224
lobe/loop see bowl
low-angle grip 17–18
lower case 175–7,222
lowering the ground 122,126–8

M 67–8,99
Maddison, Gillian 6,7
mahogany 21
mallets 19–20
  angled cutting 44–6
  raised lettering 128,138,141
  vertical stabbing 40–4,71–6
  vertical trench 46–9
matted ground see frosting
'mechanical spacing' 162
mid-line 13,224
modern roman 13,14,37,39,224
  characteristics of letters 95–106
    family resemblances 104,105
    widths 104–6
  modifications to 106–7
monogram 224

N 67–8,100
name stamp 213–15
'nibble and merge' approach 70–1
numerals 107–8

O 75,83–5,100
oak 20,21,114
oblique 12,224
oblique trenches 62–3
  joining 64–70
observation 159–60
Old English style 186–90,223
old style 13
olive ash 198
open counters 12,139,223
optical adjustment 169–70
optical spacing 162–3
outlining 35

P 90–1,100
painting 9–10,11,120,206
pen and dagger grip 17
pencil guide 199,200
Perkins, Tom 5,156,171,172,219
photocopying 160
plane, changes of 8–9
polyethylene glycol (PEG) 20
Powell, Bridget 191
preparation of wood 19,20–1,39–40,
  121,122
proportion 104–6,224
PVA wood glue 204–5

Q 88–9,101

R 91,101
Raine, Kathleen 192–3
raised lettering 9,10–11,28,109–56,
  224
  carving 115–16,208,211,214–15,
    217–18
  common mistakes 119–20
  depth of ground 111–12,128,138,
    210
  edges 116,138,223
  exercises 121–41
    grounding within a counter
      139–41
    grounding with deep gouge 122–6
    grounding to an edge 131–5
    levelling the ground 128–30
    lowering the ground 126–8
    setting in 135–9
  finishing 120,208–9,212,215,218
  ground 117–18,223
  holding work 114
  layout 113,207–8,211,214,217
  letter shaping 116–17
  projects 207–18
    breadboard 210–12
    carved and lettered sign 216–18
    large, simple sign 207–9
    name stamp 213–15
  routers 118–19
  sample letters 142–53
  texturing ground 117–18,128,154–6
  tools 114–15
  V tool 131–5,138–9,155
  wall angle 112–13
  woods 114,207,210,214,216
research 160
reversing hands 41–2,45–6
'rocking' through the cut 124,125
roman letter styles 4,161,224
  lower case 175–7
  modern see modern roman
  Trajan 4,14,173–4,202,224
Roman numerals 107–8
roman serif 14
root 12,13,224
  stabbing the root line 34
routers 10,19,115,118–19,217,224
  hand routing 119
Rust, Michael 157
rustica 182,224

S 85,87,101–2,152–3
safety 22
sanding 28–9,120,206,208–9
sans serif 14,55,224
Sanskrit 161
scrapers 117
serifs 12,13–14,38,167,170,224
  beaked 106,222
  incised lettering 50–5,57–8,63
setting in 115,119–20,131–2,135–9,
  224
shading 224
shadow, light and 8–9
shaping, letter 116–17
sharpness 18

Sheffield list 220–1
signs
  carved and lettered 216–18
  house signs 196–7,204–6
  large, simple sign 207–9
size, letter 170–1
slope 224
sloped walls 112–13
'snooker cue' grip 18
softwood 225
spacing see colour
Spielman, P. 119
spiral 74–5
square 132–5
square (slab) serif 14
square walls 112,113
squaring to the cap line 106
stabbing 32,225
  root line 34
  vertical 40–4,71–6
staining 216,218
stamp, name 213–15
stamped lettering 35
stamped surfaces 118
stem 12,225
stop cuts 32,225
straight/curved combinations 88–94
straight letters 38,40–70,165
  angled cutting 44–6
  horizontal trenches 55–7
  letters H, T, F, L and E 59–62
  oblique trenches 62–3
    joining 64–70
  serifs 50–5,57–8
  vertical stabbing 40–4
  vertical trench 46–50
stress 13,225
stroke 225
style see letter styles
suppliers, list of 226–7
surface edge 116,131,223
sweet chestnut 114
sycamore 216
symmetry, internal 33

T 59–60,102,166
table project 201–3
templates 24
text, choice of 192
textured sides 34,35
texturing ground 117–18,128,154–6
tool control 134,156
tooled grounds 117
tools 15–20,38
  carving 15–18
  efficient use 28,156
  mallets 19–20
  raised lettering 114–15,121
  see also chisels; gouges; V tool
Trajan roman 4,14,173–4,202,224
transfer lettering 1,159,204–6
transferring letters to wood 26–7,
  204–5
transitional style 13
trench 13,225
  see also horizontal trenches; oblique
    trenches; vertical trenches

U 89–90,102
U-section 34,34–5
uncial 182–5,198,225
undercutting 120,225
upright/vertical 12,225

V 67–8,102
V section 13,34
V tool 16
  incised lettering 92–4,205
  raised lettering 131–5,138–9,155
versal 178–81,193,225
vertical stabbing 40–4,71–6
vertical trenches 46–50
  junctions with horizontal trenches
    59–62
  serifs 50–5
Vogel, Karin 201

W 67–8,103
waisting 39,107,173,178,179,225
wall angle 112–13,141,222
walls 110,225
walnut oil 212
waste wood 225
  clearing from incised letters 49–50,
    76–8
  clearing around raised letters 133–4,
    135
Watzkov, H. 176
weight 13,172,225
width, letter 13,104–6,167,225
Williams, Douglas 10,36,109
woods 20–1
  density 21,114
  dimensions 20
  figuring 21
  holding 19,22
  incised projects 193,196,198,202
  inside or outside use 20
  preparation 19,20–1,39–40,121,122
  raised lettering 114,207,210,214,216
  thickness 36
  transferring letters to 26–7,204–5
words: spacing between 168
worksurface 22

X 69,70,103

Y 70,103
yew 20,196,197

Z 69,70,104

TITLES AVAILABLE FROM
GMC Publications

BOOKS

WOODTURNING

Adventures in Woodturning	*David Springett*	Practical Tips for Turners & Carvers	*GMC Publications*
Bert Marsh: Woodturner	*Bert Marsh*	Practical Tips for Woodturners	*GMC Publications*
Bill Jones' Notes from the Turning Shop	*Bill Jones*	Spindle Turning	*GMC Publications*
Bill Jones' Further Notes from the Turning Shop	*Bill Jones*	Turning Miniatures in Wood	*John Sainsbury*
Carving on Turning	*Chris Pye*	Turning Wooden Toys	*Terry Lawrence*
Colouring Techniques for Woodturners	*Jan Sanders*	Understanding Woodturning	*Ann & Bob Phillips*
Decorative Techniques for Woodturners	*Hilary Bowen*	Useful Woodturning Projects	*GMC Publications*
Faceplate Turning: Features, Projects, Practice	*GMC Publications*	Woodturning: A Foundation Course	*Keith Rowley*
Green Woodwork	*Mike Abbott*	Woodturning Jewellery	*Hilary Bowen*
Illustrated Woodturning Techniques	*John Hunnex*	Woodturning Masterclass	*Tony Boase*
Keith Rowley's Woodturning Projects	*Keith Rowley*	Woodturning: A Source Book of Shapes	*John Hunnex*
Make Money from Woodturning	*Ann & Bob Phillips*	Woodturning Techniques	*GMC Publications*
Multi-Centre Woodturning	*Ray Hopper*	Woodturning Wizardry	*David Springett*
Pleasure & Profit from Woodturning	*Reg Sherwin*		

WOODCARVING

The Art of the Woodcarver	*GMC Publications*	Understanding Woodcarving	*GMC Publications*
Carving Birds & Beasts	*GMC Publications*	Wildfowl Carving Volume 1	*Jim Pearce*
Carving Realistic Birds	*David Tippey*	Wildfowl Carving Volume 2	*Jim Pearce*
Carving on Turning	*Chris Pye*	The Woodcarvers	*GMC Publications*
Decorative Woodcarving	*Jeremy Williams*	Woodcarving: A Complete Course	*Ron Butterfield*
Essential Woodcarving Techniques	*Dick Onians*	Woodcarving for Beginners:	
Lettercarving in Wood	*Chris Pye*	Projects, Techniques & Tools	*GMC Publications*
Practical Tips for Turners & Carvers	*GMC Publications*	Woodcarving Tools, Materials & Equipment	*Chris Pye*

PLANS, PROJECTS, TOOLS & THE WORKSHOP

The Incredible Router	*Jeremy Broun*	Sharpening Pocket Reference Book	*Jim Kingshott*
Making & Modifying Woodworking Tools	*Jim Kingshott*	The Workshop	*Jim Kingshott*
Sharpening: The Complete Guide	*Jim Kingshott*		

TOYS & MINIATURES

Designing & Making Wooden Toys	*Terry Kelly*	Making Wooden Toys & Games	*Jeff & Jennie Loader*
Fun to Make Wooden Toys & Games	*Jeff & Jennie Loader*	Miniature Needlepoint Carpets	*Janet Granger*
Making Board, Peg & Dice Games	*Jeff & Jennie Loader*	Turning Miniatures in Wood	*John Sainsbury*
Making Little Boxes from Wood	*John Bennett*	Turning Wooden Toys	*Terry Lawrence*

CREATIVE CRAFTS

Celtic Knotwork Designs	*Sheila Sturrock*	Embroidery Tips & Hints	*Harold Hayes*
Collage from Seeds, Leaves and Flowers	*Joan Carver*	Making Knitwear Fit	*Pat Ashforth & Steve Plummer*
The Complete Pyrography	*Stephen Poole*	Miniature Needlepoint Carpets	*Janet Granger*
Creating Knitwear Designs	*Pat Ashforth & Steve Plummer*	Tatting Collage	*Lindsay Rogers*
Cross Stitch on Colour	*Sheena Rogers*		

Upholstery and Furniture

Care & Repair	*GMC Publications*	Making Shaker Furniture	*Barry Jackson*
Complete Woodfinishing	*Ian Hosker*	Pine Furniture Projects	*Dave Mackenzie*
Furniture Projects	*Rod Wales*	Seat Weaving (Practical Crafts)	*Ricky Holdstock*
Furniture Restoration (Practical Crafts)	*Kevin Jan Bonner*	Upholsterer's Pocket Reference Book	*David James*
Furniture Restoration & Repair for Beginners	*Kevin Jan Bonner*	Upholstery: A Complete Course	*David James*
Green Woodwork	*Mike Abbott*	Upholstery: Techniques & Projects	*David James*
Making Fine Furniture	*Tom Darby*	Woodfinishing Handbook (Practical Crafts)	*Ian Hosker*

Dolls' Houses & Dolls' House Furniture

Architecture for Dolls' Houses	*Joyce Percival*	Making Period Dolls' House Accessories	*Andrea Barham*
A Beginners' Guide to the Dolls' House Hobby	*Jean Nisbett*	Making Period Dolls' House Furniture	*Derek & Sheila Rowbottom*
The Complete Dolls' House Book	*Jean Nisbett*	Making Victorian Dolls' House Furniture	*Patricia King*
Easy-to-Make Dolls' House Accessories	*Andrea Barham*	Miniature Needlepoint Carpets	*Janet Granger*
Make Your Own Dolls' House Furniture	*Maurice Harper*	The Secrets of the Dolls' House Makers	*Jean Nisbett*
Making Dolls' House Furniture	*Patricia King*		

Other books

Woodworkers' Career & Educational Source Book	*GMC Publications*

━━━ VIDEOS ━━━

Carving a Figure: The Female Form	*Ray Gonzalez*	Elliptical Turning	*David Springett*
TRADITIONAL UPHOLSTERY WORKSHOP		Woodturning Wizardry	*David Springett*
Part 1: *Drop-in & Pinstuffed Seats*	*David James*	Turning Between Centres: The Basics	*Dennis White*
Part 2: *Stuffover Upholstery*	*David James*	Turning Bowls	*Dennis White*
Hollow Turning	*John Jordan*	Boxes, Goblets & Screw Threads	*Dennis White*
Bowl Turning	*John Jordan*	Novelties & Projects	*Dennis White*
Sharpening Turning & Carving Tools	*Jim Kingshott*	Classic Profiles	*Dennis White*
Sharpening the Professional Way	*Jim Kingshott*	Twists & Advanced Turning	*Dennis White*
Woodturning: A Foundation Course	*Keith Rowley*		

━━━ MAGAZINES ━━━

Woodturning ◆ Woodcarving ◆ Toymaking
Furniture & Cabinetmaking ◆ BusinessMatters
Creative Ideas for the home

━━━━ ◆ ━━━━

The above represents a full list of all titles currently published or scheduled to be published. All are available direct from the Publishers or through bookshops, newsagents and specialist retailers. To place an order, or to obtain a complete catalogue, contact:

GMC Publications, 166 High Street, Lewes, East Sussex BN7 1XU United Kingdom
Tel: 01273 488005 Fax: 01273 478606

Orders by credit card are accepted